T0314186

Llewellyn Castle

Llewellyn Castle

A Worker's Cooperative on the Great Plains

GARY R. ENTZ

University of Nebraska Press   Lincoln and London

© 2013 by the Board of Regents of the University of Nebraska
All rights reserved
Manufactured in the United States of America

Library of Congress Cataloging-in-Publication Data
Entz, Gary R.
Llewellyn Castle : a worker's cooperative on the Great Plains / Gary R. Entz.
pages cm
Includes bibliographical references and index.
ISBN 978-0-8032-4539-6 (hardback)
1. Workingmen's Cooperative Colony (Kansas)—History. 2. Collective settlements—Kansas—
Nemaha County—History—19th century. 3. Cooperative societies—Kansas—Nemaha County—
History—19th century. 4. O'Brien, James Bronterre, 1805-1864. 5. Nemaha County (Kansas)—
History—19th century. I. Title.
HX656.W67E67 2013
307.7709781332—dc23   2013021875

Set in Minion by Laura Wellington.

For Ocie

When you allow the justice of private property in land, you justify everything the landed interest do, both on their own estates and in the Government, for the country is theirs; and what you call oppression, is only their acting consistently with their interest.

—THOMAS SPENCE, *Pigs' Meat*, 1796

Contents

Maps

Preface

The Workingmen's Cooperative Colony — also known as Llewellyn Castle — was an obscure communal utopia that played a role in American history far greater than its size would suggest. It was an underfunded, struggling operation through its brief existence, and today its faded memory has been swept away along with so much other ephemeral detritus that America's ancestors left behind on the landscape of the American West. The few recollections remaining of the colony are shrouded in local folklore and reflect little factual history. Nevertheless, the settlement was a real place and represents an instance when a group of marginalized people challenged the status quo and attempted to demonstrate the feasibility of radical, intellectual ideas in a practical setting. It was a remarkable social experiment that resonated well beyond the life of the colony.

There have been few scholarly attempts to study the colonization efforts of Bronterre O'Brien's followers in Kansas. It is not surprising. No one directly involved with the colony and none of the colonists' immediate descendants thought its records and annals worth preserving. A few documents and newspaper reports did survive, but they are fragmentary and widely scattered across two countries. The type of ferret work necessary to uncover, unravel, and piece them back together is daunting. Additionally, because the colony was located in a remote part of northeastern Kansas and tagged with the romanticized name of Llewellyn Castle, it became relegated to the realm of historical oddity rather than a subject for serious study. Few researchers have even acknowledged its existence.

I first became interested in the Workingmen's Cooperative Colony when searching for a dissertation topic at the University of Utah. Admittedly, the linked name of Llewellyn Castle caught my eye, and the idea that someone had the ability to build a castle on the plains was intriguing. The castle proved to be a chimera. However, my interest in labor and communal history was paramount, and the working-class nature of the colony gave it much deeper roots in the struggle for human dignity than any mere architectural curiosity ever could. The colony name appeared within a handful of historical listings of communal utopias, many of which had question marks next to the dates of its existence. I made an overview of the settlement part of a dissertation that compared one example each of a political pragmatic colony, religious charismatic perfectionist colony, and a cooperative colony whose members worked together out of need or mutual agreement.

It became clear as the research progressed that there was much more to the Workingmen's Cooperative Colony than its brief existence as a political pragmatic settlement. The men and women who built the colony inherited a distinguished intellectual heritage and brought some significant concepts with them. These were beliefs and theories formulated in Chartist-era England, but ideas that any scholar of Kansas history and the Populist era would find familiar. Therefore, I continued researching the group members in order to collect their background histories and post-colony careers. The result is the story of Llewellyn Castle, from its Chartist origins to the final dissemination of its political ideas in Great Britain and the United States.

This book is unusual because it spans several distinct fields of historical study, including Chartism, British socialism, immigration, American communal studies, and late nineteenth-century labor unrest in the United States. It is a necessary overlap because the men and women who financed, built, and lived on the Workingmen's Cooperative Colony experienced and actively participated in all these arenas. My own field of expertise is in the Great Plains and American West, so the process of researching British labor history and exploring the extraordinary depth of the subject has been incredibly rewarding. Nevertheless, this remains the story of a band of British laborers who saw hope and the promise of a better life as immigrants in Kansas. They were idealists and leaders in the struggle for human rights and human dignity.

Throughout the process of research and writing there have been a number of people who encouraged, assisted, and stood by me. The creative process grows with nurturing, and I owe a tremendous debt of gratitude to those who helped me get to this point.

This book could not have been completed without guidance from both sides of the Atlantic. In the United Kingdom I am indebted to the experienced staffs of several public institutions. The National Archives at Kew; the British Library's departments of printed books and manuscripts; the British Library newspaper collection at Colindale; and the Senate House Library of the University of London. In the United States I am indebted to the accomplished staffs of a number of institutions. The Kansas Historical Society; the Nebraska State Historical Society; the Nemaha County Historical Society; the University of Michigan, Special Collections Library; the California State Archives; the Family History Library, Church of Jesus Christ of Latter-day Saints; and the Office of the County Clerk, Nemaha County, Kansas. Additionally, several libraries came to my aid whenever I needed to use interlibrary loan or required help in finding an obscure item. These include the talented staffs of the Marriot Library, University of Utah; the Mantz Library and Archives, Bethel College, Kansas; and the Richard J. Brown Library, Nicolet College, Wisconsin. I owe a particular debt of gratitude to librarians Susan Taylor, Jill Brax, and Ray Santee. These three helped me locate numerous materials and made the Miller Library at McPherson College a collegial and inspiring place for study. They understood how learning emanates from an open exchange of ideas and endeavored to maintain the integrity of a genuine academic culture in the face of obscurant austerity. Their contributions are not forgotten.

There are a number of colony descendants, some of whom have provided direct and indirect assistance for this work. These include Roy R. Bell, C. Rex Molineaux, Scott Suther, and Charles D. Terry. Of the colony descendants, I am particularly indebted to Debbie Osorio, John Radford's great-great granddaughter. The family information she provided helped tremendously in my understanding of Radford and what drove him in his quest for social justice.

Over the years there have been many individuals who assisted, motivated, and inspired me as friends and support. Some of these include Keith Sprunger, James Juhnke, and Marion Deckert of Bethel College, Kansas; Jacqueline Walker, Chong-kun Yoon, Raymond Hyser, J. Chris Arndt, and Michael Galgano of James Madison University, Virginia; Robert Goldberg, Edward Davies, Eric Hinderaker, Wesely Sasaki-Uemura, Ronald Smelser, and Dean L. May of the University of Utah. In addition, Tom Halliburton of McPherson College and Charles Sackrey of Bucknell University read and critiqued portions of the manuscript. Both offered valuable insight and useful suggestions that helped clarify my own thought.

Two people deserve special mention. Andrew Whitehead, editor of BBC World Service News, was the first scholar to give serious consideration to Bronterre O'Brien's followers in Kansas. His initial examination of the topic revealed many misconceptions about the settlers and opened the door to further inquiry. Since then he has been fully supportive of my own research, helping with a number of sources and taking the time to read the entire manuscript. It has been a privilege to know and work with him. Ocie Kilgus of Nicolet College has been the most supportive of all. She has stood by my side throughout this process, kept me focused, and critiqued the manuscript many times. She is the love of my life. I could not have completed this project without her.

Finally, I owe a debt of gratitude to Matthew Bokovoy, the members of the peer review committee, and the entire staff of the University of Nebraska Press. Their insightful suggestions have helped me think of new possibilities and moved the manuscript forward in a meaningful way.

Introduction

Llewellyn Castle

John T. Bristow was born on December 31, 1861, north of Nashville, Tennessee, in the town of Clarksville. As the American Civil War ended in 1865, Bristow's parents, William and Martha, migrated west to northeastern Kansas to escape the hardships of Reconstruction. By 1869 the Bristows had settled in the soporific little village of Wetmore along the Central Branch, Union Pacific Railroad, where William plied his trade as a tanner and cobbler. John grew up in Nemaha County, Kansas, and by his teens was no stranger to the twenty-six-mile Star mail route connecting Wetmore with the county seat of Seneca. In 1876 the young Bristow applied to deliver mail on the route despite being more than a year shy of the requisite age of sixteen to serve as a mail carrier. After receiving the recommendation of local delivery contractor Willis Coburn, postmaster Alvin McCreery turned a blind eye to the fact that Bristow did not meet the age specifications and swore the youngster into the postal service.[1]

Nemaha County was a quiet land, and McCreery had little cause for concern. In the 1850s, immense wagon trains from the freighting firm of Russell, Majors, and Waddell had lumbered across the area en route from Leavenworth to Fort Kearny, Nebraska, and in 1860 Pony Express riders had passed nearby as they galloped northward to the Marysville station. In 1862 the Confederate deserter Samuel Clemens had taken an overland stage ride through the locality on his way west to the Nevada Territory.[2] All travelers had passed safely through the sparsely populated region. In Bristow's own words, all that lay between Wetmore and Seneca was "prairie grass and wild roses and more prairie grass."[3]

The appointment of a fourteen-year-old Wetmore boy as a back country postal carrier would have been an unremarkable and long-forgotten episode were it not for the fact that many years later Bristow became a journalist and remembered, indeed, that something other than prairie vegetation had once broken the monotony of his mail route. Five miles on the path northwest of Wetmore an unusual edifice stood amidst the looping whorls of prairie wind and swaying grass: a weatherworn eight-room structure that an immigrant band of English settlers had constructed in 1869 to function as the communal home of a cooperative colony. The colony itself had been designed to serve as a pragmatic model of social and economic reform in the American West. To the wide-eyed young mail carrier, this bucolic building and the socialist utopia it symbolized made a lasting impression. Even though the colony had ceased practical operations in 1874, the former dormitory retained a striking presence on the open prairie. Bristow had attended school with some of the colony children, so the old house came as no surprise, but he nonetheless found it difficult to come to grips with the collectivist spirit that the solitary structure represented. Fifty-three years later, long after the aging dwelling had fallen into wrack and ruin and disappeared from the landscape, an elderly Bristow continued ruminating over his adolescent memories of the place. Putting his pen to work, he wrote a memoir that commemorated the building — and the colony it represented — by christening it with a flamboyant title it had never known during its existence: Llewellyn Castle. The name, a whimsical designation reflecting Bristow's boyhood imagination, was manufactured out of whole cloth, as evidenced by the response his published reminiscence received from newspaperman George Adriance of Seneca. After reading Bristow's tale, a skeptical Adriance remarked: "I had never heard of Llewellyn Castle before, although quite familiar with the English colony which settled in the Goff and Wetmore area."[4]

The abandoned settlement that Adriance referred to as the English colony was familiar to people living in Nemaha County because the children and grandchildren of many of the original colonists still made their homes in the region. Although Bristow was the first to reference the settlement as Llewellyn Castle and became its most important chronicler, previous authors had kept memories of the colony alive. These initial outlines allowed Bristow to flesh out his own story with unacknowledged nuggets of information. The earliest account appeared only nine years after the experiment collapsed. In 1883, historian William G. Cutler produced a massive multivolume history of the state of Kansas that included a rundown of the sundry towns and communities in the various counties, including Nemaha County. At the time Cutler was preparing his history, many of the original colonists were still living in the region, and a few had become locally noteworthy enough to rate biographical profiles within Cutler's community vignettes. Cutler focused his tome on boosterism and had no interest in providing a detailed overview of a failed venture, but since a number of former colonists had risen to positions of importance in their adopted home, he credited the colony as a factor in bringing the English settlers to Nemaha County. According to Cutler's summation, in 1868 John Radford and James Murray formed the "Mutual Land, Emigration, and Co-operative Colonization Company (Limited)" in London, England. Through the sale of £1 shares in the company, the group purchased a 729-acre tract of land in Harrison Township, Nemaha County. The colony began operations in 1869 with the arrival of six families from England who were expected to lease the land directly from the company. Radford came to Kansas in 1874 as the organizing agent for the settlement, but the grasshopper plague and cheap land for sale nearby defeated the colony. Cutler noted that "Mr. Wilson, a liberal-minded English gentleman," took the land off the hands of the "embarrassed colonists."[5]

Cutler's brief abstract was buried within Radford's biographical profile, which itself was a nondescript entry inside the community sketch for the town of Wetmore. The story was incomplete and remained largely unknown outside of local anecdotes. It was another thirty-three years before local newspaper editor Ralph Tennal provided an equally brief but slightly different description. Born in 1872, Tennal was a native Kansan. He had no connection to the colony but possessed a keen interest in the historical record of his home county. In 1916 he published an exhaustive account of Nemaha County that included the story of the English colony. While Tennal was interested in the entire scope of Nemaha County history, the failed colony was a minor codicil to what he saw as a narrative that celebrated progress. Therefore, rather than devote an inordinate amount of time to locating records and collecting the remembrances of as many living participants as possible, Tennal invited one individual to chronicle the colony story for the entire group. The former colonist he chose was John Fuller.

In 1916 Fuller was eighty-one years of age and an esteemed resident in the town of Seneca. He was a master tin and coppersmith and the longtime proprietor of a prosperous metalworking shop. Fuller also was an accomplished author who in 1889 composed a comprehensive treatise on his métier entitled the *Art of Coppersmithing*. Immediately upon release, the distinguished work became the definitive text on the coppersmith's craft and has remained unsurpassed in the field. Local townsfolk recognized Fuller's intellectual achievements and acknowledged him with the honorific title "Sage of Seneca." There was more to Fuller, however, than his abilities as an artisan and scholar. Born and raised in England, in 1870 he and his family emigrated from London to become members of the English colony, the colony Bristow would later identify as Llewellyn Castle, although Fuller never referred to the settlement by that name. Fuller's reflections were about his own family's experiences and a troubled colonization effort that failed to live up to the grandiose promises of its founders.[6]

According to Tennal's narrative of Fuller's reminiscences, in 1870 London-area workingmen congregated at 18 Denmark Street in Soho to discuss possible ways to alleviate working-class grievances. Among the group were three leaders: John Radford, Jim Murray, and Charley Murray, who spoke to the assemblage about plans for a colony near Goff, Kansas. Edward Grainger Smith, who managed the colonization plan, was another "promoter and prime mover" of the endeavor. Membership in the "Mutual Land Immigration Operative [*sic*] Colonization Company, Limited" came through the purchase of £1 shares (to a maximum of fifteen shares) in the colonization company. Plans for the colony called for a fourteen-room communal house, and shareholding members had the right to lease land from the company once property had been obtained in Kansas. Six families originally settled the colony, with twenty more following soon thereafter. Overall, Tennal estimated that a total of fifty families arrived. However, the project ultimately failed because there was no incentive to cooperate communally. In Tennal's words, "Anyone could have Kansas land almost for the taking at that time."[7]

Tennal's narrative of the English colony followed Fuller's recollections, and for that reason the sequence of events was incomplete and riddled with inaccuracies. Tennal had sought out Fuller precisely because of the elderly man's reputation as an author and intellectual. In truth, Fuller had not been part of the colony project at its inception and could relate little firsthand information about the company's underlying principles or the colony's *raison d'être*. The reality was that he had been little more than a transient part of the collective. Born in Horsham, Sussex County, Fuller had apprenticed in the town of Dorking in Surrey County. He did not relocate to London until after the movement to plant a cooperative colony in the American West had already begun, and he had never been an active participant in the colony's parent organization. Fuller purchased shares in the company primarily for the opportunity to migrate to the United States, and he abandoned the colony less than a year after his arrival. Because of the brevity and peripatetic nature of Fuller's experiences, Tennal's description added little to Cutler's earlier text and left more questions than answers concerning the colony.[8]

In 1931, fifteen years after the appearance of Tennal's book, John T. Bristow published his first newspaper article on Llewellyn Castle. Instead of a sketch on organized settlement, Bristow wove a tale of England's "surplus inhabitants," or people who were sent "over to this country to 'root hog, or die.'" By 1931 few of the settlers who had taken part in the cooperative experiment as adults were still living. Bristow believed he knew two surviving participants, William Conover and William Wessel, and arranged interviews with them.[9] Although he never realized it, Bristow erred in identifying Conover as a member of the colony. Conover's wife, Jane, emigrated from England and may have lived on the cooperative. William Conover himself had emigrated with his parents from Canada in 1865 and had lived on a nearby homestead but was never a shareholder or contributor in the colonization project. William and Jane were married at the time the colony was breaking apart. By 1931, however, Jane was deceased, and Bristow unsurprisingly extracted no useful information from Conover.[10]

In contrast to Conover, Wessel offered a more intriguing story. In 1931 Wessel was eighty-nine years old and resided with his daughter Emma Chase and her family in the small town of Goff, near the original colony site. Wessel was born in England in 1842 and had moved to Kansas in 1873 as a shareholder in the colonization project. He had been an agricultural worker during the final year of the collective farm and undoubtedly had an innate understanding of the colony and what its members had hoped to build on the Kansas Plains. Regrettably, Bristow demonstrated little interest in such commonplace details and instead held to his own woolly reminiscences as knowledge enough. During an interview in Goff, Bristow asked little of Wessel beyond confirming Bristow's own voyeuristic musings of hearing at one time "about a racy romance at Llewellyn Castle many years ago." Wessel gave no indication that he had any recollection of such an occurrence. To him the sketchy story of a dubious romantic tryst was negligible in comparison to his vivid memories of a group of men he identified only as "a bunch of damned rascals." Bristow never gave Wessel the opportunity to clarify exactly who the rascals were or what they may have done that was so upsetting. Instead, he abruptly dismissed the old colonist's thoughts as "living over the broken dreams of the past." Wessel could not provide the lurid anecdote Bristow sought, and Bristow assumed that he already knew the people whom Wessel was condemning. Therefore, with no further elaboration, he took his leave of the elderly man.[11]

Bristow took for granted that Wessel's ire was directed "at the shades of the original six, or, at most, only those who had actual management of the Colony affairs."[12] After all, the colony had failed, so any rascality must surely have come from those quarters. Bristow had gleaned from both Cutler's and Tennal's histories that six families originally had settled the colony. The trouble was that he really had no inkling of who the first six were, let alone the men in London who held financial accountability over the colony. At one point in his memoir Bristow confessed: "I do not choose to waste time in acquainting myself with the particulars. It takes a lot of research to do a story of that nature. And, historically written, it would be rather drab."[13] Although he wrote that statement in reference to the nearby Kickapoo Reservation and not Llewellyn Castle, his approach toward the colony reflected a similar tendency toward embellishment and a reliance solely on adolescent memory: "I grew up along with those bally English and I think I knew them pretty well."[14] Therefore, in order to avoid a colorless tale, Bristow picked six colonists he remembered and pointed an accusatory finger at George Dutch, John Fuller, Charles McCarthy, John Molineux, John Radford, and John Stowell, as "the original six to enter upon the duties of conquering this land — virgin wild land it was." By 1931 all six men were safely in their graves and incapable of raising any objection to the incriminating charges. Bristow was not entirely wrong, and he correctly identified two individuals, McCarthy and Stowell, as founding members of the colony. However, he felt obliged to exonerate only Stowell from being one of the scoundrels responsible for the colony's mismanagement and failure. Stowell apparently received Bristow's pardon because at the time of settlement Stowell had been a mere nineteen years old, but more to the point, in the 1880s he became Bristow's close friend and employer.[15] The other five men did not receive Bristow's absolution, despite the fact that Bristow erred somewhat when he haphazardly branded them all as founding settlers. Dutch, Fuller, Molineux, and Radford each purchased shares in the colonization project, and each eventually went to Kansas, but in 1869 all four still resided in England with only Radford holding a position of managerial or financial oversight.

Regardless of Bristow's fogginess in identifying the individual founders of Llewellyn Castle and who ultimately bore responsibility for tearing the colony asunder, his brief narrative provided anecdotal profiles for a small number of the colonists. His account noted the visit of company president Charles Murray, and it accurately pointed out a few external difficulties that created hardships for the group. Nevertheless, while it was true that inexperience, droughts, blizzards, prairie fires, and grasshoppers all contributed to the co-operative's collapse, Bristow again went wide of the mark when he characterized the English colony as "a glorious and ignominious failure from the very first, with romance and intrigue ever in the ascendancy." Bristow simply had no basis for his assumptions beyond the hearsay testimony of fellow Wetmore resident Tom Fish, who alleged that the colony failed because the colonists knew nothing about farming. Fish, born in 1865, had been a four-year-old living in England when the colony was founded. He may have attended shareholder meetings in London as Bristow claimed, but he would have been an inattentive child in the arms of his shareholding father, William Fish. The family of William Fish never emigrated to the United States during the colony's existence. Seven years after the settlement collapsed, the elder Fish purchased the section of the former colony grounds that included the dormitory and brought his family to Kansas. For a brief time after 1881, young Tom Fish lived in what had been the old communal building and complained about the snakes that resided under the floorboards. However, what Fish had never done was witness or take part in any of the earlier agricultural activities of the cooperative. Plus, William Wessel, John Molineux, George Cox, Robert Hill, and other former colonists who actually had worked on the collective farm went on to become successful area farmers in their own right. Therefore, what Bristow mistook as "an abiding ignorance of all things American" was in reality a resolute and unbending devotion on the part of the colony directors to remain true to their founding principles. Without knowledge of the colonists' core beliefs, however, Bristow simply presumed that a shady background combined with an unfamiliarity of local horticulture defeated the colony experiment.[16]

Had he wanted to make the effort, Bristow certainly had occasion during his lifetime to access information about the colonists' fundamental values. During Bristow's youthful days as a mail carrier, Willis Coburn offered his young apprentice the opportunity for an afternoon's conversation with one of the former colonists. The man Coburn introduced to Bristow was John Radford, who Bristow would later assume had been one of the "original six" founders of the English colony. In his reminiscences of the meeting, Bristow made it plain that he did not care for Radford and jeeringly referred to him as "Old Radidad." Radford was the only colony participant whom Bristow specifically singled out for derision. Bristow was never clear on why he disliked Radford, but he seemed to have a grudging respect for the former colonist and admitted that Radford had been an educated man with a well-developed sense of humor. He may have felt intimidated because Radford was an accomplished social radical whose "agile mind ground out astonishing facts as steadily as a grist mill that afternoon." Radford freely discussed colony matters in Bristow's presence, but the young Bristow allowed his mind to drift and admitted that he retained almost nothing of the talk. In his later years Bristow could remember only his own prurient imaginings that the discussion centered on the unlikely topic of "a racy romance that had budded, bloomed, and died at Llewellyn Castle."[17] It is perhaps just as well that Bristow had not been more attentive, because he might have gone beyond patronizing to open antagonism had he been fully cognizant of Radford's socialist convictions. As it was, Bristow was left with a vague understanding of Radford's importance. However, in his obsession over an alleged sex scandal, Bristow overlooked the fact that Radford was a central figure who undeniably knew more intimate details about the colony's philosophy, finances, operations, and ultimate demise than any other living person.

In 1948, Bristow expanded upon his earlier 1931 newspaper articles and assembled his Llewellyn Castle tales as a pair of chapters in a sundry book of local reminiscences. Bristow had learned nothing new in the intervening years, and most of his additions related to his personal recollections of the time he worked for former colonist John Stowell in the 1880s and not about the colony or its residents. The single-volume work was privately published, and Bristow reserved all copies as gifts for friends and select libraries. A few descendants of the former colonists were among those receiving his book of memories, and some of them understandably found Bristow's treatment of their family heritage insulting. For example, Alfred Molineux, son of colonist John Molineux and the last child born in the colony, was so incensed by what he read that he acquiesced to having his copy of the book burned.[18] Although Bristow had written a lighthearted account with no intent of spite, he gave his gossipy narrative an added fillip and in the end depicted Nemaha County's English colony as a lark and the colonists as incompetent fools. Thus, through no fault of the English settlers who had financially sacrificed, physically toiled, and in some instances died for their beliefs, Bristow's sequence of events trivialized their communitarian efforts and historically marginalized the colony they founded.

In 1987, historian Andrew Whitehead attempted to disabuse some of Bristow's more patronizing comments and noted that the story of the English colony in Nemaha County was not necessarily one of failure. "If the colony did not meet all the hopes of its founders," he wrote, "that does not diminish their courage in embarking on the project."[19] Whitehead was correct. The English colonists who struggled and sacrificed to establish the dream of a workingmen's cooperative on the Great Plains were audacious but not foolhardy. Their efforts merit an accurate accounting. The settlement Bristow dubbed Llewellyn Castle and that local Nemaha County residents recalled simply as the English colony was, during its brief existence, known by another name altogether. The men and women who built the colony, worked the collective farm, and financially supported the undertaking knew it formally as the Workingmen's Cooperative Colony, a utilitarian name lacking the romantic resonance of Llewellyn Castle but certainly more descriptive. It was founded in 1869 to provide a working model for the political, economic, and social ideals of its parent company, the Mutual Land, Emigration, and Cooperative Colonization Company, Ltd., of London, a joint stock organization that operated under the aegis of the late James Bronterre O'Brien's National Reform League. Although by 1874 the colony had become enmeshed in a downward spiral from which it could not recover, the undeniable truth that the cooperative had existed at all served as a remarkable testimonial to the tenacity of a group of working-class radicals determined to find a humanitarian alternative to the grinding poverty that exploitative liberal capitalism had inflicted upon England's laboring poor.

Despite the fact that it garnered little attention during its lifetime, the Workingmen's Cooperative Colony existed during what is now recognized as a transitional phase of communitarian thought and activity. The cooperative was significant because it borrowed heavily from the early nineteenth-century utopian socialist ideas of Thomas Spence, Robert Owen, Étienne Cabet, Josiah Warren, and, to a lesser degree, Charles Fourier. Its members experimented with elements of Karl Marx's scientific socialism while presaging ideas that Henry George, Edward Bellamy, and Laurence Gronlund proposed for use in cooperative labor commonwealths. The colony was a political pragmatic community of the sort that historian Robert Fogarty argues, with a few exceptions, "did not occur till the late eighties and mid-nineties."[20] Unlike many other communitarian experiments, the Workingmen's Cooperative Colony functioned through committees and lacked a single charismatic leader who could act as the public spokesperson for the group. It was neither large enough to arouse suspicions nor notorious enough to spark the popular imagination. What the English colony in Nemaha County did do, however, was weave a physical and intellectual thread that connected the utopian socialism of the early nineteenth century to the scientific socialism of the late nineteenth century. While its direct impact on international affairs may have been slight, the organization responsible for the colony linked British Chartism of the early nineteenth century with Britain's Social Democratic Federation and Kansas's Populist Party. O'Brien's followers, known as O'Brienites, held open debates with diverse personalities such as Robert Owen, Karl Marx, Henry George, and Jay Gould. They were conversant with social theorists from Jean Jacques Rousseau to John Stuart Mill, and selectively grafted ideas they found useful to the teachings of their own mentor. After the colony's demise, men like John Radford continued promoting O'Brien's philosophy while speaking on the dais alongside Mary Elizabeth Lease and other Populist agitators. Thus, if one looks closely at how the colonists came by their ideas and what they did with them after the settlement's collapse, the colony becomes more substantial than the "free-floating bits of cultural ephemera" that historian Paul Boyer maintained as the fate of isolated communitarian experiments.[21] The Workingmen's Cooperative Colony and its members were very real and contributing participants in the labor and social history of two countries. It is the actions of unknown people, like the O'Brienites, who serve as the foundation for great moments in history.

The O'Brienites originated in Great Britain during the Chartist era but wound up in post–Civil War Kansas, which necessitates a brief overview of the various causes that pushed them out of their English homes and pulled them and others toward a largely undeveloped state in the Great Plains. As political pragmatists they had been strong advocates for ballot-box democracy and had rallied for it from the Chartist era of the 1840s through the 1860s. However, as government leaders continually thwarted desires for radical reform, they began looking for an alternative outlet in which to publicize and demonstrate their ideals. As a group the O'Brienites were conversant with Marxist socialism, and in the 1860s several of the organization's leaders served as members on the International

Working Men's Association's (IWMA) General Council. For many years they had stood at the fore of London's radical organizations, but O'Brien had taught his followers to work cooperatively at the ballot box for the common good. Thus Marx's emphasis on the inevitability of class warfare and social strife had limited appeal. Despite their intimate involvement in British radicalism, the O'Brienite commitment to the commonweal may have served as a conservative brake to many of the calls for violent class action. They wanted to provide evidence that there was a viable and humane alternative to what they believed had proven to be ineffective ballot box democracy, selfish trade unionism, and Marx's revolutionary rhetoric. The O'Brienites were not armchair socialists and had an abiding commitment to fomenting radical social change. First and foremost, however, they were ordinary workingmen and women who were desperate to find something better than the degrading poverty of workers trapped in a capitalist system.[22]

Many factors drew the O'Brienites and other communal settlers to Kansas. Almost as soon as it gained territorial status in 1854, Kansas became a magnet for colony ventures. The New England Emigrant Aid Society's efforts in establishing free state settlements in Kansas served as an inspiration to many, and as early as 1855 the Vegetarian Settlement Company and Octagon Settlement Company made an effort to plant cooperatives in the region. The Civil War disrupted colonization endeavors, but once it ended, railroad advertisements and railroad-sponsored travelogues became responsible for much of the attraction. The isolation of the plains and the opportunity that the open spaces offered to separate a communal experiment from the debilitating influences of established commercial towns were appealing. As a result, by 1870 and continuing through the 1880s, writes Fogarty, "Kansas became a prime target for colony ventures and harbored more settlements than any other state." Thus, starting in 1869, Ernst Valeton de Boissiere, with assistance from Albert Brisbane and E. P. Grant, established the Kansas Cooperative Farm, or Silkville, in Franklin County. Silkville was the only Fourierist colony ever built in Kansas and one of the last at-

tempts to build a phalanx anywhere in the United States. De Boissiere selected the location for two reasons. The climate reminded
him of the silk-raising regions of his native France, and he believed
that the environmental conditions would facilitate the Fourierist
emphasis on handicraft labor.[23]

While the Vegetarian and Fourierist settlements harkened back
to an earlier age of utopian socialism, other cooperatives in Kansas
clearly intended to make a political statement. In 1871 two Russian
immigrants, William and Mary Frey, established the Progressive
Communist Community at Cedarvale, Kansas. Sometimes called
the Cedarvale Commune, this colony had some Fourierist influence but was largely designed, as Norman Saul writes, to implement "basic reforms and socialist ideals based on the example of
Russian peasant collectives." The small colony split in 1875, with
the old Progressive Community moving toward spiritualism, while
the new Investigating Community, under Frey's leadership, emphasized monogamy and communism. The collective dissolved in
1879, but during this latter period several key Russian figures spent
time as colony members. Among them was Nicholas Chaikovsky,
who later took a leading role in the 1917 Russian Revolution.[24] However, shortly after his departure from Cedarvale, Chaikovsky traveled to London where he met and debated Charles Murray, a leading O'Brienite and onetime director of the Kansas Workingmen's
Cooperative Colony.

In 1877 Louis Pio, one of the founders of Denmark's Social Democratic Party and a member of the IWMA, founded a small socialist
colony near Fort Hays in western Kansas. Dissatisfaction with the
socialist movement in Denmark coupled with pressure from police encouraged Pio to leave, and travelogues and railroad advertisements pulled him toward Kansas. Like other political pragmatists, Pio sought to prove the feasibility of socialism in a real-world
setting. Unfortunately, he had done little material preparation. One
colonist remarked "that the plans he had conceived in Copenhagen
with regard to founding a colony were 'castles in the air.'"[25] With
little advance planning, poor leadership, and a location in the heart

of one of the most environmentally challenging parts of Kansas, the colony disbanded after a mere six weeks.

In the same year, a small group out of New York established the Esperanza Community in the Neosho Valley at Urbana, Kansas. Esperanza was a progressive socialist community with a membership that gave vocal support to the Socialist Labor Party. Its fifteen-point political platform called for far-reaching legislation that included an equalization of wages for men and women, an end to child labor, and a graduated income tax. The colony's members believed that they were living in potentially violent revolutionary times, but they also had faith that Esperanza would "usher in an age in which communism would 'cure hard times, panics, starvation, and poverty.'" Regrettably Esperanza suffered from erratic and unreliable leadership. Without stability at the top to provide guidance, the colony lasted barely a year.[26]

One year after the demise of Esperanza, another political pragmatic colony appeared. Like Cedarvale, Thompson's Colony had oblique connections to members of the Workingmen's Cooperative Colony. Elizabeth Rowell Thompson of New York, a wealthy widow and philanthropist, had long been a supporter of the Co-operative Colony Aid Association, and in 1871 she had underwritten the Chicago-Colorado Colony near Burlington, Colorado. She became a patron of the elderly British reformer George Jacob Holyoake and in 1879 sponsored his speaking tour of the United States. Holyoake, who came from the Owenite tradition, had been sympathetic to Bronterre O'Brien's journalistic efforts in the late Chartist period, and in the 1850s he debated the O'Brienite Charles Murray about cooperating with the middle classes on reform issues. In his 1879 tour, however, Holyoake fully endorsed Thompson's efforts to establish cooperative colonies, and it was from this fanfare that Thompson's Colony near Salina, Kansas, was born. With Thompson's financial support, a small group of about twenty-five people traveled to Salina to cooperatively work the land. They were to demonstrate the advantages of communal agriculture while simultaneously opening up opportunities — or a safety valve — for the urban poor. Operating under strict moral guidelines, one of the major tenets of Thompson's Colony was that its members adhere to the example of temperance reform. Like many other communal settlements, the members of Thompson's Colony lacked stable leadership and a cohesive program. The colonists were unprepared for environmental conditions, and after the drought of 1880, the colony disbanded.[27]

In 1893, G. B. de Bernardi of Kansas City, Missouri, wrote the *Trials and Triumphs of Labor* in which he outlined a plan for monetary reform through a system of labor exchanges. The idea of workers exchanging their labor, or the product of their labor, for other goods and commodities was not a new one, and de Bernardi did not intend for it to be the basis of a communal movement. He saw the plan as a means of relieving economic distress among urban workers. Nevertheless, the concept sunk its deepest roots in Kansas, and de Bernardi's followers in the state used his work as the foundation for a labor exchange settlement, the Freedom Colony. Established in 1897, Freedom was an altruistic community that mixed private and communal ownership. Members owned their personal possessions and individual town lots but leased agricultural land from the exchange. The members also communally operated public utilities, the exchange warehouse, and a coal mine.[28] As the national economy improved, disagreements over ownership appeared in Freedom. The colony began to disintegrate, and in 1905 it disbanded.

There were literally dozens of cooperative colonizers and religious charismatic perfectionist colonies in Kansas as well, but of the political pragmatic settlements the Workingmen's Cooperative Colony was the first. Founded in the late spring of 1869, the colony was contemporaneous with de Boissiere's Silkville and predated the Cedarvale Commune by a full two years. It was not, however, the only British colony to find Kansas attractive. In the late summer of 1869, the Reverend Richard Wake, a former Wesleyan minister, platted the town of Wakefield in Clay County, Kansas, on behalf of the Kansas Land and Emigration Company. The company purchased land from the Kansas Pacific Railroad and resold it to settlers from Great Britain. Wakefield was a settlement with religious undertones

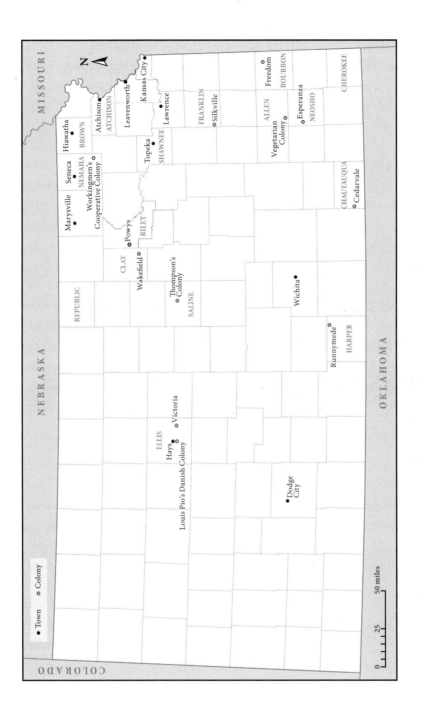

that attracted middle-class English farmers who had the wherewithal to buy land and build homes. Although it had the distinctive feature of providing refuge for orphaned boys from London, Wakefield was never a communitarian venture.[29] Another colony, Powys (later Bala) in Riley County, emerged in 1870 through the efforts of the Welsh Land and Emigrant Society of Utica, New York. Its purpose was to resettle Welsh immigrants already in the United States on land of their own in the West. Powys had cooperative elements, but like Wakefield, communitarianism was not its purpose.[30]

The other two English colonies in Kansas, Victoria and Runnymede, were never mistaken for cooperatives. In 1873 a Scottish eccentric named George Grant purchased approximately 31,000 acres of land from the Kansas Pacific Railroad east of Fort Hays in western Kansas. It was here that he founded Victoria. Grant's dream was to transform the treeless plains into an English feudal estate, "with great stone mansions, deer parks, fountains, blooming gardens, and all the other amenities of English country living." To make money he planned on raising cattle and sheep while selling individual lots of land to English immigrants from the upper classes. While Grant enjoyed some success with both, it was not enough to make the colony prosper. By the time Grant died in 1877, Victoria was already in decline. The last British colony, Runnymede, was the most flamboyant of all. Runnymede came into existence in 1887 when Irishman F. J. S. Turnly purchased land southwest of Wichita in Harper County. Turnly proposed using his estate to educate the younger sons of the British gentry in agricultural techniques. The young dilettantes who came to Kansas had little interest in agriculture and instead amused themselves with horse races, parties, and fox hunting. They did almost no farming, and by 1892 the settlement had failed.[31]

There were other group migrations from the British Isles to Kansas, but no other attempts at establishing colonies. Therefore, of all the British colonization efforts in Kansas, the Workingmen's Cooperative Colony was unique in several aspects. It was the first of the British colonies; it was the only English communitarian experiment; and it was the only attempt by members of Great Britain's working classes to build a settlement in the state. Nationally the Workingmen's Cooperative Colony stands among the first wave of post–Civil War political pragmatic communities established in the United States and the only O'Brienite cooperative colony ever attempted anywhere. The colony existed as a viable community for five years, which, according to success-failure theorists like Rosabeth Moss Kanter and William McCord, means that it did not last long enough to be considered a success. However, historian Donald Pitzer has critiqued the success-failure formula as too simplistic because it fails to account for the persevering impact of social movements, like the O'Brienites, that founded shorter-lived colonies.[32]

If nothing else, perseverance is what defined the O'Brienites. For a group that mobilized during the social turmoil of Britain's Chartist era, members continued pushing their mentor's political, economic, and social agenda well into the 1890s in both Britain and the United States. Kanter argues that "a social movement generally characterizes a social system at a particular organizational stage, namely, mobilization. Utopian communities, on the other hand, exist in a relatively established and institutionalized form." This is a curiously narrow postulate, since social movements do not end with mobilization, and utopian communities do not spring into existence as fully institutionalized bodies. Doug McAdam provides a corrective with the observation that a social movement "represents a continuous *process* from generation to decline, rather than a discrete series of developmental stages." Because the process is continuous, "any complete model of social insurgency should offer the researcher a framework for analyzing the entire process of movement development rather than a particular phase (e.g., the emergence of social protest) of that same process."[33] This is particularly true when examining a collective such as the Workingmen's Cooperative Colony because, as William Niemi and David Plante argue, "The actions of social movements are predicated on contextual collective understandings." If the background organizational stage is movement education, then radical "education is tied to the creation of an alternative ideology that opens up possibilities for collective action, identity creation, and the ensuing political consequences."[34]

A complete examination of the Workingmen's Cooperative Colony requires a look at the entire process of movement development, from education and mobilization of the intellectual ideas behind the colony, through the institutional life of the colony, and ending with the final dissemination of those ideas after the colony's collapse. Therefore, what follows is a chronological narrative of Bronterre O'Brien, John Radford, and the Workingmen's Cooperative Colony from its intellectual beginnings in the Chartist philosophy of James Bronterre O'Brien through Radford's involvement in the Kansas Populist uprising of the 1890s. The narrative is divided into three parts. Chapter 1 is set in Great Britain and examines the Chartist origins of O'Brien's philosophical ideas and how, through the National Reform League and his followers in London, his political and economic platform became the basis for a communitarian experiment in Kansas. Chapters 2-4 analyze the Workingmen's Cooperative Colony in Kansas, how it came into existence, and how the O'Brienites supported it from London. Chapter 5 explores the significance of the colony and the political contributions the O'Brienites made in both Britain and America.

While not a history of communitarianism per se, it places cooperative experiments such as Robert Owen's New Harmony, Étienne Cabet's Icaria, Josiah Warren's Modern Times, and Alice Constance Austin's architectural plans for Llano del Rio within the context of the Workingmen's Cooperative Colony. Moreover, it provides a look at nineteenth-century labor through the eyes of a group that participated in some of the most significant events of the era. While this study places the history of the Workingmen's Cooperative Colony in the larger context of the time, allowing for more than a communal history of a single cooperative, the settlement must be seen in terms of its own unique character. This small colony in Kansas was a radical O'Brienite experiment that had deep roots in British Chartism and branches that extended into modern British socialism and Kansas Populism.

Among the membership of the Workingmen's Cooperative Colony, John Radford was the one person whose name writers either disparaged or put forward as a key figure in almost every secondary account. To accomplish this feat Radford must have played a larger role than indicated because he did not sail to Kansas until 1874, which was the final year of the colony's practical existence. Radford was never an elected or appointed leader of the National Reform League and served no office higher than corresponding secretary for the Mutual Land, Emigration, and Cooperative Colonization Company. His stint as American agent of the Workingmen's Cooperative Colony in Kansas was only to oversee its demise. He was financially poor, not particularly charismatic, and made no attempt to gather a following of devotees. In fact, many of his contemporaries, like John Fuller, found him to be an eccentric zealot. Yet more than any other individual, Radford embodied both the inner spirit and the outward bravado that brought the colony into being. Radford was a polished orator, and throughout his life he remained Bronterre O'Brien's most affectionate and devoted disciple. He sacrificed everything to bring O'Brien's philosophy to life in a utopian setting and refused to surrender. Even when it was obvious that the colony was failing and former colonists were assimilating into mainstream American life, Radford soldiered on and carried the Chartist teachings of his mentor into Kansas, where he utilized them as a local stump speaker for the Union Labor and Populist Parties. Thus the history of the Workingmen's Cooperative Colony, itself a legacy of the Chartist Movement and a contributor to Kansas Populism, is intimately connected and inseparable from Radford's personal life.

Unlike Radford, Bronterre O'Brien was renowned during his own lifetime as a distinguished Chartist scholar. In fact, historian Ben Maw argues that O'Brien was possibly "the single most important intellectual of 1830s British working-class radicalism."[35] O'Brien was not a proponent of emigration and devoted his life to peaceful, democratic reform in England. Among the more articulate and educated Chartists, O'Brien's philosophy evolved out of the utopian socialist traditions of the early nineteenth century. He idolized the French Revolutionary Maximilian Robespierre, but over time his thoughts advanced from a youthful embrace of violent uprising to a more mature policy of education and moral persuasion to achieve his goals. Throughout his career O'Brien developed a clear understanding of the class struggle. Long before Marx entered the scene, O'Brien had defined a reform philosophy that embraced collective action from the working classes. In contrast to Marx's violent proletarian uprising, O'Brien sought a form of state socialism by restructuring society through overwhelming collective action at the ballot box. Once government had been equalized among all classes, then a government truly of the people could enact O'Brien's social and economic reforms. It was his social and economic concepts, designed during the Chartist uprising, that his followers tried to implement on the Workingmen's Cooperative Colony in Kansas.

1

The Sorrow of the Land

Bronterre O'Brien and the National Reform League

My Dear Schoolmaster, I esteem you above all the Chartists I know.
I have got two of your "Poor Man's Guardians," and I have just
read them. Oh! ten thousand thanks to you! I have felt my mind
enlightened — my spirits raised — my hopes strengthened, in the
love of liberty. I have followed you long.

—JOHN DUNCAN, *The Poor Man's Guardian*
and Repealer's Friend, 1843

James Bronterre O'Brien was the inspirational figure behind the
Mutual Land, Emigration and Cooperative Colonization Company and an iconic role model for those who emigrated to Kansas in
his name. Although dead and buried four years before the company
was founded, Bronterre O'Brien's formidable shadow acted as the
driving force behind its membership. In death he became the sage
upon whose altar individual supplicants vowed their commitment
to the goals and principles of the society. Had he lived, O'Brien likely would have disapproved of his name being used as an imprima-
tur for colonization. Throughout most of his life he rejected ideas of
emigration and colonization as solutions to societal problems and
believed such proposals to be counterproductive to the principles
of democratic reform. Nevertheless, it was his ideas on land reform
formulated in England during the drive for the People's Charter that
became the cornerstone of a political progressive colony in Kansas.

Consequently, before coming to an understanding of the students and their rationale for embracing emigration, it is necessary to be familiar with the mentor and the evolution of the philosophy that became the foundation for the Kansas colony. O'Brien was a radical intellectual and a popular orator, but it was his genius as an author and agitator throughout the Chartist movement that attracted his core group of devoted acolytes. He was, as his contemporary admirer Robert G. Gammage reverently put it, the "one man who wielded more of the real democratic mind than any other."[1]

Born and educated in Ireland, James O'Brien relocated to London in 1829 intending to complete his law degree at Gray's Inns. It was a stimulating time for an intellectually curious twenty-four-year-old student from central Ireland to be in the political heart of Britain. The Industrial Revolution's inexorable onslaught was ruthlessly transforming the working classes all across England. In London traditional craft and artisanal industries were confronting massive technological innovation and increased capitalist control, which led to diminished status and wages for workers.[2] During his days as a primary student at the progressive Edgeworthstown School, O'Brien had witnessed the famine and disease that accompanied the first significant failure of Ireland's potato crop. The fact, as he later testified, that he had "seen thousands of Irish who have never tasted animal food, or fish or wheaten bread, twice a year since they were born" was reason enough for entering the political arena.[3] However, while a student at Trinity College in Dublin, O'Brien also witnessed the political tumult that accompanied Daniel O'Connell's 1829 election to County Clare's open seat in Parliament. Thus he departed Ireland with an innate understanding of the interrelated problems of political disempowerment, environmental hardship, and the endemic poverty plaguing Ireland's rural communities.

For O'Brien the capitalist assault on traditional artisanal industry was an economic injustice rooted in social and political inequality, no different than the injustices meted out to the rural Irish poor. There were numerous extant proposals to alleviate the situation. The question few radicals could agree upon, however, was the methodology. How could activists compel established government officials to accept the necessity for transformational change and to implement the required reforms? As he was becoming established within London's urban environment, O'Brien began to examine the merits of three contending theories on how to foment and institute change. These theories originated with Robert Owen, Thomas Paine, and Thomas Spence and came to O'Brien respectively by way of William Lovett, Henry Hunt, William Cobbett, and Spence's aging followers.

Robert Owen was renowned during O'Brien's lifetime, and his theories were articulated in London through his follower William Lovett. Celebrated for his cooperative and communitarian experiments at New Lanark, Scotland, and New Harmony, Indiana, Owen was a utopian socialist who had an imperturbable faith in education and community cooperation as the path to a perfect society. He put little stock in political agitation and believed that reform would occur naturally and more quickly through cooperative communities. While O'Brien came to admire Owen and sincerely believed in the ends that Owenism sought to achieve, he disparaged Owen's paternalistic methods and instead saw communitarianism as the final outcome in a long process of political, social, and economic reform. O'Brien agreed with Owenism's economic and anti-capitalist analysis but went beyond Owen's limited understanding of class conflict and saw no point in withdrawing into a communitarian society without first attaining universal manhood suffrage as a bulwark of protection against the ruling classes.[4] In 1834 O'Brien wrote: "Mr. Owen and his followers may preach about co-operation till they are hoarse as frogs — but no co-operation will there ever be till the rich are stripped of the exclusive privilege of law making — this is a change which must precede every other."[5]

William Lovett, a cabinet maker by trade, was more politically active than Owen and sought to make Owenism the basis of working-class action. The Owenite London Co-operative Society was formed in 1824, and after 1825 Lovett served for a time as its storekeeper. Several other cooperative ventures followed in quick succession, all of which were forerunners to Owen's own 1832 Labour Exchange, an early attempt at trade unionism.[6] Although he remained committed to methods of education and moral persuasion, Lovett soon lost confidence in Owen's narrow views and remarked, "though mature reflection has caused me to have lost faith in 'a *Community of Property*,' I have not lost faith in the great benefits that may yet be realized by a wise and judicious system of *Co-operation in the Production of Wealth*."[7] Throughout this time Lovett had been an avid reader of William Cobbett's *Political Register*, and by 1830 he was thoroughly indoctrinated into Cobbett's ideas of reform.[8] Lovett was active in London radical reform organizations when O'Brien arrived and early on became acquainted with the young activist. By 1831 both were openly arguing for passage of the Reform Bill legislation, which was being debated in Parliament.

William Cobbett's theories of reform had a significant impact upon O'Brien's political development, as did those of Cobbett's sometime colleague Henry Hunt. Cobbett and Hunt were the elder statesmen of radical reform. Both were nostalgic for a rural, agrarian past that had been eclipsed by the Industrial Revolution. While Hunt came from the background of a gentleman farmer and Cobbett from the more modest upbringing of a farm laborer, both became politically prominent within the ferment of early nineteenth-century radical reform. Hunt, who had earned respect as a brilliant orator, gained a national reputation for militant agitation during the 1819 Peterloo Massacre. Cobbett, highly regarded as a firebrand political journalist, was a severe critic of governmental policies toward the working classes. Through his writings Cobbett influenced an entire generation of rural and working-class radicals. Both Hunt and Cobbett assailed rapacious landlords and the proletarianization of farm workers. The two men had been collaborators from time to time, but on the eve of O'Brien's arrival in London they joined together in a cooperative venture that soon drew the young activist from Ireland into their fold.

In 1829 Hunt and Cobbett took the lead in forming the London Radical Reform Association, with the purpose of organizing local pressure groups to call for annual parliaments, universal suffrage, and secret ballot elections. Highlighting core beliefs that would soon become O'Brien's own, Cobbett wrote a letter to Hunt specifying that new reformers recruited into the fold should be instructed in no uncertain terms "to listen to nobody who is not for *Universal Suffrage, Annual Parliaments*, and *Vote by Ballot.*" He went on to say that "any thing short of this would only *enable the aristocracy to rob the fundholders*, to keep their own pensions and their army, and *to continue to oppress the people for ever.*"[9] Cobbett also retained intense misgivings toward the purveyors of paper currency; "those paper-money Rooks" who were attempting to monopolize the money supply.[10] A money shortage would inflate the value of cash and increase profits at the expense of the laboring poor. He therefore placed as much, if not more, emphasis on matters of currency reform as on parliamentary reform. Cobbett had suspicions that the motives of some new members were not entirely pure, and by the end of the summer he had split from Hunt and the Radical Reform Association.

Hunt was not dissuaded, and in 1830 he was prominent in forming the Metropolitan Political Union, also known as the Metropolitan Union of Radical Reform.[11] Shortly after O'Brien arrived in the city, the Metropolitan Union of Radical Reform held a mass rally at which the radicals Daniel O'Connell, Henry Hetherington, and Henry Hunt were featured speakers.[12] For O'Brien the ideas and opinions set forth served as an epiphany that gave him a purpose in life. He never looked back. A free thinker from an impoverished Catholic background whose own experience with aristocratic and Anglican privilege sensitized him to the plight of the working poor, he soon found a new purpose in life that transcended his interest in law. O'Brien came to the conclusion that it was pointless to pursue his legal studies when the law itself was in desperate need of reform. "My friends sent me to study law," recollected O'Brien in 1837. "I took to radical reform on my own account. I was a very short time engaged in both studies, when I found the law was all fiction and rascality, and that radical reform was all truth and matter of dire necessity."[13] O'Brien became a regular attendee at meetings of the

Radical Reform Association. It was under Hunt's chairmanship and guidance that O'Brien made his inaugural appearances as a platform speaker arguing for a sweeping reorganization of society.[14]

O'Brien entered the political arena under Hunt's sponsorship, but in many ways Hunt and Cobbett were legatees of the eighteenth-century reformer Thomas Paine. Paine, famous in America for the pamphlet *Common Sense*, represented the mainstream of British radical traditions. As T. M. Parssinen concluded, Paine and those who followed in his footsteps "wanted to adjust the basic political system in order to include themselves and those for whom they spoke. Annual parliaments, proportional representation, universal suffrage, and the secret ballot were, they believed, the means of acquiring the control they wanted over the system."[15] Much of the Paineite philosophy came to O'Brien through Cobbett and Hunt and, by 1839, became manifest with William Lovett and the Six Points of the People's Charter.

Unlike Paine, who sought basic adjustments to the existing political order, Thomas Spence was an early utopian socialist who proposed an entirely new system. Born in 1750 and raised under the tutelage of the Reverend James Murray, a political and theological radical in Newcastle-on-Tyne, Spence relocated to London in 1792 and soon became a member of the radical London Corresponding Society and the revolutionary Lambeth Loyal Association. In 1793 he began publishing a penny periodical entitled *Pigs' Meat; or, Lessons for the Swinish Multitude* in which he penned articles that refined what he called his "Plan." The Plan, which was first articulated in 1775 during a lecture delivered in Newcastle, became the basis of O'Brien's own land plan and ultimately the foundation for the Kansas colony. Spence argued the rights of humankind could be protected only through common land ownership. The inhabitants of a Parish, said Spence, would form a "Corporation" that would become the sole owner of all land, including mineral and water rights, within the Parish's jurisdiction. The corporation would then lease parcels back to individuals at rates to be determined by the quantity and quality of the land desired. Rents would be remitted to the Parrish Corporation, which in turn would use the funds to finance common needs and a National Government. A minimal government was necessary to handle issues of national defense and inter-parish disputes. Because, Spence argued, corruption in government and rapacious landlords were eliminated in his system, surplus profits from the land could be divided up equally among all parish inhabitants.[16]

Although Spence died in 1814, his ideas remained relevant within Spencean Clubs, such as the revolutionary-minded Society of Spencean Philanthropists. Parssinen observes: "It is fair to say that by 1817, Spence and his followers had made known the idea of public ownership of the land. It became a part of the intellectual matrix of working-class culture that was emerging in the early nineteenth century."[17] This intellectual matrix made its way to O'Brien. As Iorwerth Prothero describes, the small but devoted following that began to coalesce around O'Brien in the 1830s was a "group of ultra-radicals centred on some Spencean veterans from the post-war period." He goes on to write: "There was some continuity between these and the group of O'Brienites who maintained a radical presence in London right through the 1850s and 1860s, and continued to push the master's ideas . . . particularly on land nationalization and currency reform."[18]

O'Brien was a deliberative thinker whose brilliance rested as much within writing as in public oratory. Early in 1831 O'Brien plunged into journalism when he wrote the first of three provocative articles for William Carpenter's *Political Letters*. Carpenter, who along with Henry Hetherington shares the distinction of instigating the radical struggle for the unstamped press,[19] was imprisoned for distributing *Political Letters* without paying the four-penny stamp tax. For O'Brien, *Political Letters* provided him with his first real public forum. He signed all three articles with the *nom de plume* "Bronterre," a name O'Brien created through a combination of Gaelic and French words that means "sorrow of the land."[20] In the first article O'Brien linked Irish land issues, with which he was intimately familiar, to the cause of political reform in England. In the second and third letters, however, O'Brien focused on reform in England and made it clear that any meaningful change would come neither from the middle classes nor from any of Robert Owen's proposals. True reform, said O'Brien, could only be achieved through the efforts of the working classes. "It is evident that such a plan of reform must invest the productive classes with real legislative power . . . with the power of gradually making whatever modifications they choose in existing institutions, and even in the constitution of society itself."[21]

While O'Brien's introductory foray into political discourse may have resembled the Paineite tradition he inherited from Cobbett and Hunt, it was Spencean ideas of land that became central to his philosophy. Like Cobbett and Hunt he saw agriculture as the cornerstone of civilized society, but unlike his predecessors he did not romanticize a return to an agrarian past. O'Brien was increasingly persuaded from his readings of Spence, who in 1794 wrote: "If then the people wish to have the government in their own hands, they must begin first, by taking the land into their own hands."[22] O'Brien therefore began to view agriculture and land reform as the fundamental basis for industrial prosperity. In 1837 O'Brien wrote: "Agriculture is moreover the most profitable occupation, as regards the whole of a community; for being the basis of all other occupations, its prosperity alone can yield the means of re-production and prosperity to all the rest."[23] From this basis O'Brien formulated his own land plan, the four points of which he advanced as the "true theory."

> 1st. The absolute dominion, or allodial right to the soil, belongs to the nation only.
>
> 2nd. The nation alone has the just power of leasing out the land for cultivation, and of appropriating the rents accruing therefrom.
>
> 3rd. The size of farms, or the portions of soil to be allotted to individuals or families; also the proportions to be devoted to tillage, pasturage, &c. — also the several other powers now possessed by individual owners, and exercised by them in the granting of leas-

es, &c. — all these are matters which it also belongs to the nation alone to determine in virtue of its rights as absolute landlord of all.

4th. Upon this theory every subject of the realm is a part proprietor of the soil. The lands being leased out by public auction, whoever bids highest for a lot should get it, because the nation would thereby be the gainer; and as population increased, and the land became in consequence more valuable, rents would increase also, and the people's inheritance be made greater.[24]

Land nationalization based on the "true theory" became a lasting component of O'Brien's theoretical canon, but, as he later wrote in the 1840s, it inextricably linked with universal suffrage. "Knaves will tell you that it is because you have no property that you are unrepresented. I tell you, on the contrary, it is because you are unrepresented that you have no property."[25] While the idea of universal suffrage had a foundation going back as far as Paine, there was much of Spence in O'Brien's statement. In 1795 Spence wrote: "You should first ask if the Landed Interest will let you have a reform, which they will take care to prevent. For a Convention or Parliament of the People would be at eternal War with the Aristocracy."[26]

The Spencean subtext within O'Brien's thought continued throughout the Chartist era. The London Working Men's Association (LWMA) had formed in 1836, and in 1837 Lovett unveiled a draft copy of what became the Six Points of the People's Charter. The petition, which called for universal suffrage, no property qualifications for voting, annual Parliaments, equal representation in Parliament, payment of members of Parliament, and vote by ballot, was an appeal to the House of Commons on behalf of the workingmen of Great Britain. The document called for peaceful reforms to adjust the basic political system. O'Brien fully supported the Charter, was an honorary member of the LWMA, and advocated that "now is the time to strike a blow for universal suffrage."[27] However, he did not view the petition as the final act that would usher in reform. For O'Brien, the middle classes had turned the government into a veritable Augean Stable on issues of equality and reform. Basic adjustments to the political system, let alone a radical reorganization of society on the scale that O'Brien imagined, could not happen through the moral persuasion of a petition. He preferred peaceful reform, but had come to the conclusion that an amoral middle class would not budge unless pressured through an underlying threat of violence. In his 1838 biography of Maximilian Robespierre, O'Brien argued that "a revolution to be effective must begin with the bottom instead of the top of society. It must originate with the productive classes, and the first blow must be struck at the profit mongers."[28]

Although O'Brien understood the usefulness in the implied threat of violence, his articulated position was that he "never recommended physical force except as a last desperate resort against tyranny, and to be used only when the popular mind has been fully enlightened beforehand."[29] Henry Jephson confirmed this outlook, stating that O'Brien "was not for employing force, not now at any rate, not until they could not do without it, and they could do with it."[30] Nevertheless, because he saw the moral reform tactics that Lovett and the LWMA were employing as ineffective, O'Brien allied himself with Feargus O'Connor and other firebrands willing to employ physical force to push the Charter through Parliament. He began writing for O'Connor's *Northern Star* and earned the sobriquet "Schoolmaster of Chartism," an affectionate title O'Brien was pleased to accept. O'Brien was at his intellectual peak and the most productive phase of his career. In the words of Alfred Plummer, "O'Brien's substantial articles in the *Northern Star* constitute the first attempt to formulate for Chartism a philosophy and a program. They were a prelude or curtain-raiser to the Chartist Convention of 1839."[31]

At the National Chartist Convention of 1839, O'Brien served as a delegate from London and several other districts. He performed a number of important tasks throughout the gathering, not least of which was to draft the convention's official stand on physical force. In addition, O'Brien was a polished speaker at this point in his career and became one of the most sought after lecturers during the convention. Flora Tristan, the renowned French radical feminist and social utopian, had the opportunity to attend an O'Brien lecture during the convention and recorded that he was "remarkable for his clear thinking, his lucidity, his self-control and his knowledge of past events."[32] Frank Peel echoed Tristan's observations and recollected that O'Brien "was one of the most eloquent of perhaps the most remarkable band of orators that ever stood on a political platform in this country."[33] This ability to draw large crowds, along with O'Brien's willingness to make provocative statements, inevitably drew the attention of the authorities. In Scotland an editorialist commented: "No man can doubt, on hearing O'Brien, that he has little faith in the efficacy of moral agitation; and that he looks to a revolution to overturn the present government."[34]

In a July 1839 Parliamentary vote the Chartist Petition received a resounding defeat, and by the end of the summer the convention delegates had little choice but to terminate proceedings. The Chartist Convention had ended, but for O'Brien and other leaders who had delivered subversive speeches the trouble was just beginning. O'Brien was arrested, tried twice on two separate charges, and convicted of seditious conspiracy in his second trial. He was incarcerated in Lancaster Castle Prison and spent the next eighteen months of his life ruminating over the prejudice of the justice system. Said O'Brien: "I was soon after locked up in Lancaster Castle for eighteen months, ostensibly for an *illegal* speech I never made, (one manufactured for the occasion), but, in reality, for many perfectly legal speeches I had made, and in which I committed the unpardonable sin of enunciating some ugly, but incontrovertible facts, touching the *virtuous* middle classes."[35]

Regardless of O'Brien's certainty concerning the injustice of his imprisonment, the deplorable conditions of his confinement left him chastened. With little to occupy his attentions, he had ample time to mull over his actions of the previous ten years and why the government prosecuted his case so vigorously. O'Brien's personal deliberations led him to abandon his embrace of physical force Chartism. Gammage reflected that O'Brien, upon his release in September 1841, resolved to no longer take part in radical agitation or incendiary meetings that the political establishment could interpret as revolutionary. O'Brien "stated his determination to attend no more processions or demonstrations of that kind, as he considered such demonstrations to be, for the present, productive of no good."[36] Unlike other Chartist leaders, he began to comprehend that there were divisions within the middle class, or what Karl Marx would later define as *haute bourgeoisie*, the capitalist class, and *petite bourgeoisie*, the lower middle class. Accordingly, O'Brien allied himself with middle-class reformers like Joseph Sturge, Richard Cobden, and John Bright to work through the Anti-Corn Law League and the Complete Suffrage Movement (CSM) to achieve a moderate restructuring of the political system.[37]

O'Brien had only modified his tactics in approaching reform, not his overall outlook or philosophy. Nevertheless, his rejection of violence and demagoguery placed him on the outside of mainstream Chartism. He maintained a small core of devoted followers who embraced his political theories of land reform, but when the second Chartist Convention convened in April 1842 O'Brien found himself roundly excoriated as both a backslider and a vicious and untrustworthy "viper."[38] O'Brien had come to the conclusion that it was preferable to proceed thoughtfully and allow "time to detach some of your enemy's forces from him, or to make them either neutral or auxiliary to you in the coming conflict."[39] In the eyes of mainstream Chartists, the Anti-Corn Law League and CSM represented little more than a diversionary tactic on the part of the middle classes, who allegedly wanted the Corn Laws repealed in order to lower the price of bread and pay lower wages to workers.[40] Since 1840 the numerous regional·Chartist organizations had been merging into the National Charter Association (NCA). With O'Brien and other regional voices for moderation marginalized, leadership of the NCA and mainstream Chartism fell firmly under the control of O'Connor and the militant extremists.

The second Chartist Convention was no more successful than the first. Upon its conclusion in 1843, O'Brien found himself mired, as he described it, in a state of "internal exile." Excluded from mainstream Chartist debates and denied column space in the *North-*

ern Star, he could only sit back and seethe as O'Connor initiated what O'Brien saw as an ill-considered and self-serving land plan. O'Connor's Chartist Cooperative Land Society, presented at the spring 1843 Chartist Convention, proposed relocating displaced factory workers to small individual holdings of one to four acres where they could practice intensive spade husbandry to earn a living for their families. O'Brien found O'Connor's land scheme to be patently absurd and ridiculed it as divisive to the cause and detrimental to the welfare of those lured into participating. In a sarcastic missive, O'Brien said it was "strangest of all that the philanthropic Feargus should have dragged millions of people after him to torchlight meetings, demonstrations, etc, all attended with great sacrifice of time and money, and caused the actual ruin of thousands through imprisonment, loss of employment, and expatriation, when all the while he had only to establish a 'National Chartist Co-operative Land Society' to ensure social happiness for us all."[41]

O'Brien feared that by distributing small parcels of land to some workers, the movement for suffrage would be split. O'Connor's landed poor would be satisfied with what they had, no longer join in collective efforts for reform, and stabilize the status quo for landed elites. O'Brien fumed: "Every man who joins in these land societies is practically enlisting himself on the side of Government against his own order."[42] For O'Brien land was the natural birthright of all men, women, and children, regardless of occupation. He saw O'Connor's plan as creating a new aristocracy and, in the language of Spence, accused O'Connor of "forgetting 'the People's Farm,'" by which he meant true public, or national, ownership.[43]

Despite his diatribes against O'Connor, O'Brien's voice was largely muted. With few alternatives available, he relocated to Douglas on the Isle of Man and began publishing *The National Reformer and Manx Weekly Review of Home and Foreign Affairs*. Although distant from the main political debates, O'Brien used his paper to dissociate himself from O'Connor while further developing his ideas of land nationalization and currency reform. Said an 1847 editorial: "Mr. O'Brien contends only for what are strictly the rights of the people and what any people may establish practically by law; whereas the systems of Owen, Fourrier [*sic*], St. Simon, &c, transcend the capabilities of all human legislature, . . . [and are] impossible of realization on a universal scale." It was a matter of common sense to O'Brien that every man "can be got to recognize his own rights, and, as a corollary, the equal rights of his neighbors." If only the people's rights could be lawfully established and "proper laws acted upon Land, Currency, Credit, and Exchanges, an unbounded field of progressive improvement and prosperity would thenceforward lie open to the people." Once true social freedom had been attained, the people "would soon discover what wonders in production, and in distribution, and in the sciences, generally, might be achieved by Associative labour, in comparison with the exertions of isolated individual labour." Only after this logical process would the "true social state" arise, which O'Brien called "the realities of socialism, as contradistinguished from the present dreams about it."[44]

While O'Brien's periodical had a small base of devoted admirers, it was not enough to sustain continued publication. When the journal folded in 1847, O'Brien gathered his family and returned to London at, as it turned out, a momentous time. Conservative governments throughout Europe had come under immense pressure to enact democratic reforms, and when the year 1848 began with a severe economic downturn, political revolutions broke out in Italy, France, and Germany. Inspired by events on the Continent, British Chartists were aroused to take one more shot at reforming the established order. Historian David Stack is correct when he states that "1848 ought to have been O'Brien's year. The convulsions on the Continent and the rising interest in socialism demanded a theorist capable of an international perspective and an understanding of social reform."[45] O'Connor was an inspiring presence in his role as leader of the Chartists, but it was an appeal built on bombast and the fervor of emotional rhetoric. He lacked the international perspective and theoretical depth that underpinned O'Brien's philosophy, but O'Brien no longer possessed the nerve, and lacked the widespread popular support, to assume any sort of meaningful leadership position.

O'Brien attended the Chartist Convention of 1848 and retained enough support within London to represent the city's workers as a convention delegate, but he was entirely out-of-step with the emotional disposition of his fellow representatives. Events on the Continent had roused the delegates to fully support O'Connor and the physical force Chartists, whereas O'Brien was part of a small minority who did not see the interests of the working classes as being honestly represented, and he urged caution. Nevertheless, because he was diametrically opposed to the tenor of the meetings and understood that he had little backing beyond his own small constituency, O'Brien recused himself from most of the debates. As a consequence, on April 13, just three days after the last great Chartist demonstration on Kennington Common, a rally in which several of his young followers took prominent roles, a motion was put forward to censure O'Brien for his frequent absences. The motion failed, and in its wake O'Brien resigned as a delegate to the Convention. However, O'Brien apparently was not humble enough in his resignation. In an effort to bestow one final humiliation, George Julian Harney, a onetime admirer of O'Brien's who had emerged as one of the most strident voices for physical force, moved for a motion to censure O'Brien for the disrespect he had shown for his fellow delegates. The motion passed, and it seemed as if O'Brien's career as a reformer was ended.[46]

As O'Brien had predicted, the tactics the physical force Chartists put forward were unwise and mistimed. The great demonstration for the People's Charter failed in 1848 just as it had been defeated on the two previous attempts to push it through Parliament. Nevertheless, whereas Chartism as a national movement fell into decline, O'Brien found himself in the unusual role of a cult hero and enjoyed an intellectual renaissance among a small group of his London followers. In hindsight it became clear that O'Brien had formulated a progressive land reform program and given the matter greater thought than had O'Connor, whereas O'Connor's plan appeared as a conservative sellout to landed elites.[47] Although he never regained the national prominence he had enjoyed prior to his imprisonment, O'Brien's fundamental philosophical principles remained unaltered, and his devotion to the six points of the People's Charter never wavered. O'Brien was intimately familiar with class oppression and, despite the fact that he switched his support from the physical force Chartists to the moral force Chartists, was consistent in his view of the state as an instrument of subjugation over the working classes. Therefore, as he had done since the beginning of his career, O'Brien promoted political parity as the means for attaining social equality. If England's laborers could be persuaded to unite fully behind the call for universal suffrage, then they would have the ability to elect a government that would be willing to use the legal power of the state to promote social justice for all citizens.[48]

The failure of the Chartist petition in 1848 coincided with the collapse of the socialist revolutions across the Continent. As conservative regimes throughout Europe effectively defended the status quo, many radical political agitators, either for their own safety or through sheer disillusionment, abandoned Europe for America. In Great Britain it was a transitional period for socialist reformers. Support for Chartist methods waned, while Marx's theory of scientific socialism began to supplant older models of utopian socialism. Bronterre O'Brien, however, never wavered. At forty-three years of age O'Brien was a political outcast with few career prospects, yet in the wake of the last Chartist petition he sought to keep alive the ideals of the Charter and the land nationalization proposals that he believed were the key to true social equality. Nevertheless, in the immediate aftermath of the Chartist movement a few of his friends and allies began to consider the emigration question and, in part because O'Brien was an ardent admirer of Maximilian Robespierre and a confirmed Francophile, the proposals they found most appealing came out of the tradition of French social utopianism. In particular, they became fascinated by a plan devised through the auspices of Étienne Cabet, a radical French reformer who in 1839 had penned a utopian novel entitled *Voyage en Icarie.*

In 1847, with the assistance of Robert Owen, Cabet had announced his intent to plant an Icarian cooperative colony in Texas. By February 1848 the first French colonists had departed for the United States. Cabet's plan for an Icarian cooperative colony was not as popular in Great Britain as it was in France, and it never captured the British imagination in the manner of Robert Owen's social utopianism. Nevertheless, Cabet did have English sympathizers willing to support his ventures.[49] Even the implacable followers of Bronterre O'Brien found the Christian brotherhood of Cabet's utopian vision appealing after the disappointing collapse of the Chartist movement. Although O'Brien's tactic of educating British working classes to press for their political rights at home remained unaltered, his lifelong fascination with the French Revolution and left-wing Parisian movements led him to commiserate with Cabet. He reluctantly conceded that emigration might be one of the few remaining methods available for British workers to obtain true social justice. O'Brien had no personal desire to partake in Cabet's experiment, but several of his followers concluded that Cabet's plan merited further investigation. In 1848 two of O'Brien's associates, John Ellis, a schoolmaster, and John Alexander, organized the North Texas Colonization Company with the goal of joining the French Icarians in America. O'Brien had an abiding interest in how this endeavor would play out. Therefore he did not vocalize any objections to his colleagues' plan, and in October 1848 he made a personal gesture of support by escorting Alexander and his wife, Sarah, to the London docks as Alexander and a number of other former Chartists boarded the passenger ship *Henry*. As he prepared to embark, Alexander promised O'Brien that he would write back to report upon the fate of the Icarian socialist venture.[50]

Born in Mauchline, Ayrshire, Scotland, in 1808, Alexander was a joiner by trade. He relocated to London in 1830, where he befriended Bronterre O'Brien and became one of his close associates. In 1848 Alexander was acting as an advance man for his organization. It was his goal to observe the progress of the French Icarians and to evaluate the suitability of Texas as a region appropriate for English labor cooperatives. As O'Brien wrote in retrospect: "He went, therefore, determined to see and judge for himself, and, ac-

cording to what he saw and experienced, to report fairly and faith-
fully for the guidance of his friends in this country . . . and of the
friends of National Reform, to whose principles he is thoroughly
wedded."[51] As an O'Brienite, Alexander was open to questioning
proposals and ideas that made little practical sense to him, plus his
fellow shipmates, with their blind faith in America and utter trust
in Cabet's promises, made such a small impression on him that he
became circumspect toward the project even before arriving in the
United States.

What Alexander found when the *Henry* docked in New Orleans on December 15, 1848, was even more disheartening. The first
wave of French Icarians had reached Louisiana in late March 1848,
where they learned from their own advance man that there was no
transportation available to the colony land in Texas. From Shreveport they would have to travel 250 miles into Texas on a footpath
known as the Bonham Road. Undaunted yet woefully unprepared
for what the Texas environment had in store, the French Icarians
set out for their promised utopia. After a summer of blazing heat
and humidity accompanied by bouts of malaria and dysentery,
the exhausted settlers gave up and straggled as they could back to
New Orleans. At least eight men died, and when Alexander disembarked in the Crescent City he found a fatigued and crestfallen
group of French refugees who were engaged in a heated debate on
whether to retreat back to France or await the imminent arrival of
Étienne Cabet.[52] While the Icarians bickered among themselves,
Alexander concluded that he had seen enough. Rather than sit idly
by and learn what Cabet might decide concerning the Icarian colony, Alexander decided to push on to Texas. However, rather than
repeat the French fiasco, Alexander headed for the established city
of Houston.

Like many who embraced the idealistic views of men such as
Owen, Cabet, and, to an extent, O'Brien, those who arrived on the
ship with Alexander labored under the illusory belief that equality of opportunity and full employment developed naturally when
governments lifted property restrictions from suffrage rights. While

more open-minded and realistic than his shipmates, Alexander was not entirely free from that delusion. Although he understood that the United States government was under the control of capitalist plutocrats, he still held out hope that the seemingly unrestricted frontier of the American West offered the best potential to find or create true social freedom. Alexander's experience in Texas, however, provided a sobering lesson that left him utterly disgusted with the United States and its citizens.

Epidemic disease, unemployment, and suffering were rampant in the Gulf Coast cities of New Orleans and Houston, and Alexander had difficulty obtaining work in either location. Freedom in this slave-holding region was evident only in the self-congratulatory press releases promoting the area, and the unquestioning praise Americans gave their government and social systems, in Alexander's opinion, only confirmed their ignorance. While Alexander was horror-struck over chattel slavery and offended by the provincialism of American religion and local government, he found himself compelled to give outward acceptance of all of them in order to survive in Texas. What he discovered corroborated what Stephen Pearl Andrews, an outspoken American abolitionist and social reformer whose writings would later become familiar to the O'Brienites, had learned five years earlier: that the denizens of Houston reacted in a violently hostile manner toward anyone brazen enough to vocalize an objection to slavery. Andrews barely escaped from Houston with his life.[53] Alexander never had to take flight, but because he was forced to acquiesce he discovered other flaws in the American system. In England Alexander had become accustomed to airing out his grievances within workingmen's associations, but Houston's slave-owning gentry would not countenance the threat of organized labor and had banned such meetings. Alexander was disconsolate and thoroughly revolted by what he witnessed. In a letter to O'Brien, Alexander wrote: "I expected to find America a few degrees better than England, but it is not — it is worse; it is, in fact, in a hopeless condition, as regards either moral, political, or intellectual progression."[54]

O'Brien published Alexander's biting critique of America in the May 1849 edition of *The Reformer* and, using Alexander's observations as verification of his earlier stance, reaffirmed his opposition to emigration. He argued that the people of the United States, regardless of that nation's claims to the contrary, enjoyed less freedom than did the British. Observing the experiences of ill-informed and poorly prepared utopian dreamers traipsing to America with thoughts of the Promised Land in mind, O'Brien felt exonerated in his belief that true freedom for laborers could not exist anywhere unless workers were educated in an understanding of their social rights and made responsible enough to hold the reins of government. O'Brien commented that democracy "without a knowledge of the true rights of property, universal suffrage, or the Charter itself, could be but a poor protection against the landlord and the money-lord."[55] With a sense of vindication stemming from Alexander's episode, O'Brien began renewing his calls for the workingmen of England to unite in the cause of social liberty at home.

In the aftermath of the failed uprising of 1848, British workers were anything but united and remained, as Malcolm Chase writes, "Chartists by conviction rather than enrolment." Ernest Jones's National Charter Association (NCA), the successor to O'Conner's old organization, struggled to keep Chartism viable as a unified movement, but the intellectual remnants of the moral and physical force Chartists fractured into numerous splinter groups, each claiming the mantle of Chartism.[56] Most were short-lived, and none outside of Jones ever managed to lay a legitimate claim upon the role of national leadership. As each of these groups dissolved, former Chartists were left feeling defeated and despondent. Many cast longing eyes toward Marx, author of the *Communist Manifesto*. One of the intellectual splinter groups, however, managed to keep the dream of the Charter alive for several decades, which was long enough for its members to play a role in shaping British, and to a degree American, political thought in the late nineteenth century. A small number of the moral force Chartists, which also attracted many who had been followers of Robert Owen, fell in behind the teachings of

O'Brien. O'Brien was less revolutionary and more inclined to raising ideas of class consciousness, but in the wake of Alexander's disastrous sojourn to America, O'Brien's following began to solidify.

During the winter months of 1848-49, Bronterre O'Brien delivered a series of lectures at the John Street Literary and Scientific Institution, an Owenite socialist organization that offered a forum to
radical speakers from differing associations. A number of former
Chartists attended these talks, but a core group of seventy-eight
regular attendees were transfixed by what they heard and wanted the discussion forum to continue indefinitely. Thus, when the
lecture series ended, O'Brien's devotees formed themselves into a
new social grouping called the Eclectic Club.[57] These men were seasoned veterans of Chartism, most young but some from the movement's earliest days, and the steps they took within the society ensured that O'Brien's interpretation of Chartist ideas would persevere
to influence the next generation of reform activists. In September
1849 club members resolved to form, in the words of Alfred Plummer, "a new propagandist body to press forward the cause of political and social reform."[58] The resolution advanced at a vigorous
pace, and by December 1849 O'Brien and John Rogers, a staunch
ally from the Central National Association of 1837 and a founding
member of the old London Working Men's Association, compiled
a summary plan of objectives of what was to become the National
Reform League for the Peaceful Regeneration of Society. This was
the body that became the institutional foundation for the Kansas
colony.

Published in 1850, the outline for the National Reform League
(NRL) endorsed the People's Charter but incorporated seven essential points that O'Brien deemed necessary to ensure real and permanent political and social justice. Although "the 'People's Charter' is a *sine quá non* with the League," wrote O'Brien, "it is, after
all, but a machinery for providing the *means* to an *end*. The *means*
is parliamentary reform; the *end* is social reform, or a reformation
of society through the operation of just and humane laws."[59] Therefore, O'Brien's agenda for the NRL was articulated as a series of sev-

en social reforms that would "ensure real political and social justice to the oppressed and suffering population of the United Kingdom, and to protect society from violent revolutionary changes."[60] The seven-point plan, disseminated in greater detail in a series of essays written during this time but published posthumously as *The Rise, Progress, and Phases of Human Slavery*, mirrored the Spencean land reform program he had advocated in 1837, the currency reform issue he had inherited from William Cobbett, and his abhorrence of the British Poor Law.

O'Brien's first goal was to equalize society, and to accomplish this he proposed eliminating the existing poor laws and replacing them with a rate system levied upon the owners of property. The collected monies would be equitably distributed among the destitute poor until such time as they could be rendered self-sustaining and self-respecting. Second, O'Brien's NRL wanted a system of Home Colonization, or a program in which the government purchased land with the express purpose of resettling the urban poor on acreage leased from the government or in industrial communities not unlike those proposed by Robert Owen. Third, a progressive tax wherein the burdens of taxation and of public and private debts would be adjusted in favor of debtors and those engaged in productive professions. O'Brien's intent was for the first three points to provide immediate relief to the working poor. Thus those points were provisional.

The final four points were designed to be permanent and make lasting, radical changes. These were the points that became the basis for the Kansas colony. Point four was that the NRL wanted nationalization of the land to be accomplished gradually. As trustee of all land, mines, turbaries, and fisheries, the government should lease the land and use the collected rents to finance public work and service projects. Fifth, it was deemed the duty of the state to provide a sound system of credit, which would allow individuals to rent and cultivate the land without being subject to the whims of the money-lords or the tyranny of wage-slavery. In a bow to Cobbett, the NRL's sixth point declared that the national currency should be based upon real, consumable wealth — the labor of its people — or upon the legal credit of the government. Basing currency upon the uncertain value or availability of scarce metals was a sham designed to benefit the speculating classes. The final point detailed a plan for a labor exchange with publicly owned stores established in every town and village. Operated by "disinterested officers," these labor exchanges would place an exchangeable value on goods and services based upon either a corn or labor standard. Depositors would receive symbolic notes, which would become the legal currency of the land and could be used to draw from the public stores to an equivalent amount.[61]

Following the counsel of several NRL members, O'Brien leased an empty chapel at 18 Denmark Street in London's Soho district. Renamed the Eclectic Institute, or Eclectic Hall, the building became the NRL's permanent home for the next quarter century.[62] On January 7, 1851, the Eclectic Institute officially opened its doors to the public as the NRL held its inaugural meeting in the new facility. In his foundational address, O'Brien renewed his commitment to the organizational objectives he had outlined a year earlier and stressed the importance of all members remaining true to the principles of the National Reform League. Although O'Brien was preaching to the choir, the NRL membership quickly followed through on his words. Throughout his career as a Chartist, time and again O'Brien had found himself frustrated over what he perceived as the apathy of London area workers or their overall inability to comprehend advanced socialist principles. More to the point, Iorwerth Prothero has argued that O'Brien was of the mind "that democracy was of no use if the people did not understand socialism and that it would even be positively harmful."[63] Therefore, in addition to organizing the NRL as a political activist group, O'Brien transformed the Eclectic Hall into an educational institution. Reminiscent of O'Brien's own schooling at Edgeworthstown, where in the monitorial system of pedagogy the advanced students taught the beginners, NRL members offered "Eclectic Young Men's Educational Classes" in English grammar and composition, French, mathematics, and sciences. O'Brien devoted his own time to raising the political consciousness of his students by delivering weekday lectures and Sunday discourses on the finer points of his philosophy.[64] Like other intellectual Chartists, O'Brien held that adult education programs, libraries, and a fluency in literature were essential to political liberation.[65]

Although O'Brien's health and relationships with other reform leaders began to deteriorate in the 1850s, the Eclectic Hall remained vibrant enough to draw the attention of Marx, who in 1852 alerted his colleague Friedrich Engels to the appearance of Ernest Jones at the institute.[66] The reality of the situation was that O'Brien's strength had declined significantly, which meant that the effective day-to-day leadership of the NRL was passing into the hands of his disciples. Nevertheless, in 1854 O'Brien remained vigorous enough to take a strong stance in denouncing Great Britain's involvement in the Crimean War. O'Brien stated in no uncertain terms that peace at any price was too high a cost for a man who believed in international socialism.[67] The Crimea, however, did not represent a case of self-defense for the British or of defending worker sovereignty. O'Brien therefore interpreted the war in terms of the class struggle and thought it a hypocritical tool designed "to rob, impoverish and decimate the industrious classes, for the gain of feudal tyrants, usurers and commercial vampires, speculating in the blood and calamities of their fellow creatures." He argued that military adventurism deterred democratic reforms while increasing taxes on politically unrepresented laborers, thus throwing more workers into debt and pauperism.[68]

With talk of the war dominating political discourse and O'Brien's access to the Chartist press in decline, a few younger members of the NRL began to grow disillusioned with prospects of reform in England. Since its inception, the NRL had been introducing O'Brien's theories of social reform to young men who had become politically active during the 1848 Chartist uprising. Many lacked the patience that comes with maturity and wanted to see their mentor proven correct in the here and now. But with the war derailing political

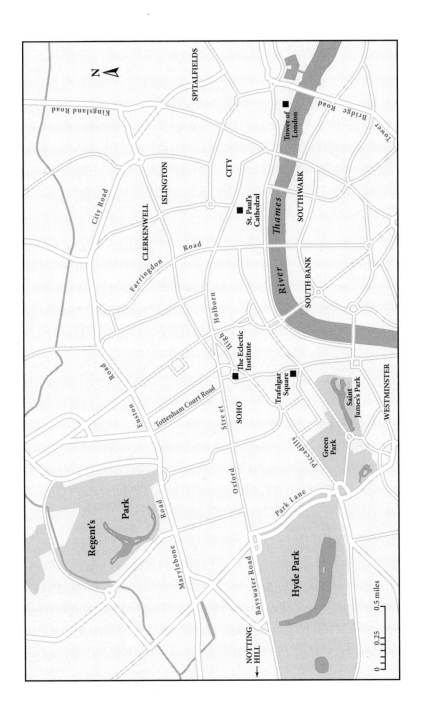

discussions of reform for the foreseeable future, there seemed little chance of progress. Therefore, without O'Brien's sanction, some of these young men introduced a motion to the NRL that it was time to reexplore the possibility of establishing workingmen's cooperatives in the United States. They did not envision Cabet's Icarian colonies as John Alexander earlier had investigated. Instead these would be colonies built upon O'Brienite principles. Consequently two men, John Days, age twenty-three, and George Murray, age twenty-two, volunteered to undertake the task of seeking out favorable locations for a settlement. They had no specific destination in mind other than to find a garden-like Arcadia somewhere in the Far West of America. According to later accounts, Murray and Days went west to locate "amidst the defiles of the Rocky Mountains some fertile valley where there could be built upon a basis of justice, a new order of society." Based upon O'Brien's principles as outlined in the NRL charter, equity rather than material profit was to be the cornerstone of a new social order that would permit subsequent ages to "be free from the corruption, vice, degradation, and misery, which enshroud the prospects of the present and future generations of England."[69]

Like Alexander's earlier foray into America, the NRL's first formal flirtation with emigration and utopianism ended in disaster and disappointment. In May 1854 Murray and Days booked berths aboard the passenger ship *Germanicus* and departed Liverpool bound for New Orleans. When the ship arrived in Louisiana on June 13, Murray, who was physically weakened from the sea voyage, fell ill. Both London and New Orleans suffered an outbreak of cholera in 1854, and it remains unclear whether Murray contracted the contagion in London, New Orleans, or onboard ship. However, shortly after docking he succumbed to the dreaded disease and died without ever leaving the port city.[70] Regardless of where the pair's original destination may have been, after Murray's passing Days continued his westward journey. He gathered himself together and traveled north to Missouri, then made the difficult overland trek to Oregon Territory. He remained only a short time and soon moved down the coast to the fertile gold fields of California. Although the official expedition died with Murray, in fairness to Days he did not capitulate to gold fever, and he sincerely worked to fulfill his mission objectives. Despite Marx's generalization that the "discoveries of immense gold-lands led to an immense exodus, leaving an irreparable void in the ranks of the British proletariat,"[71] Days did not contribute to Marx's perceived void. He settled in the mining community of Grass Valley, maintained a correspondence with his colleagues in London, and became an activist within California state politics. While trying to convince others in the NRL of the possibilities America offered, Days served as a schoolteacher, helped found a town library, and became a community organizer. No hopeful English colonists followed him to Grass Valley, and NRL members tabled proposals of building a model community in the United States for the foreseeable future.

The seeds of disorder were present within the NRL. Despite the failure of Days's mission, others within the group continued to cast longing looks across the Atlantic and dreaming of utopia. As early as 1853, NRL member Ambrose Caston Cuddon became a convert to American anarchist Josiah Warren's philosophy and went outside NRL auspices to form the London Confederation of Rational Reformers. The LCRR was a noteworthy group that adopted a reform ideal its members called "reverse of the Communistic." The organization pursued a restructuring of society through an interpretation of Warren's principles that argued against collective benefits; rather, "a *segregation*, instead of an *aggregation*" of interests.[72]

Warren, a former disciple of Robert Owen, had been a member of Owen's 1825–27 New Harmony, Indiana, experiment in communalism. He was convinced that New Harmony failed because of Owen's fixation on community instead of individual needs, which, in Warren's interpretation, exacerbated the very social antagonisms that the model settlement had been expected to remove. Therefore, Warren took it upon himself to reorganize Owen's philosophy into a program he called the "Sovereignty of the Individual." He theorized that only separation of interests, self-government, and reliance on individual responsibility could bring about an equitable society. To this he fused the idea of "cost the limit of price," which was an economic theory based upon an equitable labor exchange not unlike the system found in O'Brien's NRL charter.[73] Warren repeatedly attempted to prove the practicality of his ideas, starting after the 1827 collapse of New Harmony with a small-scale test of "cost the limit of price" in a Time Store in Cincinnati, Ohio, and culminating in 1851 when he joined the New England abolitionist Stephen Pearl Andrews in creating a utopian colony called Modern Times in Brentwood, New York. Warren's letters from Modern Times thoroughly impressed many of O'Brien's disciples within the NRL and, though few followed Cuddon into the LCRR, they eagerly sought out the American reformer's thoughts on O'Brien's social philosophy while simultaneously gaining inspiration from Warren's experience.

A crucial aspect of O'Brien's philosophical canon was universal suffrage followed by land nationalization. Presaging the American Henry George's 1879 thoughts on public ownership of the land, O'Brien taught that private ownership of the land led to monetary speculation and mass accumulations of property, by which a few privileged individuals grew wealthy at the expense of the working classes. Warren found this notion absurd and explained to Cuddon that the London O'Brienites did not "fully grasp the whole of our issue with the world's wrongs." Suggestions of nationalization, or holding all property in common, made no sense to Warren because his anarchist worldview repudiated the very idea of a nation or state. "The ownership of the soil," Warren wrote, "must be absolute in the Individual." Citizens could conduct the purchase and sale of land on the principle of cost the limit of price, which remunerated only the human labor expended in the transaction. Warren subscribed to the naïve belief that a public sense of justice would guarantee his program's success while simultaneously destroying "all landlordism, profitmong[er]ing, or usury based upon traffic in the soil."[74] Warren's radical theories failed to completely convince members of the NRL. However, for a group searching for signs of progress in the advancement of social justice, Warren's theories backed by his practical experience had a definite allure.

Although it dissolved in 1863, Josiah Warren's anarchist society at Modern Times fascinated O'Brien's London followers. They looked to it as a model worthy of emulation. Cuddon made two excursions from London to visit with Warren and Andrews and to study the New York colony.[75] He found Warren's willingness to do more than just talk about reform refreshing and expressed his personal frustration with the seemingly endless posturing of London's intellectual reformers. They comprised "the most reputable [and] most advanced minds," Cuddon wrote. While such men were capable of "some very eloquent speaking," all they aimed for was "universal suffrage [and] vote by ballot." London's trade unions and cooperative societies were equally malodorous to Cuddon, who saw them as seeking only to obtain the "profits of trade" for themselves."[76] While Cuddon's admiration for Warren and vexation with the glacial pace of radical reform in Great Britain was not representative of the NRL, it did illuminate a willingness of many remaining within the group to modify aspects of Chartist and O'Brienite principles. As late as 1867, four years after the demise of Modern Times, NRL member George Harris disseminated a narrative article to praise the colony and ensure that the lessons of this "equity village" remained alive. Harris wrote that what Josiah Warren accomplished at Modern Times was "better than the so-called reformers *pretending* to something higher, nobler, better [than] themselves." He lauded Warren's comment that the colony "was one step towards developing means and modes for the relief of the suffering classes, by opening opportunities for them to get bread, and by degrees to obtain a successful life."[77] Cuddon, Harris, and others never addressed their frustration toward O'Brien by name. Throughout his life O'Brien had remained faithful to Chartist demands and distanced himself from those who were willing to settle for the lesser goal of organizing workers into a pressure group on liberalism's radical left wing. However, the message was unmistakable. Certain members of the NRL were ready to approach reform from a different direction.

In the mid-1850s leadership of the NRL was transitioning to a younger generation of reformers, and during this time, in the words of Margot Finn, Charles Murray emerged as the group's most "vociferous critic of liberal economics."[78] Charles, who was born in 1823 or 1824, and his brother James F. Murray, born in 1830, had risen to distinction during the final Chartist uprising in 1848. James had been one of the young O'Brienites delivering fiery speeches during the last great Chartist rally on Kennington Common. Within the NRL, however, it was Charles who assumed the more prominent position. As the Crimean War distracted workers from issues of reform, and as O'Brien's health continued to falter, Murray provided focus for a group that was vacillating from O'Brien's lessons and threatening to splinter apart. Rather than seek out new land or philosophies in America, Murray reminded his colleagues that O'Brien's teaching on land nationalization at home provided the key to political and social reform. Using O'Brien's own argument from 1849 Murray wrote: "I defy all the genius and statesmanship of the world to save a population from being the slaves of the middle class vampires so long as land is private property."[79]

Emigration solved nothing and left the middle classes unchallenged as they exploited those workers who remained behind. The solution, said Murray, was reform at home where the "Political and Social Rights of the People must be recognized" and the people should be educated in their "Social Rights relative to Land, Currency, and Equitable Exchange." As far as land in England was concerned, Murray minced no words. "It is not the subdivision of the soil, that is required, so much as the right of occupation; let the land become National Property, on the principle of Government compensation to existing holders; abolish private ownership of the soil, and you thereby destroy the power of one Class to make slaves of another."[80]

Again quoting O'Brien, Murray lamented that he failed to understand how it would be possible to "be extricated from poverty and premature death in this country without a radical reform of our land and money laws, unless there be a general scramble for property, to be followed by a re-beginning of society, *de nova*, which, in my estimate, would amount to a massacre of one-half of the population, and a launching of the other half upon an unknown sea, without chart or compass." Despite this pessimistic outlook for the future, Murray used the light of O'Brien's philosophy to illuminate the path to salvation. "But if a few honest laws upon Land, Credit, Currency, and Exchange would at once stop social misery and social murder on the one hand, and guarantee the owners of property on the other, against spoliation and anarchy, *ought not every honest man, of every class, to give me his aid to create a public opinion in their favour?*"[81]

Murray's single-minded contempt for the middle classes mirrored O'Brien's own and helped center a group that might otherwise have drifted apart. O'Brien was no longer a high profile activist, but his earlier work of establishing the NRL's Eclectic Hall as an educational center for young workers now seemed prescient and was beginning to reap rewards as new adherents lined up behind Murray. A leading light among the acolytes joining the group during this period was John Radford, who would become a significant figure in the later Kansas colony. Born in Devon, England, on March 23, 1834, Radford was the son of William Radford, a shepherd. Little is known of John Radford's early life, but in later years he related that he relocated to London in 1846 and lived the hardscrabble existence of a boy trying to survive on anything honorable "by which he could turn a penny." While he likely witnessed the final rally for the People's Charter in 1848, there is no record of his having been an active participant. Instead, Radford began attending "night schools, lyceums, and mechanics' institutes" and soon found his way to the Eclectic Hall. He became learned in a trade, and for "seven long years he was apprenticed to an enameler and engraver, at which trade he worked twelve years in all."[82] In 1856 he married Mary Days, the sister of NRL member John Days who had gone to California, and soon thereafter he was collaborating with the Murray brothers in the NRL.

The Murray brothers were far from quiet and, as Stan Shipley notes, saw no good reason to apologize for being working-class men. A prime opportunity came in May 1857 when Robert Owen, who celebrated his eighty-seventh birthday that month, convened in London a Congress of Advanced Minds of the World. In a nature versus nurture debate, Owen's premise was, as it had been for many decades, "that the character of man is formed *for* him, and not *by* him." The middle and working classes must unite, and competition must be abandoned "in the production of the necessaries of life." For Owen the only conclusion was that the millennium of harmonious cooperation between the classes "would only be reached with the help of Spiritual Manifestations." Owen's belief system had remained unchanged for many years, and Charles Murray was ready for him. Murray found the concept that all of mankind was by nature good to be absurd. He rebutted Owen with the flat-out statement that middle-class capitalists were not crafty, callous, and covetous because of corrupting influences; they had become capitalists precisely because they were by nature evil men. Murray fully understood that he was making a sweeping generalization and, as he detailed in his earlier letter to Holyoake, confessed that "men of soul — men of heart — men of principle" could be found within the middle class, but such individuals were "noble exceptions" to the general rule. With no small hint of irony, Murray wanted it clearly understood that "I do not blame the individual members of those classes for being such: because it is an unjust and tyrannical form of society, and every man born to it must either be a victimiser or a victim."[83]

The Murray brothers found a kindred spirit in Radford. The young neophyte fully embraced Bronterre O'Brien's radical philosophy and was willing to stand up in defense of the ideals he had come to admire. While Radford was not up to the level of publicly debating a legendary figure like Robert Owen, by January 1858 he was honing his oratorical skills and had readily taken his place on the platform alongside other NRL members. In what was one of his earliest public addresses, Radford made it plain that he "deprecated any alliance with the middle classes until they recognised the rights of labour. To

unite with them in giving a small measure of reform would be suicidal; for it would give them more power than ever they possessed
to tyrannise over labour."[84] The sentiment was vintage O'Brien and
certainly in agreement with the model Charles Murray had established for the NRL to follow. Murray took the young activist under his wing, and in 1859 Radford was lodging in Murray's household.[85] O'Brien certainly had reason to be proud of both Murray's
and Radford's efforts, but as Radford was becoming increasingly
active within the NRL, O'Brien entered into his final decline.

Bronterre O'Brien never regained his health, and his financial
poverty meant that his family lived on the edge of desperation.
He remained active through the 1850s, and as late as 1858 O'Brien,
Charles Murray, and others in the NRL were reiterating calls to support the People's Charter through the National Political Union.
Marx did not respect O'Brien as a political operative, and the old
reformer's stubborn dedication to the Charter prompted Marx to
snipe in an 1858 letter to Engels that O'Brien was "an irrepressible
Chartist at any price."[86] O'Brien remained attentive to current political developments and could, at times, be as sharp as ever. However, he could not work on a daily basis, and his mental agility was
diminished because of the physical wreck he had become. Industrial London, particularly in the working-class districts where O'Brien
resided, was a crowded nightmare of dark, unsanitary streets and
an atmosphere thick with coal smoke. O'Brien had lived a hard life
deprived of comfort and medical care. The end result was that by
1861 bronchitis had embraced him in its fatal grip. David Stack records that in 1862 O'Brien once again contemplated emigration, but
his chronic bouts of bronchitis and increasing inability to get out
of bed would have made such a move impossible.[87]

For O'Brien, who by this time was lodging with Charles Murray,
the end was neither merciful nor quick. His bronchitis grew progressively worse until 1864 when it developed into what doctors diagnosed as "dropsy of the pulmonary circulation." Finding it ever
more difficult to breathe, O'Brien could no longer lie down and
spent the final, painful year of his life propped upright by pillows.

After months of suffering, on December 23, 1864, he passed away. Upon learning of O'Brien's death, the French poet Victor Hugo eulogized: "Progress, democracy, and liberty have lost much in losing the valiant and generous man whom you deplore. Let us not, however, mourn without hope. The dead, such as O'Brien, live, for they leave behind them their example."[88]

Charles Murray took charge of the funeral arrangements and scheduled the burial for December 31 in Abney Park Cemetery. Abney Park was the perfect choice for a figure like O'Brien. Established in 1840, the cemetery was designed specifically as a nonconformist garden open to people of all religious and political persuasions. The intent was for Abney Park to be a landmark of religious toleration, and the grounds were never consecrated by any sectarian group. The unconventional, egalitarian nature of the cemetery made it attractive to secular radicals like the O'Brienites, and Bronterre O'Brien subsequently become one of the more notable individuals interred on the grounds.

The O'Brienite faithful gathered in the small chapel on the grounds of Abney Park Cemetery for the interment. It was an intimate affair and devoid of the massive crowds that marked the funerals of other Chartist leaders. In O'Brien's instance, however, the number of attendees was not what made the services significant. While the mourners paid tribute to O'Brien the man and grieved over the loss of a "revered teacher," they celebrated his commitment to the People's Charter and vowed to remain faithful to his principles. The NRL was well represented at the memorial service. John Rogers, who had known O'Brien since the 1830s, and John Radford, who represented the next generation of reformers, were among those given the honored duty of delivering eulogies over the gravesite. With the final ceremonies concluded and the body laid to rest, the attendees performed a significant act of supplication: "a large proportion of those assembled walked up to the grave, and, with hands extended over it, pledged themselves in the most solemn manner to a lifelong adherence to, and zealous propagation of, the doctrine of the deceased."[89]

Passionate devotion to O'Brien's principles was an oath that members of the NRL ardently fulfilled. The O'Brienites were vocal in their support of international republican movements throughout the 1860s, and when the International Working Men's Association (IWMA) formed in September 1864, O'Brien's followers were there. The IWMA was notable for the prominent role Marx and Engels played in its development and stands as the symbolic beginning of the modern international communist movement, but for many English workers at the time, the International represented a continuity of the ideals they had been fighting for since the days of the People's Charter. In reality the IWMA was a loose and argumentative alliance of socialists, anarchists, trade unionists, utopian idealists, and mutualist reformers who joined to overthrow the capitalist system. The NRL was certainly involved at the creation and, even as O'Brien lay on his death bed, several high-profile O'Brienites assumed key positions in the IWMA. While Marx became leader of the IWMA General Council, NRL members Charles Murray, Martin Boon, George Harris, and George Milner took seats on the council. Two other O'Brienites, William Townshend and Alfred A. Walton, later served on the council. More than individual members, the NRL as an organization affiliated with the IWMA and, by doing so, lent a sense of continuity to the proceedings. The NCA had ceased operations in 1858, which meant that by the time of the International the NRL was the sole surviving Chartist association and provided the IWMA with its only organizational link to the Chartist era. The NRL's influence was genuine, and after 1867 meetings of the London section of the International were held in the Eclectic Hall.[90]

Members of the NRL were deeply involved with the IWMA and conversant with Marx's concept of the dialectic. However, they refused to fall into lockstep with Marx and were adamant that fulfillment of the O'Brienite principles they held dear remain paramount. In fact, a decade later Charles Murray reflected that O'Brien's doctrine of "just laws on land, credit, currency, and exchange" were "identical with those on which the international was based."[91] This devotion to O'Brien's philosophy exasperated Marx, who at one point complained: George Harris and Martin Boon "belong to the sect of the late Bronterre O'Brien, and are full of follies and crotchets, such as currency quackery, false emancipation of women, and the like."[92]

Marx had little tolerance for ideas that deviated from his own, and as the International progressed, he began to suspect that Harris and Boon were engaged in unauthorized correspondence with the anarchist-minded Section 12 of the IWMA in New York. His wariness was not without justification. Section 12, established in 1869, was headed by former Modern Times colony cofounder Stephen Pearl Andrews and American feminist leader Victoria Woodhull. Andrews had been part of the IWMA from the beginning and, through his affiliation with Modern Times, was friendly with Harris and other O'Brienites. Section 12 irritated Marx because Woodhull and Andrews had the temerity to amend his labor doctrine with statements of support for women's suffrage, free love, and Andrews's concept of a universal language.[93] Marx had less patience for anarchist ideas than he did for the "follies and crotchets" of the O'Brienites, and he worked to expel Section 12 and other anarchist groups from the International. Unlike the despised anarchists, he was inclined to put up with O'Brien's followers because, as he conceded, they constituted "an often necessary counterweight to trade unionists on the Council. They are more revolutionary, firmer on the land question, less nationalistic, and not susceptible to bourgeois bribery in one form or another. Otherwise they would have been kicked out long ago."[94] The truth was, as Edward Royle found, that the O'Brienites "provided Marx with the most ideologically aggressive members of the International."[95]

Marx's inability to countenance interpretations of socialism other than his own ensured that the NRL would not relinquish its distinct identity by giving unquestioning support to the IWMA. O'Brien had designed the NRL to educate British workers in matters of political equality and social reform so that collectively they would have the means and understanding to rise up peacefully through the ballot box. His disciples in the NRL remained committed to this ideal after the death of their mentor and, while dedicated to wresting government away from middle-class control, never fully embraced Marx's call for an international communist revolution. Harris gave voice to the group's sentiments when he opined: "There is a trite saying that those who wish reform, must first *begin at home.*"[96]

NRL delegates serving in the IWMA were disappointed with Marx's obstinacy to issues they held as sacred. Years later Townshend, a man who spent ninety sessions on the IWMA General Council butting heads with Marx, recollected that the author of *The Communist Manifesto* "thought us valuable members of the Council in order to counterbalance the Capitalist-Liberal influence of some of the Trade Union members, but he rather made fun of currency reform." He went on to lament, "I wish Bronterre O'Brien had lived a few years longer; he would have been the man to argue currency reform matters out with Marx; none of us could."[97] Realistically, there was scarcely anything groundbreaking that Marx could offer the O'Brienites concerning the role of capitalists in worker oppression or theories about the class struggle. In his 1859 dissertation on Robespierre, O'Brien wrote: "For, let me here, at the outset, apprise the reader that no truthful history of the revolution has yet appeared, nor ever can appear, until there be another revolution, which shall rescue the populations of Europe from the fangs of the middle classes, whose present social position gives them both the will and the power to effectively crush all such attempted publications, and all who may be daring enough to undertake them."[98] O'Brien had already defined the class struggle for the NRL, and no argument from Marx could sway them to a different interpretation.

Because of O'Brien's emphasis on removing the despised middle class from its position of privilege, the O'Brienites remained involved in all aspects of reform, and this included the Reform League. The Reform League had formed in the aftermath of Giuseppe Garibaldi's 1863 visit and remained active and resolutely committed to universal suffrage and vote by ballot. The 1865 victory for the Union in the American Civil War and the fall of chattel slavery, the vilest form of worker oppression, provided no small measure of inspiration for democratic movements. Bowing to the pressure, in 1866 William

Gladstone, leader of the majority Whig Party, introduced in Parliament what has since come to be known as the First Reform Bill.[99] The O'Brienites supported the measure, but when it was killed in Parliamentary committee, James Murray of the NRL spoke for many reform advocates when in September 1866 he said: "Let no man believe . . . any social reform possible until the House of Commons is rescued . . . through the enfranchisement of the adult males of the population."[100] Massive protests followed, and when accompanied by a severe economic downturn, Chancellor of the Exchequer Benjamin Disraeli of the new Tory government introduced the Second Reform Bill. The Reform Bill of 1867 passed and did enfranchise all male householders with twelve months residence, but in order to garner support from conservatives the bill contained redistribution clauses that left rural areas overrepresented in Parliament. The bill ensured that an expanded urban vote would do nothing to undermine the influence of landed interests. The intent was to water down the bill's effect and protect conservative power in government from radical working-class influences.[101]

The Tory Reform Bill effectively doubled the electorate but did so by undercutting liberal efforts to make government more democratic and ensuring that the status quo would remain unchanged for the foreseeable future. The Reform Act of 1867 was a disappointing piece of legislation, and in its wake members of the NRL once again began to consider ideas of emigration and building utopian colonies modeled on O'Brien's philosophy. Throughout 1867, George Harris had been publishing articles in the *Working Man* in praise of Josiah Warren and what he accomplished at Modern Times. Harris's infatuation with Warren was more apparent than with any other O'Brienite, and this was reflected in his rhetoric. In the midst of the Reform Bill debate, Harris stated: "The sovereignty of the people must remain a mere phrase until the *Sovereignty of the individual* is recognised and developed. It must be the sovereignty of the *units* that shall perfect the sovereignty of the aggregate." After passage of the Reform Act, Harris suggested: "Where there is 'union' there can be no freedom — no liberty; and whenever there is an absence of these, there can be neither truth nor justice."[102] Harris mixed Warren's terminology with his O'Brienite sentiments and argued that no reform could take place until the government recognized the suffrage rights of all. While he stressed a harmonization of interests, his pessimistic outlook that truth, liberty, and justice were absent from Britain was a sentiment shared by many in the NRL.

Three years after O'Brien's death, members of the NRL had a great deal of which to be proud. They continued to honor the Chartist tradition and adhered to their mentor's philosophy with gritty determination. The NRL enjoyed the prestige of being the sole surviving Chartist organization still operating in London and maintained a successful educational center at the Eclectic Institute. Its members retained prominent positions in the IWMA and on its General Council. They were at the forefront of radical political agitation throughout the period. From their perspective, however, any sense of accomplishment may have seemed small. The 1867 Reform Bill was an unsatisfactory piece of legislation that fulfilled none of the NRL's stated objectives, and in the IWMA Marx remained obtuse toward their ideas on currency reform and other aspects of the O'Brienite canon. Yet they remained steadfast in their beliefs and refused to give an inch. Thus, as the year 1867 came to a close, members of the NRL were as determined as ever to prove to the world that, if given the proper setting, the economic and social philosophy of Bronterre O'Brien could succeed. All they needed was an opportunity.

2

High Moral Chivalry

———∞∞∞———

The Mutual Land, Emigration, and Cooperative Colonization Company

Once allow the soil of a country, which God made for all its
inhabitants, and for all generations born upon it, to be bought up,
or otherwise monopolized or usurped by any particular section
of any one generation (be that section large or small), and that
moment your community is divided into tyrants and slaves — into
knaves who will work for nobody, and drudges who will have to
work for anybody or everybody but themselves.

—JAMES BRONTERRE O'BRIEN, ca. 1850

For many working-class radicals, particularly those who had labored
in the field of political equity and social justice as long as members
of the National Reform League (NRL) had, the reform legislation
of 1867 was deeply frustrating. The O'Brienite members of the NRL
were resolute in the belief that Bronterre O'Brien's philosophy held
the key to economic prosperity and social happiness, but without
the political means to enact their program there were few signs of
progress. They continued hosting the London section of the International Working Men's Association (IWMA) at the Eclectic Hall and
pressed the NRL's agenda in IWMA General Council meetings with
Karl Marx, but to little avail. A peaceful transformation of society at
home through a workforce united at the ballot box, nationalization
of the land, and currency reform that would end predatory, speculative practices continued as the NRL's utmost priority. Regardless
of their own association's principles or how steeped the O'Brienites

had become in Marx's scientific socialism, theirs was the only Chartist organization that remained active, and their mentor's philosophy, in many ways, was reflective of what Friedrich Engels derided as utopian socialism. The NRL was not above dabbling in utopian ideas, and O'Brienites previously had made two abortive attempts to plant a utopian colony in America. It had been many years since the NRL's only sanctioned effort in 1854, but following passage of the odious Reform Bill, a colleague from the past came back to reignite the group's passion for communitarian experimentation.

When the NRL sent John Days and George Murray to the United States in 1854, it had been with the intent of scouting out suitable locations in the Rocky Mountains for a workingmen's settlement. The colony never materialized. Following the death of Murray immediately upon the duo's arrival in New Orleans, Days relocated to Nevada County, California. The mission seemingly terminated at that point, and the NRL tabled the issue. Days, however, had not conceded defeat. Although no one followed him to plant a cooperative colony in California, he did maintain contact with his London colleagues. Despite the allure of the California gold fields, Days remained true to his O'Brienite instruction. He became an educator and labored for many years on behalf of miners in his adopted home of Grass Valley. By 1867 Days had won election on the Union Party ticket as a representative from Nevada County to the California State Legislature. Over the course of Days's elective career he fought corruption in the Insurance Commissioner's office, advocated for the protection of mine laborers, called for the removal of the word "male" from the state constitution, and pressed for the O'Brienite-style reform of breaking up large landholdings.[1] In June 1868, following his first year in office, Days made a triumphal return to London and earned the adulation of his old friends.

Members of the NRL held a soiree for Days at John Radford's residence in London's Clerkenwell district to pay tribute to his success in California. Radford, as chair of the meeting, immediately made note of the "remarkable and interesting circumstances of the occasion." In congratulating their guest, Charles Murray spoke for the group when he praised Days's ongoing commitment to O'Brien's philosophy. Murray stated that the NRL "expresses its admiration and satisfaction at his continued and unswerving adhesion to early imbibed principles from that great man, and for his active propagation of those principles in the distinguished and influential position he now fills by virtue of the votes of his fellow citizens in the great republic of America." The reception and testimonials gratified Days, but he had come for more than simply to renew old acquaintances. Fourteen years earlier he had been appointed as an advance scout to evaluate the American West on its suitability for a workingmen's colony and was back to deliver his recommendation. While Days was moved to find so many of his old colleagues "and fellow disciples of their beloved teacher, Bronterre O'Brien, still united, and actively doing battle in the good and great cause of human advancement and liberty," he had not come to rejoin them. Days had responsibilities in California, but before leaving he had to answer the question of colonization. His response was that working conditions were difficult in America, particularly in the mines. Nevertheless, Days believed that American workers possessed many political and social advantages over their brethren in Great Britain, his own rise up the political ladder being a case in point. Days's final judgment was that the NRL should move forward, find a suitable location in the United States, and plant the colony it had first discussed many years earlier.[2]

In 1870, while reflecting back on the 1868 meeting with Days, Radford recalled: "Thus, the hopes which had smouldered for fourteen years were again revived, and resolute action was immediately taken to put the same into operation." The conversation with Days electrified the group. According to Murray, after discussing "the advisability of the emigration of advanced reformers to favourable spots in America, and the advantages of colonisation upon the basis of the principles contained in the seven propositions of the National Reform League," members of the NRL found themselves receptive to the proposal. The meeting attendees therefore "unanimously resolved to communicate with the United States Government upon the subject of the acquirement of land." Radford waxed a bit more poetic and stated that the information Days delivered to the NRL led those in attendance "to devote their lives to the founding of the colony in the Far West of the United States, where the political rights guaranteed under the 'Stars and Stripes' would enable intelligent and just men to organise a better order of social existence than now prevails."[3]

Before adjourning, the members chose an executive committee and elected Edward Grainger Smith to take a prominent role as corresponding secretary. His first duty was to open a line of communication with government officials in the United States. Smith had been with the NRL only since the early 1860s but was a seasoned veteran of the Chartist era. Born in 1815, Smith earned a living as a carpenter and cabinetmaker. He resided in London and, although not counted among the speakers, was likely in attendance at the last great Chartist rallies of 1848. He became one of many who grew disillusioned with prospects for reform in England and in 1852 emigrated to New York. He spent eight years in America, but after 1860 he returned to London and soon became active with the NRL. It was in deference to his several years' experience abroad that Smith received the responsibility of corresponding secretary. A focused individual devoted to O'Brien's philosophical canon or, as Radford described, "one who had lived to advance the cause of human freedom," Smith was a solid choice to act as the committee spokesperson.[4]

Smith's appointment as corresponding secretary demonstrated that members of the NRL were not oblivious to the mistakes they had made fourteen years earlier. Rather than send a small scouting party to wander around in a blind search for an ideal spot, Smith led the committee on a determined investigation of potential locations based upon emigration literature obtainable in London. What the group started out with was the knowledge that they wanted to go to one of the western territories of the United States, preferably one that was largely unsettled but still had arable land and access to transportation networks. The Great Plains fit the bill, and it was not surprising that the immense grasslands of the West caught their attention. Little information about the plains region had been available in England before and during the American Civil War. Displayed on maps as the "Great American Desert," the treeless prairie was considered a barrier to settlement and received little attention on either side of the Atlantic. After the Northern victory in the Civil War, however, the last political restraints on railroad expansion disappeared. With construction of a transcontinental railway across the West, settling the plains became a realistic consideration. What had once been disparaged land suddenly became marketable, and a flood of promotional materials designed to lure prospective settlers to the region came pouring into England.

For the working-class members of the NRL, information about the Great Plains arrived primarily through the deliberate publicity efforts of American railroad companies, in particular the rapidly advancing Union Pacific (UP) transcontinental railway.[5] Rail lines such as the UP enjoyed generous government subsidies while building across the West, but to survive for the long term a railroad company needed homesteaders to produce grain for shipment. Marketing agents were aggressive in their drive to recruit settlers for the railroads, but in 1868 few rail conglomerates were as eager to develop a population base along its tracks as was the nearly completed UP and its eastern branch, the Kansas Pacific (KP). Promotional tracts from the UP were widely available in England. Members of the NRL were voracious readers and accumulated material from both railroads and travel journals for their reading room in the Eclectic Hall, although no member of the group ever credited a railroad pamphlet in the selection process. The information they did recognize as having influenced them the most came from the personal testimonies of former colleagues, in particular John Days. When he repatriated to London for a brief visit, Days spread the news about "the Great Union Pacific Railway, which with its various branches was about to open up the all but boundless and beautiful 'Far West' to settlements."[6]

Nebraska, which had attained statehood in 1867, had the most extensive tracts of farmland available within the UP's territory. Among the travelogues available in the Eclectic Hall reading room that the group cited was the Reverend R. Wake's 1867 emigrant's guide to Nebraska. Wake's tract discussed southeast Nebraska near the town of Rulo "at the mouth of the Great Nemaha River." He described the region as rich in coal and a land of plenty where everything imaginable grew. The NRL members also quoted a specific passage from a series of articles that Bayard Taylor had written in 1866 for the *New York Tribune*. In his essays, republished in 1867 as *Colorado: A Summer Trip*, Taylor stated: "I consider Kansas and Nebraska, with the western portions of Iowa and Missouri, to be *the largest unbroken tract of splendid farming land in the world*." Thus, with Days's assurances backed up by the published testimonials of Wake and Taylor, it was to the region west of Omaha that Smith and other representatives on the executive committee turned their attention.[7]

By the end of the summer Smith, Charles Murray, and James Flexman had drafted a prospectus on behalf of the executive committee to form an ad hoc organization called the Mutual Land, Emigration, and Colonization Company. O'Brien had taught them that communitarian settlements were an admirable end to the class struggle but not a practicable means to attain political equality. Plus, emigration had the negative effect of removing some of the most radical workers from the fight at home, which only served to strengthen middle-class power. The group was deviating from O'Brien's prescribed methods and rationalized:

> The state of society in which we live has long been regarded by us as one entirely antagonistic to the welfare of the producing classes, and in fulfilling the duty urged on us by that conviction, we have stood by the side of those who have protested against the system, whereby the majority are doomed to toil for the privileged few, and have assisted in the propagation of principles which by peaceable means would entirely change the system; but we find all our efforts unequal to the task, and we are therefore willing to throw our energies and lives into the promotion of an enterprise, which shall transfer the arena of our action to a spot more favourable for the accomplishment of objects which we deem to be the sacred duty of our lives.[8]

The group members sincerely believed that if they could establish a colony based on O'Brien's principles of social equality, they could secure the produce of the land to the producers and aid "in one of the noblest enterprises ever committed to man's care." The company would hold the land, preferably an entire township of thirty-six square miles, as a common inheritance. The committee believed that this would allow for the settlement of 576 families on forty-acre plots. They saw the land as a never-failing source of abundance that, if properly tended, would "augment the wealth of the colony, as well as enrich the individual members." Money earned from the cooperative would be used for taxes, interest for money advanced, infrastructure improvements, aid to individuals in emigrating or building cooperative enterprises, and finally dividends to shareholders. If everything was conducted properly, the committee members were confident that neither poverty nor the fear thereof would ever be known in the colony. Nebraska, they concluded, was centered on the necessary combination of resources essential to success. It was there that the world would see "the visible results of our mission in the gardens that bloom where the wilderness or the prairie existed before."[9]

On October 19, 1868, Smith wrote a candid letter of inquiry on behalf of the newly named company to Nebraska governor David C. Butler. He made no attempt to disguise the NRL's socialist convictions and forthrightly proclaimed that their plan was to build a colony based upon "the most advanced principles of Mutualism, viz — by holding the Land as common property, in contradistinction to the old feudal right of every man holding it for himself." A board of directors would hold title to the land and manage its improvement for the mutual benefit of all who purchased shares in the endeavor. The main goal, wrote Smith, was for the settlement to serve as a model "for the further development of all those social, political, and moral rights inculcated by many of the great reformers, dead and living, but more especially the teachings of the late Bronterre O'Brien, upon whose principles *the Colony* will to a great extent be founded." Smith made certain to assure the governor that he and his colleagues would conform in every way to the constitution and laws of the United States and that the proposed colony would have nothing to do with anarchism, free love, or religious idiosyncrasies. He and his colleagues wanted to live in harmony with their neighbors and help "develop the material and moral well being of the community." Furthermore, wrote Smith: "we are entirely unconnected with any of the parties who would wish to interfere with the marriage laws — *as the Mormons — the Shakers* and others."

Smith proceeded to explain to Governor Butler that each worker investing in the colony would have a collective right to share in the profits of the entire estate. At the same time, in strict adherence with O'Brien's plan, each shareholder would have the right to "hold a certain portion of the land under a two-life lease, at a nominal rent — which would always pay the Land tax, and other assessments taken from the land." In this scaled-down version of nationalization, the company would assume the role of the state and retain ownership of the soil while leasing out small tracts to shareholding citizens. No speculator could amass large swathes of land, and no family member could inherit large holdings because the two-life lease, defined as sixty years, could not be passed down from parent to child. The acreage reverted back to the company at the end of the lease, with just compensation provided for buildings or other development. Profits from the land would be "expended by the Company in the making roads, Bridges, and other improvements for the benefit of all."

Smith proposed an initial contingent of between six and twelve men to begin preparatory cultivation but anticipated rapid growth. He estimated that "many thousands in a year or two" would follow. In order to make such a grand scheme succeed, the company Smith represented would need a significant area of land. However, land required financing, and this was a group that had found it difficult to raise the money necessary to support their revered founder O'Brien in his infirmity. Because cash was not readily at hand, what Smith and his colleagues were most "anxious to know" was "whether there exists any facilities for our obtaining a sufficient amount of land there, which we could enter by purchase on time of the State, or of the United States, whether we could enter, and occupy under the Homestead, or Pre-emption Laws those lands by trustees." Smith was well aware that his request of government financing was unlikely to succeed and was uncertain about regulations governing the Homestead Act, so he inquired into the railroad land grants. He asked if the railroads were "capable of affording us the desired tract, on extra pay being made, for deferred payments — the rent of the land would meet the payments for the company." The rent would be steady and, in Smith's optimistic view, all but guaranteed since "the whole estate would be leased to the shareholders, and held only in trust for the Company, — no monopoly, or unjust rental could be expected."

If the government or railroads were willing, Smith desired a parcel of land large enough to prevent speculators from taking predatory advantage of the company's hard work by swooping in and exacting a high price for future expansion. Therefore, in order to properly develop the colony, Smith requested an area of land "a few miles square — (say a Township)." He admitted that his company would not be able to use so much property at first but wanted "to have some promise that we should not be shut in by speculators — we would desire neighbors, and not too far out to be in danger of Indian outrages, as at first we may not number many — but in a few years tens of thousands." This was a matter of some urgency to Smith's company, and he appealed to the governor for special consideration. Conditions for working men in England were bad at the present time, said Smith. It was important that the governor understand "how her population are starving — her trade is declining, how her finances are deranged, and panic stricken, how her lands are locked up in the hands of the few territorial lords of the country, how powerless the people are to redress their grievances." Whereas England was heedless of its peoples and their basic needs, Smith hoped that the Nebraska governor would be conscientious and assist Smith and his colleagues to "found a Home, or Colony, in that highly favoured Country under the benign influence and protection of the glorious *Stars* and *Stripes*, and help to be the means of adding another *Star* to that galaxy of the Great Republic."[10]

What Smith and his colleagues on the executive committee could not have known was that political pressures occupied Governor Butler's attention in 1868 and left him little time for a small group of British socialists. Born in Indiana in 1829, Butler moved to Pawnee City, Nebraska, in 1859 to become a cattle trader. He was elected to the Territorial Legislature in 1861 and, with Nebraska's ascension to statehood, became the first elected governor. As governor, Butler used his position and influence to advocate relocating the seat of government from the old territorial capital of Omaha to the planned city of Lincoln. In 1868 Butler was campaigning for reelection, but his questionable ties to Lincoln area land speculators, alleged misuse of state school funds to purchase lots in Lincoln, and controversial support behind moving the state administrative offices opened the door to the beginnings of a political scandal that would culminate in impeachment.[11] The internecine battles in Nebraska were far more serious to the Butler administration than what must have appeared as an insignificant bit of correspondence from an obscure group of impecunious English workers. Furthermore, regardless of the specifics surrounding the Butler administration, state and territorial governors across the West routinely received hundreds of requests from groups and individuals seeking information on land availability and prices. Butler was no different than any other governor and rarely responded to such inquiries without additional motivation, which ensured that Smith's letter would go unanswered.

Butler's lack of response troubled Smith and other members of the executive committee. Since determining to go forward with the project, NRL members had been using the Eclectic Hall to lecture on the proposed colony and recruit potential emigrants. They had made optimistic promises of cooperative prosperity through land in America and, even though the endeavor was less than six months old, the executive committee felt pressured to demonstrate some visible progress. By the end of December, Smith and the executive committee decided it was time to give Governor Butler the additional motivation necessary to elicit a response. On December 28, Smith composed a second letter of inquiry for the Nebraska governor. The second dispatch was an abridgment of the group's September communication and reiterated their desire for land and cooperative plans for the colony.[12] However, no longer content to entrust their ambitions to the vagaries of the international mail or the ambivalence of a distant politician, Smith and the executive committee marched en masse to the American embassy in London.[13] Their goal was to meet with the ambassador, explain their proposals, and seek advice on how to proceed.

In December 1868 the American ambassador to the Court of St. James's was a career politician named Reverdy Johnson. Born in Maryland in 1796, Johnson was a lawyer and Washington official with a noteworthy background. A former attorney-general in the Zachary Taylor administration, Johnson had been a member of the Whig Party but was not in full agreement with the Republicans of the 1850s and switched to the Stephen Douglas wing of the Democratic Party. In 1857 he stood before the U.S. Supreme Court and argued for the defense in the *Dred Scott v. Sanford* case, and in 1865 he defended Mary Surratt in her trial as one of the conspirators in the Lincoln assassination. Johnson was a staunch supporter of President Andrew Johnson, and in 1866 he was an influential member of the Union Convention backing the president's policies. His loyalty to the president was rewarded in 1868 with an appointment as minister to the United Kingdom.[14] Johnson's personal history was not one of great sympathy for working-class issues, yet when the delegation from the NRL arrived at the embassy to request an appointment, the ambassador agreed.

Reiterating much of what was contained in the letter to Butler, Smith and his companions explained to Johnson how they believed that the middle class used its control over the British government to ensure the continued impoverishment of English workers. They proceeded to outline the company's proposal for an American colony and, with the proper respect due an invested ambassador of the United States, presented Johnson with the second letter and requested that he deliver it to Butler via diplomatic channels. Johnson fulfilled his ambassadorial role and expressed a judicious amount of consideration for their cause and even went so far as to encourage them. As members of the working class, said Johnson, they would be welcomed with open arms in America. "The fact is," he continued, "all in the United States belong to that class, and I do not think any man has any motive to live at all who has no work to do or is incapable of working." The ambassador expressed an appreciable amount of concern over their plan to purchase and administer land as a collective and was uncertain whether this would be permissible under American law. Nevertheless, he was convinced that Smith and his colleagues could obtain property individually under the Homestead Act and, if they so desired, unite to become joint proprietors. Johnson may have had reservations about communal property, but the one thing he had no doubt over was a guarantee of success. "If you go to America," concluded Johnson, "you may be sure that the prosperity of yourselves and your children will be secured beyond doubt." Johnson was engaging in national boosterism without consideration of any consequences that his assurances might create, but his rhetoric was exactly what the NRL deputation wanted to hear. As they handed their letter to the ambassador, Johnson gave his solemn pledge that he would see it delivered to Governor Butler through official State Department channels.[15]

Members of the NRL considered the meeting with Johnson a success and believed it demonstrated progress toward the stated goal of building a colony in the United States. Nevertheless, the NRL was not the agent for the colony, nor was it meant to be. The executive committee of the informally organized Mutual Land, Emigration, and Colonization Company was promoting the proposed colony, but without the NRL and its established facilities, the colonization company had very little to offer. In point of fact, before any such endeavor could move beyond the talking stage, the organizers had to raise operating capital. They were aware of the financial realities of the situation, and since announcing the plan, the executive committee had been admitting anyone into the membership who was willing to pay a nominal application fee of one shilling and an additional subscription of six pence per week, all of which went toward the purchase of £1 shares in the company. Early in 1869 the colonization company was still an informal organization, and its founders in the NRL had yet to draft a set of rules and regulations that would make a professed adherence to Bronterre O'Brien's political philosophy a requirement for joining. The inevitable result was that individuals who desired an opportunity for land in America but did not necessarily endorse the company's objective of collective ownership began to purchase shares. These shareholders expected a tangible return on their investment, and some began to question the motivation and abilities of the company leaders when the expected benefits did not appear soon enough.

The first broadside struck on February 13, 1869, when a disgruntled subscriber took issue with what he perceived as a disorganized company and misuse of shareholder funds. Before being lured into this scheme, warned this anonymous shareholder, the public needed to be aware that "they are but simple working men with good intentions, no doubt, but totally incapacitated for even the commencement of such an enterprise." The directors in the executive committee had failed to organize their company in accordance with British law, they were not collecting nearly enough money for emigration purposes, and they barely had the funds necessary to cover their weekly operating expenses. Without factoring in the price of land or supplies, the unsigned author of the letter calculated that the cost of transporting a workingman with his family to Nebraska would amount to an average of £40 and, according to his assessment, the company reserves totaled £6 in hand remaining from £25 subscribed thus far. This nameless critic was more pessimistic than the organizers and scolded the group for failing to acknowledge that unforeseen difficulties would be inevitable and cash reserves would be necessary to meet them. The company directors may not have cared to hear it, but he felt it was reasonable to ask: "I should like to know in the name of common sense how it is possible, considering all the drawbacks which will necessarily follow, how this affair is to be a success." The anonymous shareholder concluded this scathing assault by verbally assailing any laboring man foolish enough to give his hard-earned shillings to such an impracticable scheme when it "ought to be used for the benefit of his poor children."[16]

The gauntlet had been thrown down, and Smith could not allow the allegations to go unanswered. The anonymous critic actually did the company a favor. O'Brien's followers in the NRL excelled in debate, and to counter the former shareholder's argument Smith publicized the nascent emigration company's current progress, finances, and long-term goals. He pointed out that since taking the initial steps toward forming a company some six months earlier, the company directors had sponsored thirty public meetings around London with fifteen additional lectures on the emigration topic held in the Eclectic Hall. At each of these gatherings one or more of the company directors would elucidate the seven fundamental principles of the NRL and outline the group's colonization plans. The membership financed these gatherings by passing the collection plate among the attendees, while the money obtained through shareholder subscriptions had been used to print handbills, pay for postage, and give the corresponding secretary a modest compensation for his time with a five shilling weekly salary. Smith conceded that the company had but £13 4s remaining out of £20 16s that had been collected from the sixty shareholders who had thus far subscribed to the enterprise. It was a small amount when compared to the immense sum necessary to purchase land and build a colony in Nebraska, and Smith freely pointed out that the money actually subscribed was less than what the detractor had estimated. Rather than allow one's expectations to run wild, he advised persistence in seeking goals and patience in awaiting outcomes. Smith proclaimed: "We don't expect to convert the world to-day, nor to found a colony in six months; as we are conscious of progression and that's enough, and that we have not wasted either our time or others, nor yet their money."[17]

Smith believed that the anonymous letter writer was a shareholder who had invested a mere two shillings in the program with no intention to pay any more. He suspected, "from the style of writing and animus shown," that it was a disgruntled subscriber "who wanted to be nominated by the directors, on his own personal recommendation, to be sent out as one of the pioneers." The directors were not yet ready to nominate anyone to be among the first group of settlers, which had angered the shareholder and left him disappointed because he wanted his hard-earned shillings to guarantee him one of the initial slots. As far as the competence of the men serving as directors was concerned, Smith argued that "the fact of it is not only being commenced and progressing well daily, numbering sixty members, and each day bringing fresh inquirers, new members, and giving general satisfaction, is a conclusive proof that if we can keep such men out as your correspondent we shall not only go on but cannot fail to work out successfully this novel scheme." The scheme, of course, was based upon "common property in land, equitable labour exchange, a currency based upon labour, and a system of credit co-equal with the wants of the community." This was to be an experiment is social reform, in proving O'Brien's philosophy in a practical setting. Said Smith: "The principle, mutually and co-operatively applied to society, with emigration as the forerunner and colonisation as the result, will at least show that we are not fools nor rogues, neither do we expect to see it grow up like mushrooms, or that all the shareholders will prove equal to the task before them. We shall feel satisfied ourselves if we can gather sufficient number of the good and brave to form the nucleus of a grand experiment."[18]

The company directors had yet to determine where in Nebraska this grand social demonstration was to develop, but Smith contended that since going public with their plans certain interests in the United States had offered the group more than three million acres of property at reasonable rates. Smith was cagey about the identity of these interested parties with land to offer, but such proposals could easily have come from railroad agents or land speculators because by this point news of the colonization project had hit America. Reverdy Johnson was true to his word and had sent a telegram message to Governor Butler shortly after the December meeting with Smith and the company directors. As early as December 30, 1868, the *Omaha Weekly Herald* announced: "Reverdy Johnson received a deputation of artizans [*sic*] desirous of founding a colony in Nebraska. Johnson encouraged them." Smith had no desire to conduct business with speculators and, beyond holding up such offers of land as tantalizing bait, he ignored them in anticipation of Butler's long-awaited response. By the end of February Smith learned that Johnson had sent the company's actual letter to Nebraska via State Department channels and reported receiving an offer of "immense tracts of land in Southern States."[19] The big news finally arrived in March when John Radford took the podium during a shareholders' meeting to read Governor Butler's personal acknowledgment of their query. The tone of the governor's letter was encouraging and gave the assembled listeners "great satisfaction," even though Butler made no specific promise of land and could offer counsel only on acreage available through government homesteads or railroads. Nevertheless, a positive response from an elected official in the United States left the group more determined than ever to proceed with their colonization program.[20]

Plans for a colony now moved forward at a dizzying pace. The group still had little money and no guarantee of land, but such matters were of minor concern as members were encouraged to study the works of Josiah Warren and Stephen Pearl Andrews for inspiration.[21] What the directors had gleaned from Butler's communication was that the company would have to establish a physical presence in Nebraska if its shareholders wanted to have legal access to acreage via the federal Homestead and Pre-emption laws. Their immediate reaction was to organize a small delegation of two or three advance settlers who would travel to Nebraska, select the land, and send word for the rest to follow. A small scouting party, however, was too similar to what the NRL had attempted in 1854 with John Days and George Murray, and nobody wanted to risk having the whole operation collapse if one of the advance men died en route. Therefore, fully confident in their ability to make an initial settlement succeed, the company directors resolved to send a substantial party of men, women, and children as part of the first contingent of "pioneers," as they referred to those who would go first. Based upon the numerous offers and assurances of abundant and affordable land that Smith had received since the beginning of the year, the directors anticipated that their pioneering group could easily find and secure an estate large enough for themselves and thousands of future shareholders wanting to escape from the misery of London's working-class districts.

In early April, Radford ascended the platform in the Eclectic Hall to address a gathering of shareholders. His purpose was to explain the reasoning behind organizing an emigration society and provide further details on how and when the directors would select the initial band of colonists. Radford accentuated the incorruptible character of the enterprise currently before them, which, in his view, distinguished it from the emigration schemes that lesser reformers and profiteers had so often in the past "trailed before the oppressed people of England." What other emigration society, asked Radford, could possibly boast of such a moral force? "Here we have that 'faith' which will ultimately move mountains — 'faith' of working men in integrity of one another — going forth to meet the array of nature's forces with the full assurance of conquering nature's greatest general, ere they can hope to destroy their arch enemy, man, in the covetous institutions of their native country."

Paying homage to Bronterre O'Brien, Radford acknowledged that emigration was not what the NRL was about and that forming the new colonization company had not been their first choice of action. However, after the Reform Act of 1867, the company organizers concluded that prospects of advancing meaningful reform in Britain were nearly nonexistent. Working and living conditions in factories and slums throughout England made life intolerable for laboring men and women, and government officials had become inured to their pleas. Radford believed the daily reality that British workers faced to be utterly shameful, which led him to proclaim that he "owned no country that did not recognise his rights as a citizen." After denouncing the British government, Radford deflected accusations that he and his fellow company directors were unpatriotically abandoning their country and emphatically declared that it was their sovereign right to decide what course to pursue. In no uncertain terms Radford insisted that he "recognised no country that only allowed him to toil out a life with a vagrant submission to every dignity. The law of nature would allow him something more than a servile nationality in Africa, in Australia, and other parts of this ball of earth." In order to transcend a life of servility, Radford stipulated the necessity of all good workingmen to demonstrate patience, perseverance, and, above all else, moral resolve.

Radford assured his listeners that the company directors had determined to prove the viability of O'Brien's social and economic theories in the United States because of that country's genial climate and reputation for political equality. Due to the "depravity of the wealthy classes" and the "brutish turpitude" of paid political functionaries, it was impossible for workingmen to have any real power in England. Therefore, the directors had determined to pin their hopes on a future in America, regardless of any obstacle put in their way. Within the month, announced Radford, the directors intended to select from the qualified shareholders an initial group of ten pioneers who would soon leave Great Britain "to found a new birth unto righteousness" in a land five thousand miles away. He stipulated that only those possessed of "high moral chivalry" and dedicated to O'Brien's cooperative ideal would qualify to lead the first assault for freedom. These chosen few would be men and women of the utmost integrity, individuals whose faith in the group's collective abilities would carry them through as they advanced into the wilderness of the American West. Radford concluded with a stirring testimonial, stating: "Their forces would multiply as they went on gathering up genial spirits, whose souls were above slavery, and as time rolls on, our little stream shall widen into a mighty river, as it approaches the great ocean of social justice."[22]

The unpretentious spirit behind Radford's blossoming skills as an orator made an impression. Prior to this meeting, Radford had been a stalwart member of the NRL and faithful adherent to O'Brien's teachings but had rarely stepped out from behind the formidable shadow of the Murray brothers. He was thirty-four years of age at this point and ready to take on a higher profile role. An observer at the meeting remarked that "Mr. Radford seems to be a man of earnest, energetic thought, destined from the very intensity of his honest aspirational nature to be a worker, not a common mechanical worker — but a worker who is very likely to sacrifice self for the good of others." Such a description could easily have been made of O'Brien in the 1830s, although Radford likely would have demurred over such a comparison. As it was, the reporter saw something special in Radford. "Such workers are few," he said, "and need encouragement and husbanding."[23] The membership of the NRL recognized it as well, and of all the shareholders, Radford was the most vociferous in his support of the colonization project.

On April 13, 1869, the company directors completed work on a code of rules, or Articles of Association, and formally registered their organization under the Joint Stock Companies Act of 1862 as the Mutual Land, Emigration, and Cooperative Colonization Company.[24] The word "Cooperative" was added to the formal company name as a linguistic symbol that cooperative colonization was the ultimate objective for everyone involved. The new company did not supplant O'Brien's NRL, nor was that the intent. The NRL continued operating as a Chartist political protest organization and the Eclectic Institute persevered as an educational center for young workers. However, the Mutual Land, Emigration, and Cooperative Colonization Company, with Charles Murray elected to serve as its president, operated under the aegis of the NRL and used the Eclectic Hall as its base of operations. It was out of this forum on April 16 that the shareholders held a public meeting to select the first contingent of ten pioneers. By virtue of his previous experience in the United States, the shareholders elected Smith to become the company's first land and colonizing agent in America. Smith accepted the honor and immediately resigned his position as corresponding secretary. John Rogers, O'Brien's old Chartist colleague, succeeded Smith in the secretary's office. As duly appointed leader of the expedition, Smith was the only shareholder guaranteed to travel with the first contingent of emigrants. Being among the initial group of settlers was not possible for every member. The spirit of equity demanded a general election among all eligible shareholders, but the company directors restricted the remaining slots to qualified individuals who possessed the agricultural and building skills necessary to establish the colony and support themselves until the project could become self-sustaining.[25]

A large, celebratory crowd gathered for the election of colonists, and an intense competition ensued among the shareholders to be among the first to flee "England's social wilderness, and plant the seeds of justice in the Western States of America." Sympathetic to the overwhelming desire of so many men and women to escape "from England's helpless and hapless future," the company directors debated, but decided against, the possibility of adding two more positions to the expedition roster. Charles McCarthy, a thirty-year-old common laborer, chaired the meeting and delivered an opening oration that detailed the history and progress of the young company. "Their mission," he said, "was specific, and they were prepared to carry their object out at the cost of all sacrifice." Company president Murray, Radford, Rogers, and Ion Perdicaris, a young American dilettante who had been dallying about the Eclectic Hall for several months, all offered encouraging remarks to the assembled crowd.[26] After the vote, Harris read a brief farewell address as the honored selectees were roll-called onto the platform to receive the congratulations and well wishes of their fellow workers. In addition to Smith, the chosen colonists included John Coney, age twenty-one; Robert Hill, age fifty-six; William Jenkins, age twenty-nine; Charles McCarthy; Felix McCarthy, age twenty; Josiah Morley, age fifty; Charles Sargood, age twenty-one; James Sargood, age twenty-eight; and John Stowell, age nineteen. This group of ten consisted of five carpenters, two painters/paper hangers, two common laborers, and one bricklayer. With the inclusion of wives and children, the entire party numbered eighteen. As the "Spartan band" of pioneers assembled on the platform, the company directors revealed that arrangements had been made for the group to depart from the Victoria Docks on April 24 aboard the steamship *Paraguay*. From this point forward, however, the selectees were on their own and could count on little to help them beyond the expectation that the legitimacy of O'Brien's principles would enable them "to erect for themselves a citadel of social justice" on the Great Plains of the American West.[27]

The company's financial outlook had experienced only slight improvement since January, and all available funds were reserved for making a down payment on the proposed land purchase in the United States. Therefore, before the directors accepted any of the selected pioneers as official members of the first party's companionship, each colonist had to sign a contract specifying that he would bear the whole of his own and any family member's transportation expenses to Nebraska. In addition, because there was no established colony to receive them, and because the company had yet to acquire a single acre of land for settlement, each emigrant consented to seek out some form of interim employment for the mutual support of the entire group. Finally, once Smith located and finalized purchase of a suitable parcel of land, the chosen pioneers agreed to donate another £5 apiece for purchasing lumber, seeds, implements, and provisions. It was a significant physical and financial sacrifice for the ten working-class colonists to make, but every one of the group endorsed the agreement. They were confident that collective efforts in labor and finance would "crown their efforts in a more genial country." Once the initial financial problems had been overcome, they could then afford to subsidize transportation expenses and allow their less solvent colleagues to join in the grand experiment.[28]

On Sunday, April 24, the company directors and, according to Harris's estimate, five to six hundred artisans took a holiday to escort the pioneer band of emigrants to London's Victoria Docks, where the chosen few prepared to board the steamship *Paraguay*, bound for New York via Le Havre, France. They were on a mission "to seek a *locale* in the Nebraskan territory of the U.S.A. previous to founding a settlement based upon the principles of the late Bronterre O'Brien." Harris observed a scene he described as both joyous and sad, "and yet no coward's tears or regrets could be seen or heard, although in the eyes of many a stalwart 'brother' could be detected in unutterable silence — which ofttimes speaks more potently of truth than the tongue." With each farewell embrace the colonists found a few extra shillings pressed into their hands. Given the size of the crowd, Harris anticipated the extra coins would add considerably to the group treasury, "which must facilitate the company's operations in the matter of deposits in the true banking up of the land." During the intervening week since the pioneers had been chosen, one man, an unemployed and penniless tanner named John Shallis, had beseeched the company directors to subsidize his passage to America. His case must have been persuasive because they succumbed to his entreaties and dipped into their own meager reserves to help pay for his ticket to New York. However, they could not take Shallis any further west and made certain he understood that he was on his own if he wanted to bring any family members or join the colony in Nebraska. Beyond the addition of Shallis and the minor drain he added to their resources, on that bright Sunday afternoon it seemed as if nothing could go wrong. The emigrant band began boarding the ship at noon, and by late afternoon the vessel with its hopeful passengers cleared the docks. Those who remained behind, wrote Harris, went home "to watch this unpretending movement to see what labour can do for itself when freed from the false teachings of a specious and spurious economy."[29]

The ship steamed across the English Channel toward France, and Smith took advantage of a port of call in Le Havre to dispatch a short letter to his expectant colleagues in London. As a prelude to a scheduled address from Charles Murray on the program and objects of the company, Rogers took the platform at the Eclectic Hall to read Smith's letter before an assembly of shareholders and potential subscribers. Smith reported that spirits remained high and all in the pioneer band remained devoted to O'Brien's spirit of cooperation. To illustrate the emigrant group's positive morale and mutual force of will, Smith related a shipboard incident where he and his companions had organized a successful protest demonstration against the questionable arrangement of berths aboard the *Paraguay*. This, wrote Smith, was "an attempted infringement of the Passengers Act." Murray took the podium next and seized upon the episode to delineate the advantages of an O'Brienite education. Cooperative projects and collective efforts provided for the good of all and were beneficial to society as a whole, unlike schemes initiated for selfish, speculative reasons.[30] The confidence level of those in the Eclectic Hall remained upbeat, but Murray's assessment of success came a little too soon. The *Paraguay* still had a lengthy voyage ahead, and the colonists on board had many long hours to dwell upon the uncertainties awaiting them in America.

In the midst of the passage across the Atlantic, Smith came to the unfortunate realization that some of the pioneers in his group were not as devoted to O'Brien's principles of cooperation as he had been led to believe. All ten selectees had freely signed a contract pledging to donate £5 that would go toward the purchase of the colony's initial stores of provisions, seeds, and tools. The money had not been collected in advance, and when Smith went through the group asking if each individual was prepared to make his contribution, Charles and James Sargood balked. Whether they misunderstood Smith's request or never had any intention of paying is unknown. However, when queried about the money, the two siblings became angry and accused Smith of deceiving them. The Sargood brothers came from the Notting Hill section of London and were two of the five carpenters on the voyage. They were chosen for their construction skills, but were now building animosity with the allegation that Smith had demanded they hand over all their money so he could use it to purchase land for the company. Moreover, at this point the Sargoods began protesting that they had never been informed of the company's policy of collective ownership and believed they should have full title to any acreage they settled rather than simply a shareholder's right to lease. Unless they had been randomly plucked off the street, the two brothers were being disingenuous as it would have been impossible to attend any shareholders' meeting without knowing the communal objective of the colony project. As it was, the disagreement divided the travelers. The Sargoods had approximately £13 between them and could have fulfilled their obligation or possibly have negotiated an agreement with Smith to pay later after they had gained employment and earned some extra money. Instead the siblings would not be reconciled, and they bolted from the expedition. They later claimed that two others defected with them but never identified any such companions.[31]

So long as the *Paraguay* was in transit, the company directors in London remained oblivious to any dispute that may have divided the pioneering group. Even as Smith and the Sargood brothers were clashing, Radford stood before the shareholders in the Eclectic Hall and praised those traveling to America for their unanimity of purpose and special abilities. When asked what qualities the first wave of ten emigrants possessed that earned them the honor of going first, Radford replied it was because of their varied skills and ability to work together. He highlighted Smith as "an inventor and good mechanic, who had an experience of seven or eight years in the backwoods of America." Robert Hill, who earned credit as an "excellent mechanic," had, like Smith, lived for a number of years in the United States "and was deeply involved with a love of justice and right." Josiah Morley, the group's bricklayer, was "an old East End co-operator" and a man who had "worked his way from agriculture to a position in the building trade." Radford cited Charles McCarthy as an "engineer who had worked his way from a boy at 4s. per week, into a position as foreman at 45s. per week." McCarthy was, however, a man who "preferred social justice to his employers' entreaties to stop with them at an advance pay of 50s. per week." Radford made no reference to others in the group and instead drew the attention of his audience to the "geographical and climactic advantages" of choosing "Kansas and Nebraska over the

Canadas." Canada was too cold and dismissed for political reasons because "British rule was growing hateful in every intelligent breast." Radford mentioned Kansas for the first time in this speech but still cited "the land report of Mr. Wilson the United States surveyor" to argue in favor of Nebraska.[32]

More than any other O'Brienite, Radford was sorely disappointed when he finally learned that an argument over filthy lucre had divided the party during its voyage to America. He thought that those who professed a belief in O'Brien's teachings had advanced beyond such middle-class money grubbing. Like his mentor O'Brien, Radford sincerely believed that a united workforce had the power to achieve a gigantic growth and could not understand the selfishness that drove fellow workers to undermine those efforts. Nonetheless, he and the other company directors were glad to be rid of anyone unwilling to contribute to the greater good of the cooperative. One week after the *Paraguay* made port in New York and news of the voyage had reached London, an unambiguous statement from an anonymous writer posing as Bronterre O'Brien appeared. The unnamed author conjured O'Brien's ghost from the grave to chastise those who would abandon his principles. "Unless you forsake profit-mongering, usury, and land monopoly, ye cannot be my disciples," said the contrived phantom, reflecting the sentiment of the group toward any Judases, like the Sargoods, that might still be lurking among them.[33]

Charles and James Sargood had already concluded that they would be better off fending for themselves. On May 17, when the *Paraguay* reached safe harbor in the United States and its passengers disembarked at the immigrant processing center in Castle Garden, New York, the Sargood brothers walked away from Smith and the other colonists. Shallis, with no money for a train ticket and unable to continue with the others, also took leave of his companions and melted into the urban metropolis in search of employment. The remaining pioneers had severely limited funds and no time to procrastinate, but Smith was familiar with Castle Garden and knew where to find railroad agents. Smith never recorded with whom he met and talked while in New York or when he made the decision to alter the group's course from Nebraska to Kansas. As late as May 16 in London, John Radford had mentioned Kansas but was still touting Nebraska as the preferred haven. However, the immigration officials who processed Smith and his colleagues through Castle Garden on May 17 recorded their declared destination as Kansas.[34] The entire party purchased train tickets for Atchison, which suggests that Smith encountered a land agent for the Central Branch, Union Pacific Railroad (CBUP).

Founded in 1859 as the Atchison and Pikes Peak Railroad, the railway initially existed only on paper and had no physical infrastructure until Senator Samuel C. Pomeroy invested in the company and helped secure it the right to be one of the four proposed branches of the UP Railroad. Construction on track leading west out of Atchison began in 1865, and in 1866 the company changed its name to the CBUP. By January 1868 the railroad had reached the Little Blue River, one hundred miles west of Atchison, and qualified for its full subsidy of $16,000 per mile in government bonds, plus 187,608 acres of land. The CBUP had intended on making a connection at the Republican River with the Kansas Pacific as that railroad made its way to Kearney, Nebraska, and the main UP trunk line. However, several years earlier the KP had successfully lobbied for permission to continue west toward Denver along the Smokey Hill River instead of turning north toward Kearney. With no link and unable to obtain further federal subsidies to continue building, the railroad halted construction on the CBUP at the Little Blue River and went no further. Nonetheless, the CBUP had a tremendous amount of land, including access to property from the Kickapoo Indian Reservation left over after allotment. All western railroads advanced their economic position by actively encouraging agricultural development along their routes, but because of Major William F. Downs, few could match the CBUP for aggressiveness.[35]

Born in Seneca Falls, New York, in 1837, Downs moved to Territorial Kansas in 1857 and quickly established himself as a political operative. When the Civil War broke out in 1861, Downs relocated to Washington and worked for the Lincoln administration as chief clerk in the Treasury Department's Bureau of Internal Revenue. In 1865 Downs used his political connections to win appointment as land commissioner for the CBUP, which allowed him to return and administer the railroad's government land grant in Kansas. Downs was the first railroad land commissioner to perfect an efficient system of surveying and disposing of government land grants while maintaining proper records. His system worked so well that it was imitated by several Western land grant railroads. By 1868 Downs had been promoted to general superintendent of the CBUP, and it was from this position that he boosted his company's economic prospects by establishing land offices in New York. In 1869 Atchison had seven thousand residents and was pushing to become a major rail hub in northeastern Kansas. Therefore, Downs's actions were designed to lure new immigrants to CBUP property west of Atchison. Immediately prior to Edward Smith's arrival in New York, the *Atchison Daily Champion and Press* boasted that Downs was "doing great work in attracting emigration to Kansas."[36]

Whether it was through the personal efforts of Downs or one of his aides, Smith and his traveling companions were en route for Atchison to examine land Downs had advertised as being "100 miles long and 40 miles wide,"[37] which was a size that neatly fit Smith's bill. In London the shareholders were exultant. The company's success in launching a pioneering band of colonists and good tidings of their safe arrival in America, the Sargood defection notwithstanding, emboldened the movement. The first direct news from Kansas arrived on June 27 during a shareholders' meeting. That evening James Murray opened the proceedings by whipping the assembled crowd into an emotional frenzy worthy of a religious revival. After analyzing the underlying problems with British society and explaining the reasoning behind why they found it necessary to form an emigration organization, Murray demanded that his listeners stand up and be a part of the solution. "Equity was their war cry; justice their determination. In these they would realise the teaching of Christ — viz., 'Seek you first the Kingdom of Heaven, and all these things shall be added unto you.'" Radford next stood before the anxious gathering and announced that he had just returned from Mortlake, where he visited with Edward Smith's wife, Elizabeth, and was given a letter Smith had sent to her from America. The letter, dated June 12, detailed that Smith's party had arrived in Atchison and had commenced the search for land. Radford said: "With the exception of Mr. Smith's health, which was suffering from over-fatigue, everything was going on prosperously and well, and that soon a locality would be decided on." With that information in hand, Charles Murray revealed that it was time to send the second wave of colonists. Since April the company had generated considerable excitement among London's workers, and the company directors eagerly accepted new shareholder applications. The accumulated subscription funds enabled the directors to provide Smith with an extra infusion of cash and labor. John Trent, a twenty-year-old plasterer, and Edward Rooney, a thirty-two-year-old warehouseman, were elected mission leaders entrusted to deliver the company treasure. Beyond the announcement, there was considerably less fanfare in launching the second party of settlers. How many others traveled with Trent and Rooney is unclear, since no other names received direct mention, but there may have been as many as fourteen who departed Liverpool's Albert Docks on June 30 onboard the steamship *Manhattan*.[38]

As per Radford's report, Smith, once he regained his strength, engaged in a determined search for a suitable estate. Downs ran an efficient land office and extended every courtesy to his clients. When the English settlers stepped off the train in Kansas they discovered that everyone "in and about Atchison had heard of their coming, and since their arrival had shown them every hospitality and kindness." As soon as he arrived, Smith began receiving offers from speculators touting land that ranged anywhere from one to twelve dollars per acre. While the colonists were pleased with the countryside and anxious to get started, they were aware that they had arrived "too late in the season to crop the land for this year's return." Smith believed that the region promised everything the company had wanted, but saw no reason to hurry through a transaction and refused to bite on the first property dangled before him. Instead he adopted a methodical approach that allowed him to inspect as much of the area as possible before coming to a final decision. However, it was railroad land that most interested Smith. By this point he had acquired a CBUP real estate booklet and believed "the book description seemed to answer for the purpose of the company."[39]

Downs ensured that Smith had ample opportunity to view the land for himself. Smith received a pass to travel on the CBUP to inspect the various parcels of acreage the railroad was offering for sale, and for three weeks he traveled up to fifty miles a day on the rail line. Downs was too busy to accompany the English settlers as they made their examinations, but Smith did not mind as he waxed poetic over a prairie panorama that he described as "enchanting." After weeks of nearly non-stop traveling, Smith luxuriated in what he believed was a balmy and salubrious climate. Both the vista and the weather heartened the small band, and Smith's conversations with local residents gave him renewed confidence in his choice of Kansas. "The country looks beautiful," wrote Smith to his colleagues in London, "the climate is cool and bracing, and there is nearly always a breeze, and sometimes pretty stiff, even in the warm days." Smith's letter was from mid-June, and in it he assured his fellow shareholders that the "heat is not oppressive, there appears plenty of rain, and, from what I am told, they have drought very seldom, once perhaps in a dozen years." The Kansas winter was tolerable as well, wrote Smith. "The winter is short, and if you don't mind the wind, which is cold, you may work out of doors in your shirt sleeves; this is what I am told by men on the prairies." Such a land had to be good for the soul, and Smith found that all the people looked robust and vigorous. "I believe myself it is a very healthy place, and beneficial to life."[40] Smith's description of CBUP land was reminiscent of the advertising picture Downs had painted of the property the railroad was peddling. Wrote Downs: "And such a country! A climate full of health and strength; an air bright, balmy, and pure; a soil whose richness centuries of cultivation could not exhaust; a landscape fair and lovely to look upon; gently undulating prairies; streams of pure water, their banks fringed with trees."[41]

To bargain for CBUP land, Smith had to deal directly with Downs, but Downs was exceptionally busy and difficult to nail down. Smith complained of spending many "days waiting my opportunity to see the Commissioner of the railway, who has a vast amount of business to attend to." While anxious to move forward, Smith reported: "I have attended the office four or five days, and not got much further on the negociations and settlements about the land, although every information was afforded by the Commissioner and his courteous clerks." Downs was unusually pressed for time because Smith's decision to make a purchase happened to have the bad luck of taking place just as Senator Pomeroy decided to return to Atchison for a visit. Pomeroy served on the CBUP board of directors and owned a one-sixteenth interest in township sites along the rail line, so it was no coincidence that the railroad superintendent's time was fully consumed. Downs was responsible for making certain the senator was comfortable, arranging rail tours of CBUP land holdings, and organizing formal receptions, all of which left precious little time for negotiations with Smith.[42] Nevertheless, Downs respected Smith's position and certainly did not want to lose his custom. Downs's well-mannered demeanor likewise impressed Smith: "Mr. Downs, the railway land agent here is a most gentlemanly and courteous man; whenever he has had an opportunity of introducing me to any of the persons frequenting his office, he has always done so and spoken of me as the agent of an English company, whose headquarters are in London, England, and who is likely to send out a large number of settlers to Kansas."[43]

Smith's potential for bringing in future business was not lost on Downs, who took the opportunity of Pomeroy's visit to introduce Smith to the senator. According to Smith, Pomeroy "shook hands in a most cordial manner, and wished us every success in our enterprise."[44] It is unclear whether Pomeroy was informed of Smith's socialist principles or proposal to develop a commune in the senator's home territory. However, never a man to let social or political convictions interfere with profits, Pomeroy doubtless meant what he said since he stood in line to receive dividends from Smith's purchase and development of CBUP property.

Regardless of the senator's disruptive presence, Smith managed to complete his negotiations with Downs and on June 14 made a partial down payment on an entire 640-acre section of land. The property, on maps as section 25, was located in Harrison Township, Nemaha County, forty-eight miles west of Atchison and three-quarters of a mile north of the railroad tracks.[45] Nothing but prairie grass covered the treeless parcel of ground. Smith realized that the colony was going to require a source of timber and therefore committed the company to purchasing an additional forty-acre lot, or the southeast quarter of the northeast quarter of section 19 near the Nemaha River. The 40-acre section was not contiguous with the colony grounds but was nearby and contained a few essential cottonwood groves.[46] "I walked about up to my knees in grass, saw nothing, except to admire," rhapsodized Smith about the company's new Eden. "I have been over it three different days; it is covered with beautiful grass, about two feet high, which, if we could cut, would produce many tons, and sell at a profit of several thousand dollars." Smith overestimated the market value of Kansas grass but was more interested in the soil those grasses produced. The "soil is excellent," he said, "being black friable mould, the result of years of rich grasses being produced and burnt on the ground equally, and spread over the vast extent of the prairie." Smith went on to describe the beautiful prospect from which a person could "see more than ten miles" from the center of the property. He assured anyone retaining misgivings about relocating to the prairie wilderness that vicious animals were not a concern and that other settlers near the company's land were pleased to hear of their coming. They "express a desire for our welfare," remarked Smith, "and the success of our Christian work."[47]

Property along the entire one hundred mile stretch of the CBUP railroad averaged $7 per acre, but given variables such as distance to the tracks, soil quality, and other considerations, it could range

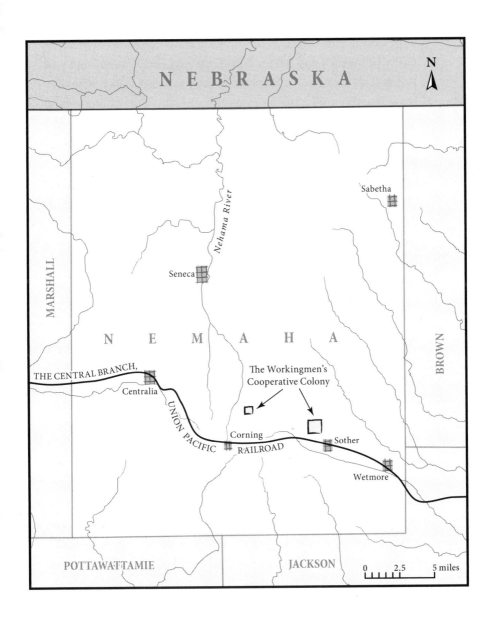

in price anywhere from $1 to $12. Real estate in the immediate vicinity of Smith's procurement usually fetched between $3.50 and $7 per acre. Smith may have been a crafty negotiator, but more likely Downs was willing to bargain given the size of Smith's purchase and prospect of attracting more land-hungry English settlers. The price Smith and Downs agreed upon was $3.50 per acre for the 640-acre section and $5 per acre for the wooded forty-acre section. In total Smith obligated his company shareholders to a $2,440 purchase price, which was a considerable sum for a group of radical agitators who suffered from chronic monetary shortages. Nevertheless, Smith had no trepidations for the future. "I am not in fear of failure now I have secured a piece of land for our operations to be commenced upon," he mused. "I never felt more confident in our company than I do at the present moment."[48]

Official news of Smith's land purchase arrived in London on a Sunday evening in mid-July when the company shareholders gathered to hear a lecture from George White, an old firebrand Chartist colleague of O'Brien's recently repatriated after a twenty-year exile in the United States. White commended the assembly for their colonization project, which he viewed as purely an educational movement. "Education," he said, "was and is the motor-power of all social, industrial, political, moral, and economic advancement," and the company's plan to build a model community based upon equitable principles would provide just such an education. "Emigration would aid them in the immediate adoption of their plans by transferring them to the more congenial soil of America, where labour and land could be more effectually united than it possibly can in this country." Land was the root of all true educational improvement, he said, and only in the free institutions of the United States would they find "the commercial, political, and moral bearing" necessary to succeed. White was familiar with the Latter-day Saints and highlighted the successful Mormon settlements in Utah as a source of hope and inspiration for company members. These religious communalists had separated from the established civilization yet had used cooperative principles to irrigate the desert and prosper in the

American West. He believed that if the Latter-day Saints could make the barren desert bloom, then surely the O'Brienites and their advanced social theories could do the same on the Great Plains.[49]

After White concluded his encouraging remarks, Radford stepped forward amidst the cheers of the crowd to share the news of Smith's land purchase in Kansas. Through Smith's informal correspondence with his wife, Elizabeth, the company directors had known that a deal was close at hand. However, Radford's announcement was the first official news that the company shared with the public. Knowing the shareholders would be curious about where the land was and what everything looked like, Smith sent his colleagues a map of the CBUP territory, with their new acreage clearly marked, and a daguerreotype image of Atchison. Most important of all, he forwarded a receipt for the deposit he had paid on the land. While everyone in the crowd got a turn to look as the items slowly made their way around the room, Radford declared that "all the preliminaries are now negociated, and the estate," consisting of 640 acres of fertile land about fifty miles west of Atchison, "awaits the fructifying hands of the pioneers." George Harris wrote the news release on the meeting and added that the "O'Brien principles are eagerly sought after, and inquired into, and the people generally speak approvingly of the aims and objects of the colonists." The people of Kansas recognized labor "as the only true dignity," waxed Harris, "and there are no merchant millionaires nor aristocratic blockhead princes in the locality to devour the people's industry."[50]

Radford and Harris had a difficult time containing their enthusiasm, but the reality in Kansas was that most of the scattered residents in the vicinity of the new colony lands were indifferent to the project and scarcely noticed the arrival of Smith and his intrepid band of cooperative pioneers. Several of the men in the pioneering group had taken work in Atchison while waiting for Smith to complete the transaction, but all were ready when the day came to start building. The troupe boarded a CBUP train in Atchison and traveled to an unmanned flag stop called Sherman Station. There was no town or station at Sherman Station. The only thing at the stop was a wooden post marking the fifty-mile point between Atchison and Waterville. In 1871 the CBUP renamed the spot Sother and proposed building a small post office, but it remained little more than a flag stop. Wetmore, the closest settled town, was five miles east of the stop. In 1869 Wetmore was a village of roughly thirty-five inhabitants. John Stowell, the youngest shareholding member of the colony group, later reminisced that when he and his companions first arrived at Sherman Station, the train unloaded them "on the plains in a city with no inhabitants and not a building of any description." As the locomotive pulled away, these lifelong urban dwellers stood alone along the tracks and stared out toward the distant prairie horizon. As they did, the full realization of what they had done may have struck them for the first time. Stowell recalled how impossible it would be "to convey the feeling of loneliness that came over the party."[51]

Smith and his settlers brought only enough money to make a partial down payment on the property and had little remaining to begin the physical construction of their utopia. Moreover, it was too late in the season to plant a crop, and the colonists would have to wait an entire year before seeing any meaningful income or food production from the land. This meant that the English settlers could not maintain their unity and soon had to scatter around the countryside in search of employment to support the colony. Most found work as agricultural laborers with local farmers and earned little more than room and board, although Josiah Morley managed to do some jobs for the CBUP. Smith and Charles McCarthy remained on the land and began work on a dormitory building. On August 6, a cotton broker identified only as Mr. Bryan, who had met the Sargood brothers in St. Louis and learned about the Kansas colony project from them, rode out to have a look at the settlement. He witnessed Smith and three others working at the dormitory, but looked in vain to find evidence that the soil had been tilled. They did intend to plow and plant a crop soon, reported Bryan, but "I don't think they will be able to stand the winter on their land; having nothing ready, they will freeze up."[52]

Had Smith and his colleagues been able to plant a crop of late season vegetables, then they likely would have done so. The problem for the colonists was not in the will but in the means as constant money shortages continued to plague the group. All their capital had gone to the CBUP for the land purchase, and they had insufficient reserves to obtain a plow or draft animals. The company directors in London were acutely aware of this problem. They had already sent out Trent and Rooney with some extra cash, and in late July they began issuing urgent appeals "for aid to assist the pioneers and to keep the movement from being compromised with 'extraneous indebtedness.'" Secretary Rogers spoke for the company directors on this issue. He avowed that if workingmen and women "ever meant to lift themselves up from the social thralldom they must not care so much about savings' banks, but apply their own resources to effect the remedy." The object of the company was to found a new social order based on O'Brien's principles of mutual aid and cooperation, and in order to accomplish this feat every member had to learn to respect and believe in their own and each other's abilities. "Those who held the land could feed, and those who held the food of a people could govern," argued Rogers. "The time had come when proletarians must show a better order of life by striking at the root and destroying the evil." Rogers exhorted his listeners to stop viewing money as the measure of value and its accumulation as the highest commercial virtue. He believed instead that if they used their combined funds to supplant the present system with "a more rational and scientific arrangement of equivalents — issuing notes upon labour," the company would thus render "every man in their new colony his own banker."[53]

Charles Murray concurred with Rogers and backed up the secretary's statements with some conceit of his own. Murray advised all who "were desirous of helping themselves, to come forth and join this society, and, by their subscriptions, to place the company in such a position as should, within a very short space of time, return them the compliment with a four-fold bounty." He emphasized that they were not a company of capitalists and that those looking for easy money were bound to be disappointed. They were a company of O'Brienites and, with land securely in the shareholders' possession, it was "time that the men struggling for the rights of industry in all nations should be able to illustrate by example the truth of principles now deemed theoretical." Murray concluded that the Workingmen's Cooperative Colony Smith was establishing in Kansas would provide that shining example. "This enterprise, great in its objects, and we hope glorious in its results, is intended to solve the possibility of the actual producers realising all the advantages of their toil." He reasoned that British laborers needed to bear the burden of sustaining the pioneers for only a single season before the operation of high moral principles could "secure that for which so many noble men have struggled and suffered in all nations, 'liberty in right, equality in law, fraternity in interest.'"[54]

The entreaties achieved the desired results, and the company directors were able to collect enough capital to keep Smith and the colonists ahead of their debts for a short while longer. Trent and Rooney's expedition had arrived at Castle Garden on July 13, and within a short time they had joined Smith on the colony grounds in Kansas. The money Trent and Rooney brought enabled Smith to complete the down payment on the land with a surplus for essential tools, a plow, and team of horses. Though it was too late in the summer to start any crops, the colonists could barely contain their excitement and gleefully began breaking the soil in anticipation of the next year's planting season. The infusion of supplies meant that work on the main communal building could continue, while Rooney and Charles McCarthy took advantage of some new picks and shovels to begin digging a well. The directors in London understood that the Kansas settlers would need additional funding for livestock and implements before attaining self-sufficiency. Nevertheless, the shareholders felt assured that they had successfully launched the colony and were safely on course to prove the validity of O'Brien's principles to the world. George Harris summed up the effort when he wrote: "Work was their birthright, and work was their object, and now their colony had a 'local habitation' in which they proposed to have their future home, and thus relieve themselves by mutualism and self-help from the degrading work of the English Sisyphus."[55]

The time between John Days's visit to the Eclectic Hall in June 1868 and Edward Grainger Smith's purchase of land in Kansas was exactly one year. The very act of advancing the idea of a cooperative colony beyond the talking stage was a remarkable feat for a relatively small group of London workingmen. According to Stowell, their plans for the colony constituted nothing less than "to form the nucleus of a scheme to change the whole system of land tenure in the United States and the world in general."[56] Planting a colony on the Great Plains may have been a brash move, and one that saddled the company with debt, but it was a step that reflected the absolute confidence members of the NRL and, by extension, the Mutual Land, Emigration, and Cooperative Colonization Company had in Bronterre O'Brien's reform program. If their plans proceeded without difficulty, the settlement had a chance.

3

An Honest Social State

—⁂—

The Workingmen's Cooperative Colony

If it be said that such application of public property would benefit
the poor only, and be an injustice to the rich, the answer is that the
lands so purchased would not be the property of the poor, but the
property of the whole nation — rich and poor; and that, inasmuch as
the rents accruing therefrom would be applicable to public uses only,
the whole public, and not the poor alone, would have the benefit
in the remission of rates and taxes. The only disadvantage the rich
would suffer from such reform is that it would gradually emancipate
industry from their iron grasp.

—JAMES BRONTERRE O'BRIEN, ca. 1850

Most O'Brienites shared John Stowell's conviction that the colony he
had helped establish in Kansas was to form the nucleus of a grand
experiment that would radically alter the form of land tenure in the
United States and, ultimately, the world. While a few skeptics in
the group were apprehensive about ignoring O'Brien's admonitions
against emigration, most embraced the project and readily supported the experiment in communalism. Nevertheless, establishing the
colony saddled the shareholders of the Mutual Land, Emigration,
and Cooperative Colonization Company with a financial burden
that they could scarcely afford. How quickly they could make their
colony self-sufficient and retire the debt would determine whether they could even take the first step toward transforming the nascent settlement into a model community.

With every confidence that the Workingmen's Cooperative Colony in Kansas was stable and ready to move forward, the company directors in London had little difficulty soliciting subscriptions for new shares. The extra income enabled the company to send small remittances to Edward Grainger Smith, the American-based superintendent, during the colony's early months. By early October John Radford reported that the group had collected and sent a total of £104 from the National Reform League's Eclectic Hall to Kansas. From its humble beginnings of about sixty-five shareholders in 1868, the company had grown to more than two hundred subscribers and seemed to need only time before its colony could be weaned from investor support. In November Smith reported that he had used the money received to purchase a yoke of steers, a cow that was in calf, a second plow, a wagon, a few hand tools, and twenty bushels of potatoes for use as food and spring seed. He had put the colonists to work clearing the land, cutting fence posts, digging a well, constructing a stable, and completing the central dormitory. Radford believed the steady investment in time, money, and labor "would return them four-fold next year."[1]

Not everyone associated with the National Reform League (NRL) shared Radford's optimism. Since the beginning of the colonization project, Martin Boon, an ironmonger from London's Clerkenwell district, had opposed the scheme. Boon was devoted to Bronterre O'Brien's political program and was counted among the NRL members serving with Karl Marx on the General Council of the International Working Men's Association (IWMA). He was also a devotee of Robert Owen and a vocal proponent of land nationalization. Nevertheless, he stood firmly against emigration proposals and believed that abandoning England was not the answer. True social and economic reform, as O'Brien had preached before him, had to begin with political reform at home. In October 1869, Boon became a founding member of the Land and Labour League (LLL). Closely affiliated with the IWMA, the LLL was composed of workers who were incensed over the results of the Reform Act of 1867 and wanted to continue pressing for expansion of suffrage rights at home. In advocating for complete suffrage, the LLL focused much of its agenda on the land nationalization issue, and Boon was its loudest propagandist. There was nothing inherent in the LLL that contradicted O'Brien's thoughts on land nationalization, and other NRL members, such as Charles Murray and John Weston, were also active in the league. However, it was Boon who used his position in the LLL to denounce emigration companies like the Mutual Land, Emigration, and Cooperative Colonization Company. Boon agreed with William Cobbett's invectives of a generation earlier, as perpetuated through O'Brien, against the vices of city life. He supported home colonization on nationalized land, not emigration, as the solution to the debilitating effects of large-scale industrialization. Our colleagues, Boon wrote, "Who are so earnestly advocating emigration schemes . . . are unknowingly committing a serious wrong to our fellow countrymen." Boon sympathized with workers who had grown weary of capitalist oppression and acknowledged that thoughts of emigrating to a new land and a fresh start held certain attractions: "These men sigh for peace and tranquility, and when they are told of the prairie lands in America . . . they long to get away from their native shore." Nevertheless, in his view emigration proposals were chimeras that offered nothing of substance capable of aiding or advancing the class struggle. There was no escape, cried Boon. "Peace to the cottage — war to the palace — again lifts its voice, and republicanism, hand-in-hand with socialism, strives to elevate itself as the only thing to cure the ills of society."[2]

Boon's condemnation may have irritated some of his colleagues, but it did little to slow down the Mutual Land, Emigration, and Cooperative Colonization Company. The colony effort pressed on. Those who had invested in the company were more interested in whether it would succeed rather than in debates on whether they even should have undertaken the project. Most early news was cautiously optimistic, although not everything ran according to plan during the fall season. The colonists' inexperience with rural life and the prairie environment created setbacks as well as successes. Stowell, for example, recalled a botched effort to split some posts and rails during the fence building project. The settlers had pounded iron wedges into green wood until the tools became hopelessly stuck. They ruined the wood and damaged several expensive axes in the effort to extract the splitting implements. The fencing problems led the company to send shareholder George Cox, who had some fence-building experience, to the colony during the winter. Cox encountered an entirely different set of difficulties on the cooperative, but for the moment he remained quiet. A more immediate issue was fire. Prairie fires were a constant threat on the dry grasslands of Kansas, and the settlers spent four days in November trying to keep a wildfire from destroying all their hard work. The buildings survived, but the group sacrificed three ricks of hard-earned hay, which they valued at £8, to the Great Plains "fire king."[3]

The colonists were entering their first winter season on the Kansas plains. They had worked diligently to make their settlement as comfortable as possible, but, other than seeking off-colony employment, they had no income and relied completely on the goodwill of their comrades in London. Without a wealthy patron, the company directors had to cultivate the generosity of workers still in England who hoped someday to move to the colony themselves. If the organization lost that support, particularly at such an early date in the cooperative's development, the entire effort would collapse. A critique from a detractor like Boon, even though he was a respected activist, could be brushed aside as the remarks of a cynic who had never been to Kansas and did not want to participate. More difficult to disregard were criticisms coming from Charles and James Sargood, men who had been intimately involved with the project. The Sargood brothers, who had been, in their words, two "of them so-called pioneers" accompanying Smith the previous spring, repatriated in the fall of 1869 to England. On December 6, they went public with a scathing attack against working conditions in the United States and a blistering condemnation of the company directors.

In *Reynolds's Newspaper*, the Sargoods contended that they "joined that scheme" only because Radford and other directors had duped them with an exaggerated depiction of American prosperity. The brothers wanted everyone to understand that they had been willing participants and "were anxious to be off, to build up this happy colony, which was to be the best of all organizations, and a pattern to the world." However, according to their version of events, while on board the *Paraguay,* Smith heard a rumor that the brothers had brought £40 each. The Sargoods accused Smith of approaching them about the cash and insisting that they turn it over to him so he could add it to the funds reserved for the land purchase. Furthermore, they alleged that Smith stated there was not going to be enough money for a substantial estate. Any shareholder in Kansas would have to subsist on two acres for two years, after which time said shareholder would earn the right to a lifetime lease of forty acres. The Sargoods claimed that this last bit was just too much. To work one's life on a leased parcel of land, making improvements, "and then to fall into the Company's or director's hands [sic]," and have the property "disposed of as they think proper. I cannot describe how I felt when I first heard this statement from Secretary Smith."

After besmirching Smith's integrity, the Sargood brothers made the worst accusation possible and indicted the company directors in London for trying to profit from the shareholders and their labor. "What a boon to offer," they exclaimed. "To leave a home and family, give up one's entire life savings in order to help buy land, labor on it for two years in work of the most difficult sort, and all for the benefit of whom?" The Sargoods asked the question, and they supplied the answer. Everything was for the company's benefit. It was this alleged disclosure that led to dissensions in Smith's group and, according to the brothers, "four of us pioneers left when we arrived at Castle Garden. We were afraid we should be too happy in such a millennial state, and thought before we participated in these blessings we would retire." In New York the brothers observed that John Shallis stayed behind while Smith and the remainder of the pioneering group left to book train passage west. Shallis had been a charity case from the beginning. He had no money, and Smith could not afford to subsidize his travels any further. Therefore, as per the agreement struck in London, Shallis stopped in New York to look for work. The Sargood brothers, however, either misunderstood or chose to ignore why Shallis had accompanied the group in the first place. They now complained that the company's action of taking a man from England, where he had a wife and children, and abandoning him in New York with nothing in his pocket was "the cruelest act of all." While their hearts may have belatedly gone out to Shallis, at the time the brothers made no effort to help their fellow worker in his hour of need. Instead they departed of their own accord to search for work. From New York the Sargoods traveled west to Indianapolis and Kansas City, after which they started working their way back east. In St. Louis they discussed Smith and the colony project with Mr. Bryan, the cotton broker, then moved on to Pittsburgh and back to New York. The siblings never lingered in a single place long enough to obtain employment beyond casual labor but blamed this on American employers rather than their own transient existence. The Sargood brothers attested that few good jobs existed for outsiders in the United States, and every American they encountered seemed conditioned to point newcomers west while taking advantage of every opportunity to swindle them out of their money. The message they wanted English workers to understand was that the social and economic environment was "not all honey in America." In New York the Sargoods witnessed immigrants starving to death because jobs paying a living wage simply were not available. The brothers recommended that British workers stay away from the United States, if indeed the goal was to improve their economic condition.

Charles and James Sargood had no personal reputations as reformers and no appeal as public figures, but there was such intense worker interest in the company that their polemical letter created a tempest capable of knocking the company directors back on their heels. Shortly after publication of the Sargoods' correspondence, Radford traveled to Portsmouth to promote the company before an assemblage of interested laborers. He was on a fund-raising tour and under normal circumstances needed only to highlight the colony land and the improvements Smith and the colonists were making, but in Portsmouth Radford found himself deflecting questions about the Sargood brothers and their allegations. To his credit, Radford denied the truthfulness of what the siblings had said and refrained from publicly criticizing his former comrades or their methods. Instead he defended Smith's character and urged his listeners to examine the empirical evidence. The company had successfully established a workingmen's cooperative in Kansas, on land that had the advantage of being near railroad and river highways, which connected the commune to all parts of America. The quantity of land to be allotted to each shareholder, said Radford, "will be what it has always been represented — 'as much as he can cultivate,' which has yet to be determined by experience." Radford avowed before the workers of Portsmouth that his company's program "would ensure the union on an equitable basis in land, labour, and capital; and though their enterprise may be young today, it has a power of achieving a gigantic growth." He appealed to his Portsmouth audience to rise up and aid the workers of London in attaining their economic independence and give absolute proof of "the power of united labour combined."[4]

The other company directors adopted a similar approach during shareholder meetings in the Eclectic Hall, although Charles Murray's response was more caustic than Radford's. Murray stated that he would have nothing to do with "the wantonness and freaks of temper of these young men" and would rather "deal with the facts of the case as it affected the company." The Sargood brothers had taken out shares in the company under the pretense of recognizing its O'Brienite principles. They had signed a contract pledging to act in harmony with the other pioneers and in accordance with the company's articles of association, yet "ere they arrive in New York, all devotion to their former profession vanishes, and then return to give public evidence of their own folly." According to Murray, the Sargoods had paid but six shillings toward their shares and were in arrears to the company even before departing for the United States. But this was all beside the point, said Murray, who proceeded to illustrate just how far the company had advanced in a few short months. Would it have been possible to establish a colony in Kansas and begin the work of developing it, asked Murray, if all the pioneers "had acted as the Sargoods have acted — men devoid of principle?" George Plowman stood to commend Smith, "whose character had been publicly maligned," and James Murray regaled the crowd with a presentation of the contract bearing both Sargood brothers' signatures. Radford closed the proceedings by reading letters from Charles McCarthy and other colonists in Kansas testifying to "the unequalness of the tempers and manners of the Sargoods on their voyage out."[5]

The verbal rebuttals served well enough among the company membership, but the Sargoods had created a far greater disturbance that threatened future subscriptions. The directors were uncomfortable in the given situation and asked two of their more distinguished members, Charles Murray and John Rogers, to prepare a direct refutation of the Sargood brothers and what the directors saw as libelous accusations leveled against the company. Murray and Rogers agreed and subsequently published their response on December 12 in *Reynolds's Newspaper*. The company, they wrote, had been formed by "social reformers of the Bronterre O'Brien school." It was their profound belief "that the chief causes of the evils here from which the emigrant seeks to escape, grows out of the vast monopolies of the land and money-lords, which are secured to them by self-privileged class legislation." Through many years of experience dating back to the Chartist era they knew as well as anyone "how slow is the progress of reform in the teeth of opposition of united and powerful action, and unscrupulous vested interests." Murray and Rogers wrote that they "naturally looked across the Atlantic, where free institutions and ample opportunities" continually invite immigrants "to come and share in their enjoyment." Nevertheless, the decision to emigrate was neither impetuous nor malevolent. It was only after long and anxious consideration that the promoters became convinced that the time had come, "though the evils and disappointment inseparable from emigration might be considerably mitigated, if not altogether avoided," by means of cooperative efforts.

Murray and Rogers recalled the 1868 visit John Days made to his old colleagues in the NRL. Men like Days, they said, "returned on short visits, and without selfish ends to subserve, frequently exhorted them not any longer to waste time and means in vainly endeavouring to obtain reform here at the expense of years of struggling, and the sacrifice, perhaps of vigour and health." They believed that all the rights denied to them in England, and all the advantages of access to natural resources, were available in the United States and open to all comers. Among the most important of recent developments in America was the construction of the Union Pacific Railway, "which with its various branches was about to open up the all but boundless and beautiful 'Far West' to settlements." In the West one could find abundant land, rivers, minerals, "and every assorted requisite to sustain in happiness hundreds of millions of human beings." Above all else, however, the people settling the lands of the West "share in the enjoyment of the freest, most popular, and cheapestly-administered Government on the face of the earth." All these things, said Murray and Rogers, received consideration in the nine months between Days's visit and when the company was formally incorporated.

Since the Sargood brothers had questioned the motivation behind the company's stated goals, Murray and Rogers detailed the group's chief objective and what they hoped to accomplish. They were out to acquire land, but not for reasons of profit. The company property in Kansas was established as a freehold estate jointly held by all the shareholders and to be developed "by means of capital equally subscribed by all, either in money or labour." Their plan was to emigrate from England and settle in this and future colonies "by means of mutual cooperation." Murray and Rogers said that the company directors were emphatically opposed to land monopoly and for this reason "inserted in the rules of the company clauses that in their operation prevent the first settlers becoming the land-lords of after comers, by forbidding re-leasing by individual shareholders, and by making all rents the property of the entire body." Money collected from rents did not go into the company coffers for the benefit of the directors. Rather it could be disposed only through "a vote of the majority, and available as a fund, out of which to assist all in turn to prosecute, by temporary advances, every kind of useful occupation." The company's Articles of Association clearly stated that shareholders were guaranteed "only the occupation of such lands as may be acquired in farms or town lots upon reversible leases, in such sizes as they themselves may determine." Cooperative emigration and settlement in colonies founded on O'Brien's principles was the goal, and the directors believed that in this method families who otherwise could never emigrate could now go to Kansas using the combined resources of every subscriber.

Because Murray and Rogers had not been witness to events onboard the *Paraguay,* they could only repeat anecdotal reports of what had transpired. Nevertheless, given the weakness of other evidence the Sargoods had presented, they had no difficulty defending Smith's actions. "We will," testified Murray and Rogers, "be bound for Mr. Smith that he made no unreasonable request, or other than in accordance" with the contract the Sargood brothers signed. As far as dissensions tearing the pioneering group apart and causing others to leave with the Sargoods, Murray and Rogers asserted that such a statement was "contrary to all the letters that have come to hand since, including Mr. Smith's relation of the affair in his first letter from New York." The case of Shallis was a separate issue, but Murray and Rogers testified that the directors had helped him to New York "on the condition that he should support himself there, and afterwards work his way up West." They had since been in communication with Shallis and could give evidence that "he obtained immediate employment, at more than double the wages he earned here. His wife and family have joined him three months ago." If this was what the Sargoods considered an act of cruelty, then Murray and Rogers were proud to claim it.

Unlike the Sargood brothers, said Murray and Rogers, Smith and the other members of the pioneering group proceeded with their mission in an honorable manner. They secured ample land for the company to proceed and have since "acted like heroes; and, in spite of scarcity of funds, have overcome all difficulties, and are manfully prosecuting the work of preparing the way for the spring emigrants." The company had furnished them with money, which they had used to purchase tools, livestock, and provisions. As winter was settling in on the Kansas colony, the settlers had completed a common "dwelling of three rooms, in which are lodging Mr. Smith and two shareholders." In addition to the central dormitory, Charles McCarthy and his brother Felix built a house where Mary McCarthy and the four McCarthy children lived. All correspondence coming from Kansas indicated that the colonists were moving ahead, and being "provided with food, dwellings, and fuel, there is no fear that they will 'freeze up' this winter."

As for the disparaging statements the Sargoods made about working conditions in America, Murray and Rogers would not comment directly because they had no firsthand experience and felt it had nothing to do with what the company was trying to achieve. Nevertheless, they contended that anything the Sargood brothers said about what an immigrant could expect in the United States was "calculated to mislead" and insinuated that whatever difficulties the two siblings may have encountered were undoubtedly of their own making. After all, out "of the hundreds of thousands who have emigrated to the States during this year, it is only to be expected that some get left behind in the race after competence." Murray and Rogers nonetheless could not imagine the democratic United States having the same callous disregard for the working poor as aristocratic Great Britain and too easily dismissed the Sargoods' assertion that immigrants could starve on the streets of New York. Murray and Rogers said that no person "expects to hear that any one of these alien-born people will be allowed to starve to death, as the born subjects of Queen Victoria do in Britain and Ireland."[6]

The company directors would have preferred to put the Sargood incident behind them, but the brothers had opened a discussion that intrigued English workingmen. A lively debate ensued in the press, and many wondered whether immigrating to another land would do anything to address their most basic grievances. One fellow named

Thomas Harvey wrote that conditions in America were as horrid as the Sargood brothers claimed, whereas another, identified only as "a pioneer," agreed that life was hard in the United States but there was abundant opportunity for those willing to labor. Neither correspondent was affiliated with the company, but the unnamed pioneer had been in Kansas and argued that with an outlay of £10 for six months of supplies, a man, "if he is worth anything, he will have built himself a house and stables, grown his first crop, and generally in a good way make his mark."[7] Individuals like the pioneer provided indirect support for the company. However, as far as the company directors were concerned, the public discussion had shifted away from the credibility of their colony project in Kansas and refocused on laboring conditions in the United States. This sort of a dialogue was acceptable, since their purpose in establishing a cooperative was to supersede such conditions.

The Sargood brothers were not content to drop the matter and carried a vindictive grudge against the company directors. In an effort to redirect suspicions on the company and its chosen colony site, the brothers launched a visceral condemnation of Kansas and the people who lived there. The Sargoods expressed astonishment that anyone would defend the idea of immigrating to Kansas and stated: "If it was not from the vivid recollection I have of Kansas, I should certainly think that I had not been there." From their experience the siblings no longer believed "the garnished accounts of paid lecturers, and advertisements in American papers, and paid lecturers from railway companies here in England for that purpose, to sell their large tracts of land along their lines granted them by Congress." None of the hype was true, they said, and anyone who believed in it did so at their own peril. "Kansas State, I have no hesitation in saying, from what I saw, is peopled with the scum of mankind of America." The Sargood brothers related that "a railway company turned out a lot of homestead settlers, whilst we were there, stating that Congress had just granted them the land." Settlers in the region resisted and "burnt all the railway plant they could, and when we left, were playing with each other with revolvers."[8] The Sargoods were referring to the Neutral Land League in Cherokee County and the controversial sale of the Cherokee Neutral Tract in the southeast corner of the state to James F. Joy, Chicago agent of the Missouri River, Fort Scott, and Gulf Railroad.[9] The two siblings had been in Kansas City at the time the conflict in southeast Kansas broke out but were not witness to any of the events. Furthermore, the discord had no bearing on the Central Branch, Union Pacific (CBUP) or the Workingmen's Cooperative Colony in northeast Kansas, but the Sargoods used the incident to belabor the point that they believed the company had made a catastrophic error in choosing to settle in such a violent region.

For the Sargood brothers, a state peopled with rogues, corrupt railroad companies, and the disturbing level of violence that accompanied both was a compelling argument to avoid Kansas altogether. They alleged: "There is in reality no law or order in Kansas State; murder is common, and robbery is more so; little notice is taken of a murdered body. It strikes one with horror to see this reckless disregard for life." Such was the way it had always been in Kansas, they said. During their journey a "Tennessee gentleman" informed the Sargoods "that for years before the civil war the greatest scoundrels in America were sent there for political purposes." As disagreeable as Kansas residents were revealed to be, the Sargood brothers made certain to expose the natural environment to an equally unfavorable light. They had been told by lecturers in London that the weather on the Great Plains was remarkably dry and comfortably warm. Instead "we found it flooded in June, and it was so for six weeks afterwards," and just to add a bit of sarcasm the brothers added, "but I suppose that was merely accidental. We were glad of our greatcoats." Their final bit of advice was that no person, "except he wished to mix with the worst kind of men," should go to Kansas at any time in the foreseeable future.[10]

There was little the company directors could do to reduce the effect of the Sargood brothers' allegations. The Sargoods had not traveled to Kansas with the pioneering group, which meant that the directors had no specific knowledge of events the two siblings encountered on their journey. Moreover, the company had no reports, not in letters from the colony or in U.S. newspapers, of any growing animus being directed toward its cooperative efforts in Kansas. What the directors could do, however, was go to their most knowledgeable member, their American superintendent, and ask him to provide a direct rejoinder to what the Sargoods had said about the voyage from England, the colony, and Kansas. The directors had made certain that Smith received the December issues of *Reynolds's Newspaper* containing the incriminating articles, and Smith, in correspondence cosigned by his fellow colonists, was only too happy to clear his good name and the company's reputation.

In response to the first charge, that he had demanded £40 from the Sargood brothers while onboard the *Paraguay*, Smith flatly denied that such an event ever occurred. According to Smith's letter in the February 6 *Reynolds's Newspaper*, he approached the two brothers and inquired if, after purchasing railway tickets west, they would still have £5 "to lay down, or expend in cooking-stove, provisions, &c., as agreed to by them in London before the directors, and all the other pioneers, and gave their signatures to this agreement." Nothing was ever said about Smith needing the money for land because "all knew that I had received from the company money for that purpose." As to how much money the Sargoods actually admitted to carrying, Smith said that everyone in the group could "testify that they answered, £13 between them; and nothing was said about £40." On the second charge, that a shortage of land would limit each colonist to a single two-acre lease from the company, Smith had an explanation. During the voyage across the Atlantic, when it was still uncertain as to how much land the group would be able to acquire, the pioneers discussed different possible scenarios. In one instance Josiah Morley opined "that in case we had to purchase a quarter section, or 160 or 180 acres of Government land to commence our experiment upon, or to purchase an improved farm, we might then have two-acres each on a lease for house and garden lot." Suggestions such as Morley's represented nothing more than the intellectual bantering of a group trying to idle away the hours at sea. At no point did Smith indicate, either through word or deed, that he considered it a viable option.

Had the Sargood brothers remained committed to O'Brien's principles, they too could have enjoyed the benefits of the Kansas cooperative. As per Smith's report, how the land of the company's 640-acre estate was to be divided between the shareholders had yet to be determined, but a division into two-acre lots was not a consideration. Nevertheless, as it stood at the beginning of 1870, the colonists in Kansas had each taken ten acres on lease, "leaving plenty for each new-comer and for cooperative purposes." With the amount of land in the company's possession, said Smith, "each shareholder will have all he can cultivate comfortably, with all other shareholders' interests, and the amount of land held by the company." Practically all the acreage was fertile and arable, he gushed, "with not five acres of useless land out of the whole." Twelve acres had already been plowed and only awaited spring planting. In addition, the colonists had completed "a well-built house and off-set, capable of accommodating a dozen persons" as well as a separate dwelling for the McCarthy family. Smith also boasted of a stable still under construction, posts set for a cattle lot and awaiting only the fencing boards, and "a first-class well of splendid drinking water, forty feet deep, rocked all round from top to bottom by two of our hardy pioneers." After going through a laundry list of animals, implements, and cooking utensils the group had purchased, Smith gratefully acknowledged that none of it would be possible without the money his comrades in London had sent during the colony's first six months.

Smith felt that most of the other comments the Sargood brothers had made were unworthy of a response and believed that the true "facts are beyond denial." The company directors had fully explained the Shallis episode, and those who had continued to the colony were prospering. The Sargoods had openly pitied the women in the group and considered it a travesty that they should be forced to endure such deprivation, but Smith scoffed at this notion and thought it more a case of envy. Smith wrote that the women did not need anyone's pity. They "are well and happy, and have never wished themselves back, nor regretted the heroic step they took in coming with the first party, well knowing that they would have many difficulties to contend against." All the women, said Smith, had borne their duty nobly and, unlike the Sargood brothers, "stood by the party." As for the other colonists, Robert Hill and his daughter Sophia were employed fifty miles distant from the colony, most likely in Atchison, and the Josiah Morley family was working "on the Branch Pacific Railway, about forty miles away from us." All were expected to return to the colony grounds in the spring.[11]

Smith wrote with the authority of a person who lived on the Kansas cooperative and had reliably followed through on his word. His defense of the colony project effectively defused any lingering controversy and left the Sargoods to fade into obscurity. Letters that subsequently appeared in *Reynolds's Newspaper* roundly condemned all the Sargoods had said about Kansas and working conditions in America.[12] Smith emerged from the debate as the more believable party, but in truth his assessment of the settlement tended to emphasize the positive successes while glossing over potential discord.

George Cox was a case in point. Cox had come to Kansas specifically to oversee the fence building project but arrived at the start of winter when the ground was beginning to freeze. Like most colonists, Cox came with little more than what he could carry and had no money on which to survive. He was completely dependent upon the colony resources during that first winter but found to his dismay that Smith was a stickler for O'Brien's ideas on currency and labor exchanges. Cox discovered that if he wanted to draw any food from the communal larder he first had to perform an equivalent value in labor. Therefore, in the dead of winter, Cox went out with pick and shovel to dig postholes in the frozen ground. Cox was a hard worker and willing to do what was necessary to survive, but he was not an individual to be abused. When spring came Cox moved off the colony. He took up temporary residence with a local farmer but soon had his own homestead and traded away his own greatcoat to pay someone to break the ground for him.[13]

News of discontent in Kansas did not reach London, or if so the directors chose to suppress it. In high spirits after the Sargood controversy had passed over, the directors focused on the good news that twelve acres of colony ground was plowed and ready for spring planting. They eagerly anticipated the halcyon days when the cooperative could be weaned from the company's financial support. In February the shareholders gathered in the NRL's Eclectic Hall for an annual celebration to commemorate the birth of their exalted founder, the late Bronterre O'Brien. While congratulating themselves for creating a company that offered cooperative advantages for workingmen desirous of emigrating from England, the directors began laying the groundwork to expand their mutual operations and attract new subscribers. They were making preparations to send another group of colonists out to Kansas, but in an ambitious move the directors announced that they were opening a cooperative store in London to make foodstuffs and other necessities of life available to shareholders at affordable rates. Money from new subscriptions would pay for the inventory while profits gleaned from shareholder purchases would be applied to a fund to assist emigration to the cooperative colony in Kansas. John Fuller, a thirty-five-year-old coppersmith, exemplified the confidence of his fellows when he exhorted the group to remain united "in the object for which they were organized; perseverance to achieve the end they had determined on; and charity for each others' failings."[14] Fuller's sentiments were noble, but he was a new subscriber and had never been part of the NRL. It was yet to be seen if his convictions would match his rhetoric.

One disconcerting rumor that could not be concealed was the state of Smith's deteriorating physical condition. The cooperative settlement was still in its infancy, and its future success depended on Smith's ability to manage colony affairs and keep every colonist working toward a common goal. Smith never had the charismatic authority of a leader like O'Brien, and evidence from the Sargoods and Cox indicated he may have had a pugnacious personality that grated on some people's nerves, but he was an effective administrator who could keep the settlers in line and the company books in order. However, the American agent's westward journey the previous spring had left him physically exhausted, and his subsequent hard work on the open prairie had done nothing to improve his well-being. As the colony was nearing the first anniversary of its existence, Smith's health was failing. His correspondence from Kansas regularly noted that his vigor was improving, but such assurances occurred with enough frequency that the directors resolved to assist him in his duties and give him the opportunity to truly regain his strength. To help nurse their agent back to health, the directors arranged for Smith's wife, Elizabeth, to depart from Liverpool at the end of February to join her husband in Kansas. Furthermore, they elected Fuller to lead another band of five families, totaling seventeen colonists, to the colony. The directors formally appointed Fuller as Smith's assistant agent in America.[15]

News from Kansas was pouring into London. While much of the correspondence had no direct relation to the colony, so much of it was positive that it seemed but a matter of time before everything on the cooperative bloomed. What the directors failed to consider was that some of these reports were just too good to be true and likely came from the hand of railroad agents or speculators. For example, in April 1870 a letter appeared in the *Penny Bee-Hive* from an English settler in Republic County, Kansas, that boasted of all the free land anyone could want. A person could "go where you like and choose your own land." It was the best land possible, loaded with game beyond description and fertile beyond imagination. People in Kansas "can sow two bushels of wheat and grow fifty from it. They can grow potatoes as big as mason's mallets, and grapes 3½ lb to one bunch, peaches in abundance, and everything grows very plentiful." The climate was beneficial to the point that "nobody ever dies, it is so healthy." The letter writer urged everyone to come to Kansas "to be their own Boss, and have a nice easy time of it." Kansas, he wrote, was "called the Working Man's Paradise, and the name is certainly appropriate."[16] While the anonymous letter was, at best, an exaggeration, its tale of a heaven on earth reflected what potential emigrants signing up for shares and established subscribers in the company wanted to hear.

In April 1870, one year after the initial pioneering band departed from London, Fuller led his group of hopeful colonists to Liverpool where they boarded the steamship *Java*, bound for America. The *Java* reached Castle Garden on May 4 and, after passing through the immigrant processing center, the party headed west. From New York, the Fuller contingent traveled for Kansas by way of Elkhart, Indiana, and Chicago, Illinois. Fuller's reminiscences of the journey across the United States corroborated some of what the Sargood brothers had said about the character of Americans. In later years he recalled that "thieves and sharks were all along the line to victimize the emigrants." In Elkhart the group encountered a streetwise immigrant boy from Kent who agreed to escort them through Chicago. The band had to change trains in Chicago, and the Kentish boy fulfilled his duty by standing watch to "protect them from depredations," while they huddled for the night in a noisome freight depot. Despite their apprehension, the Fuller expedition arrived safely in Atchison but without enough money to finance the final fifty-mile leg of their journey to the colony grounds. Fuller appealed to the good offices of William Downs for assistance. Downs, as gracious and accommodating as he had been with Smith, gave the group a free pass on the CBUP and rode the train with them to make certain they could find the Sherman Station flag stop and the colony.

The new colonists immediately took up their ten-acre allotments and went to work on the settlement. Fuller purchased the lease to Stowell's partially improved ten-acre tract for two dollars, while the unmarried Stowell went looking for employment to help sustain the cash-poor colony. The Fuller family's experiences on the cooperative were illustrative of the problems the company was having in achieving the oft-stated goal of self-sufficiency. Smith's health was progressively declining, and without firm supervision the colonists drifted from company objectives. Most worked diligently to develop their own ten-acre allotments, or on jobs outside the settlement, but few devoted much time to work in the common fields reserved for support of the entire enterprise. Adding to the colony's difficulties was the group's overall agricultural inexperience, a shortage of accessible tools, and the devastating reality that by the start of summer they had to sell or lease their prized livestock and larger implements to neighboring farmers in exchange for food or money to buy food. Ann Fuller recalled trying to plant seed corn on as much of her family's ten acres as possible using nothing but a hatchet to dig furrows in the ground. She was on her own because to earn an income her husband, who was expected to serve as Smith's assistant supervisor, was compelled to become a migrant worker. John Fuller earned money while near the colony by sawing wood for CBUP locomotive boilers but spent most of his time tramping between Atchison, Leavenworth, and Kansas City in search of casual labor.[17]

The lack of proper tools and scattering of labor meant that when the English settlers could find time to plant the communal crops, they first had to work for their neighbors in exchange for the right to borrow oxen and implements to till the land. The settlers managed to sow only twenty acres of wheat in 1870, and as fall harvest neared it was evident to everyone that there was no hope of realizing financial independence for another year.[18] Instead of using the colony profits to fund additional emigration from England, the directors had no choice but to ask the shareholders once again to take out subscriptions on additional shares and aid the colonists for another winter.

During the spring of 1870, well before news of any poor harvest reached London, the company directors were broadening their operations and entertaining utopian designs of transforming the Kansas cooperative into a model town. In April, just as the Fuller party was departing for America, the directors invited Colonel Henry Clinton of Earlsbury Park in Hertfordshire to speak at the Eclectic Hall on the topic of "Associated Homes." Clinton, who envisioned a circular, geometric space, came specifically to provide an outline for a utopian village. Well aware that he was in an O'Brienite enclave, Clinton used Bronterre O'Brien's own poetry to remind the shareholders of why they had purchased land in Kansas. Clinton quoted:

> To every hearth might comfort be brought home,
> Did each but feel for all, and all for each;
> Then o'er earth's globe, where'er our steps might roam,
> We'd find a paradise within man's reach.
> Ah! with what ease might wealth and wisdom bring
> Home to hearth — now drear — now desolate —
> The joys that from content and plenty spring,
> Would they but link their fate to other's fate,
> And help to found an honest social state.

To O'Brien's verse Clinton added a rhyme of his own: "But foresight must regulate all; what *can* be arranged in advance must wisely be ordered — not left to caprice or chance." Clinton's doggerel was intended as a warning shot across the company's bow. It was one thing to buy land and start a cooperative colony in a far-off country, but to succeed, the shareholders had to have the foresight and consideration to develop a concerted plan of action.[19]

Clinton's proposal established a blueprint for what the directors hoped to accomplish in Kansas. According to Clinton, large cities such as London were breeding grounds of vice and social unrest. In this he agreed completely with O'Brien who, in his 1836 translation of *Babeuf's Conspiracy for Equality*, argued that in large cities greedy capitalists, landlords, and unscrupulous merchants formed a rotten center around which gathered petty criminals, debauchers, and other freeloading sorts who were easily beguiled by the siren call of money. Such a system fed off the misery of the honest workingmen, and vice became the wedge splitting apart unity of opposition.[20] The solution to the problem, Clinton said, was to do exactly what the O'Brienites had done, establish "a joint-stock company of limited liability, which might be called a 'Home Company.'" There might be any number of such companies, but once formed the directors must be cautious and not admit just anyone. The membership must be limited to "such a number (as might seem desirable) of shareholders, heads of families, consisting of persons, of, as much as possible, *congenial*, dispositions." Once a group of shareholders had been established, the company would engage in every type of agricultural, commercial, and manufacturing activity necessary to provide useful and rewarding employment for its members while simultaneously giving them "all the comforts, and all the luxuries, of life, at the least possible charge." No one was to be stuck for life in a distasteful job. Every village had jobs often deemed repulsive yet remained necessary for the welfare of all. Therefore, in order to provide variety in a worker's life, occupations should be varied so everyone takes a share of the unpleasant tasks.

There was nothing in Clinton's plan that deviated from what was in the company's own articles of association. Providing agricultural jobs and homes on O'Brien's cooperative principles, however, was where the company stopped. Clinton went further and told them exactly how they were going to have to build their city in Kansas. The imagined space of his associated village started off on a block of land anywhere from 160 to 640 acres, which was exactly what the company had available. An impressive edifice serving as the main administrative and civic center would stand as the hub of a massive wheel. The central building would have a rounded shape and contain all the offices of the company directors and village administrators. The building would house the library, public records office, and the cooking and provisioning gathering place for those living in the heart of the complex. Expanding out from the innermost administrative building on a radial street system were five concentric circles, each with its own designated specialty. The first circle of buildings would house cooperative shopping arcades, lecture rooms, educational facilities, and other accommodations as required. Clinton designated the second circle of buildings as places of indoor exercise and amusement, segregated by sex and age. The third circle of buildings was residential and would contain twenty to thirty dwellings, each with four rooms per floor. Every house would be surrounded by its own garden on one acre of ground. Clinton said the fourth circle was optional. It too was designated residential but would be built only if the population was large enough to warrant the extra housing. The fifth and final circle surrounded the entire village. This was intended as a greenbelt, an area that would contain farm buildings, workshops, warehouses, and any other utilitarian structures that might be needed. Open fields in the outer greenbelt could be used for cricket grounds, recreational parks for outdoor exercise, and volunteer militia training grounds.

Clinton envisioned a symmetrically ordered world in which rural farming villages surrounded small, widely dispersed manufacturing towns. The population of each town would be limited in size but at the same time spread out over a wide area. Therefore, covered tramways "would convey field labourers, and workers in factories, to and from their respective places of occupation, daily, and at all times, all returning, by the same means, each evening, to their homes, in their respective dwelling places." Pneumatic tubes would provide a communication link to every building, and each floor of every home would come equipped with hot and cold running water, baths, and gas hookup. Steam heat would ensure that every home and office building in this self-contained facility would stay warm all winter while eliminating the filth and soot associated with fireplaces and chimneys. The company, in the role of the state, would oversee all employment and ensure fair remuneration as compensation for work completed. This naturally was in addition to every worker being "entitled to enjoy the inestimable privilege and advantage of being supplied, by the company, with all the requisites of life (according to the means of each member) at the lowest possible charge."[21]

With Clinton's fanciful blueprint in hand, the company directors had an ideal plan to parade in front of potential subscribers and a dream for the distant future. They sincerely desired a cooperative village in Kansas, but were never so naïve to think that they could go out and immediately start construction on the central administrative edifice. According to Smith's correspondence, the colonists had expanded the central dormitory building in Kansas so it could accommodate twelve persons. The small wood-frame structure was a far cry from the grandiose administrative complex that Clinton envisioned. It was diminished even further when company directors exaggerated its actual size. John Fuller recalled the directors promising him lodging in the colony's "fourteen-room house," but upon his May arrival in Kansas Fuller had to shelter his family in an unprepossessing "frame room fourteen by ten feet, with a leaky roof over it."[22] Throughout Smith's tenure as the company's Kansas agent, the directors always made an effort to be straightforward and honest about their assets and liabilities, but their utopian plans and constant emphasis on future prosperity may have inadvertently misled certain shareholders into thinking that paradise was just around the corner. Fuller, among other colonists, felt disillusioned upon discovering the reality of the colony. The directors were aware of this problem, and Radford callously observed that some weak-willed settlers had become dismayed by the difficulties and disappointments that necessarily accompany emigration to another land. Such people, he said, "either return or sink under their prospects; or, if successful, become entangled by new associations and affections, and probably lured into the 'broad path' where the multitude are insanely hoping to overtake the will-o-the-wisp happiness of dollar hunting."[23]

From the perspective of hindsight, prospects for the Kansas colony appeared grim. However, in 1870 there were enough signs of progress that the shareholders remained upbeat. By the end of the summer there were five residential buildings on the grounds. Of even greater symbolic significance was the first birth on the colony. Jane Bielby was pregnant when she departed from England in April, and Mary Anne Bielby was born in May. The successful delivery of one baby girl signified nascent life for the colony and was a cause for celebration in both Kansas and London. During the same month, Radford and James Murray began publishing a monthly labor periodical designed to promote the colony effort and promulgate the philosophical ideals of Bronterre O'Brien. The periodical, confidently named the *New World*, was a publicity arm of the

Mutual Land, Emigration, and Cooperative Colonization Company. It provided curious readers with news from Kansas while advancing cooperative emigration and colonization as the solution to emancipating labor from the "domination of landed and monied capitalists." One reviewer called it "a *bona fide* sign [and] manual of the times." Radford, who had succeeded John Rogers as the company's corresponding secretary, had primary responsibility for the journal. It reflected his unbridled confidence that perseverance along with a commitment to O'Brien's principles would undoubtedly succeed.[24] Nevertheless, the difficult summer months amply demonstrated the problems inherent in transforming the Kansas colony into a self-reliant cooperative and revealed how much work the company yet had to undertake.

As upbeat as the directors had been in the spring, by the end of the summer their outlook was decidedly less sanguine. Even before news of the meager fall harvest filtered back to London, a new disaster rocked the entire group and left the colony leaderless. In September Smith succumbed to his illnesses and died. Fuller, who by default became colony agent, built a rude coffin for Smith but had no means to convey the body to its place of interment beside a schoolhouse two miles distant. The colonists were so destitute and had so few resources at this point that circumstances reduced them to borrowing a wagon and horses from neighboring farms in order to bury their leader. Forty to fifty settlers, colonists and neighbors, from the surrounding area gathered at the gravesite to mourn their fallen comrade. Fuller, a member of the Odd Fellows society, donned his fraternal regalia and performed an Anglican funeral service from memory. One of the nearby homesteaders stepped forward and assured Elizabeth Smith that her husband had been highly regarded and that she "had the sympathy of the inhabitants of the locality." Smith's London colleagues mourned: "Amidst such a scene, upon the Prairies of Kansas, were the remains of him we knew and appreciated so highly conveyed to their last resting place."[25]

Smith had been the linchpin of the colony project. Respected for his devotion to O'Brien's reform philosophy, Smith, when healthy, was unencumbered by family concerns and able to devote his full attention to colony operations. His death was a crippling blow to the cooperative, as no one of a similar stature was on hand to take his place. Smith's fellow directors in London eulogized him as a martyr whose sacrifice would be remembered through the ages:

> An intelligent thinker, an earnest worker, and a devoted martyr to the cause of humanity, he accepted the position assigned him, as the pioneer of our enterprise, never faltered in the path of duty, faithfully fulfilled the great trust reposed in him, and died at the post of duty. When our enterprise has successfully encountered the difficulties inherent in such an undertaking, and happy homes and flourishing settlements, founded on social justice, shall cover the prairies of the West, the name of EDWARD GRAINGER SMITH will be revered as the founder of our first colony.[26]

Henry Burton, a shareholder from Nottingham, proclaimed that Smith was "the Bronterre O'Brien of our Colony — the man whose exertions, integrity, and judgment materially aided in overcoming the difficulties of organisation, and shared an example worthy of our esteem." As a fitting tribute to Smith, Burton suggested using shareholder money to erect a monument to Smith on the colony grounds in Kansas. The directors appreciated the sentiment but had a more practical mark of respect for the former agent. As they conveyed to Burton, "the best tribute they can give to his memory is to help on the undertaking with good wishes, active operation, and support, both moral and pecuniary."[27]

The company directors had trusted Smith implicitly and were fully cognizant that his passing represented a serious setback to their plans. The Kansas cooperative had progressed far more slowly than anticipated, and with Smith's demise it seemed appropriate to carry out a thorough examination of the colony operation and an audit of its books. The directors did not take this matter lightly and appointed their most distinguished member, company president Charles Murray, to travel to the United States and undertake a complete inspection of the colony. With another winter approaching, morale among the colonists was beginning to slip, and it was Murray's duty to re-invigorate the settlement and remind everyone of their cooperative responsibilities. Above all else, Murray wanted to see for himself exactly how money was being spent, make necessary adjustments, and put the colony back on the path toward sustainability.

On October 4, Murray and five new colonists, four men and one woman, traveled to Liverpool and boarded the steamship *Calabria* for its voyage to America. The ship arrived in Castle Garden after a difficult crossing of twelve days. The passage was particularly wearing on Murray, who was compelled to rest in New York for a few days to recover his strength. Once able to resume his journey, Murray traveled by rail to Kansas. He found the train ride across the United States invigorating and commented that the country was "most beautiful, the weather delightful and warm, [and] the sun shining brightly." Autumn in America was, he said, "just like July in England." Murray arrived in Atchison on October 24 and stopped long enough to make an appointment with CBUP superintendent William Downs. He very much wanted to discuss the company's payment schedule with Downs and gain a precise understanding of land taxes and other such matters that Smith had handled in the past. Late in the afternoon Murray's party boarded a CBUP train and headed west on the last leg of their journey. The locomotive stopped in Wetmore, five miles east of the colony, and the group took advantage of the opportunity to look around the small town. Many years later an elderly reporter from Wetmore recalled this day and claimed that Murray was a raconteur who "partook freely of Johnny Clifton's 'alf- and-alf.' He was a free spender and made friends here readily." In England Murray was highly regarded in the ranks of the London Boot-Closers Society, the International, and the NRL. Such success within organized labor associations required that an individual be intelligent, expressive, and good-humored. Murray had led mass demonstrations in London's Hyde Park. He knew how to handle a crowd and to assess the mood of the local population toward the cooperative colony. His stop in the Wetmore saloon represented an effort in cultivating goodwill.[28]

From the beginning, the company directors emphasized praxis over philosophy and expected the Kansas cooperative to demonstrate the validity of Bronterre O'Brien's social and economic theories by becoming a self-sufficient showpiece. However, the artisans transplanted to the Great Plains were in an unfamiliar environment and attempting to become agriculturalists without the resources needed to carry out the task. This was an issue that became readily apparent to Murray when he arrived on the colony grounds. Smith had gotten the colony started, but his months of declining health and eventual demise had created a leadership void among the settlers. Fuller had been sent to Kansas precisely for the purpose of relieving Smith and had been expected to assume the agent's responsibilities. Unlike Smith, Fuller was a young man with a wife and six children under his care. He was not going to sacrifice his family for the sake of the colony and had to earn money away from the settlement. Fuller was unable to take on the agent's duties, and no one else was prepared or willing to step forward and replace Smith in the months preceding his death. Thus, when Murray arrived, the colony administration was in a state of disarray. It was an embarrassing situation for the hapless colonists. They realized the directors were disappointed, but understood better than Murray just how difficult life on the prairie had been. The settlers were reluctant to open the colony books for inspection.[29] Nevertheless, Murray was not a man to be denied and started the auditing work.

In November Radford submitted a financial accounting of money spent and a prospectus for the company. He apologized for the colonists because they no longer "had the advantage of having the use of horses belonging to the Company, yet they have labored part of the time for neighbors, and obtained in exchange the use of cattle and implements." Because of this extra effort they were able to sow twenty acres of wheat, which Radford believed signified a good start on a "provision made for a crop of *breadstuff* next season, which, converted into flour at some neighboring mill, would be sufficient to sustain at least a dozen families during the next year." For Radford the twenty acres of grain was a symbolic triumph and a necessary step "in the founding of our Colony." As far as money was concerned, Radford explained that at the time of Fuller's departure for the colony in April the company in total had collected £503 from share subscriptions and loans. Colony expenses had consumed most of the treasury funds, leaving £22 on hand. Looking over the colony assets and prospects for 1871, Radford calculated that the shareholders could, if they followed "a judicious business plan of operation" during the coming season, realize a surplus by the end of the summer, "from the Company's farm alone, after paying all expenses and liabilities, nearly equal to the whole of the share subscriptions from the commencement of the Company."[30]

In the company's prospectus Radford estimated that the group could raise a working capital of £5,000 from the sale of five thousand shares at £1 apiece, "with the power to increase to £50,000." To make the operation affordable to workingmen, Radford's plan stipulated that shares could be subscribed for an application fee of one shilling per share, with weekly payments of sixpence. Every shareholder, regardless of how many shares owned, received one vote in the company operations. This was an egalitarian operation where management of the company was "absolutely under the control of the shareholders." The company, as guided by the directors, acted as "agent in many ways calculated to achieve the personal independence of its shareholders and increase their material prosperity." To encourage the material development of the Kansas colony, the directors were willing "to act as agent between any shareholder and trade societies or other corporate bodies willing to advance their funds the means (on loan) to such shareholders to emigrate and settle on the Company lands." The upshot, however, was that the company was "established by working men for working men. Its dogma is, labour is omnipotent; its motto is, liberty in right, equality in law, fraternity in interest."[31]

Radford delivered a rosy prognosis for the Kansas cooperative's future, but external events beyond the company's control intervened to a detrimental degree. O'Brien had been a devoted Francophile, and since his passing members of the NRL continued paying careful attention to left-wing political agitation in France. Radicals exiled from Louis Napoleon's Second Empire often found a welcome embrace in the Eclectic Hall. When the Franco-Prussian War broke out in July 1870, members of the NRL joined other workers in cheering for the Germans against the despised regime of Louis Napoleon. However, with the decisive German victory at Sedan in early September and the fall of Louis Napoleon's empire, English workers began cheering for the new Third Republic of France as the hope for Continental republican ambitions. The International Working Men's Association went so far as to pass a resolution urging armed British intervention on the side of the French. Reminiscent of the mass rallies supportive of Italian and Polish republican movements in the early 1860s, London workers again gathered in places like Hyde Park and Trafalgar Square to back the French Republic. Republican clubs sprang up throughout London, and working-class efforts to embrace republicanism and enact meaningful democratic reform in England found new life.[32]

After the French surrender in January 1871, the German army insisted upon a triumphal march through Paris that humiliated residents of the city. Angered over the inability of the Third Republic to stop the Germans and frustrated over the monarchical pretensions of the National Assembly, in March 1871 Parisian workers rebelled against the conservative regime and established the independent Paris Commune. It was an invigorating moment, and London workers were swept away in the torrent. There were voices of moderation, such as Charles Bradlaugh, a journalist and longtime NRL sympathizer. Bradlaugh served as president of London's Republican Club but argued against using the red flag of the Commune at gatherings in England lest it spark a violent conservative reaction. At a rally in Clerkenwell, Irish republican sympathizers warned that too much attention focused on foreign politics distracted workers from necessary reform work at home. In the intoxicating atmosphere of the moment, however, few listened, including members of the NRL. Speaking before an East End republican meeting in April 1871, NRL member John Weston attempted to insert O'Brienite sentiments into the debate when he proclaimed: "A republic, to be of any use to the masses of the people, must deal with the social questions affecting their interests."[33]

In April, James Murray approached the IWMA requesting support for a public demonstration of solidarity with the Paris Commune. In contrast to his brother Charles, James Murray did not serve on the IWMA's General Council. Instead he came as a representative of the International Democratic Association, which, unlike the NRL, had refused to affiliate with the IWMA on the grounds that Marx's IWMA did not go far enough in its advocacy for international socialism. Although his O'Brienite colleagues on the General Council supported the request, Murray's proposal was voted down. It made no difference. In a massive April procession, James Murray, accompanied by a marching band and thousands of protesters dressed in red caps of liberty, proceeded to a demonstration in Hyde Park. Once there he and other O'Brienite speakers, including John Radford, expressed their sympathy and support for the Communards. Murray was the leader, but it was Radford who stood before the crowd and, in the official address, declared that the workers of London recognized the people of the Commune as "the pioneers of progress and the architects of a new and purer social state."[34] Regardless of the international attention it garnered, the Commune did not last long and fell in May when Adolphe Thiers brutally repressed the uprising.

The existence of the Paris Commune was detrimental to the Kansas colony. There was no direct link between the two, but during the Commune's existence NRL members became thoroughly swept up in the political fervor. News of the colony disappeared from the London press while publicity and fund-raising for the Mutual Land, Emigration, and Cooperative Colonization Company all but ceased. Experienced NRL members like James Murray, who normally would have been out working on the colony's behalf, was utilizing his spare moments in support of the Commune and republican reform efforts. Radford's struggle to maintain a monthly periodical to promote the colony folded in February, and the company's cooperative store in London likewise disappeared. Charles Murray remained in Kansas and worked through the winter in an effort to put the colony on a steady footing, but with attentions diverted and support fading in London, his labors became that much more difficult.

Shareholders continued to emigrate to the Kansas colony as individuals, but there were no more celebratory send-offs of large groups from London. Charles Murray managed to keep the colonists organized and working on the land during his months on the settlement, but morale remained distressingly low. In March 1871 another prairie fire swept through the area immediately west of the colony grounds. It destroyed a neighboring settler's stores of hay and threatened timber belonging to the CBUP, but a joint effort by everyone residing in the region quenched the flames and saved the cooperative. The near disaster marked an inauspicious beginning of the spring season. With prospects continually looking bleak and little money coming from London, some of the colonists gave up and began abandoning the settlement. John Fuller was prominent among the deserters. The man who one year earlier had implored his colleagues to remain united and have charity for each other's failings now announced that he was tired of "raising nothing but weeds." Fuller quit the colony and moved his family first to the nearby town of Centralia and then to Seneca.[35]

Murray also discovered that the company's plan for turning the workingmen's cooperative into a model town was due to receive some unexpected competition. In May a Congregationalist group that formed in Northampton, Massachusetts, in 1830 under the tutelage of Elijah Smith announced it was relocating to the fifty-mile post on the CBUP to build a religious settlement called the Memorial Colony. The group had been residing in Princeton, Illinois, but in the fall of 1870 the sons of Elijah Smith came to Kansas and agreed to terms with the CBUP on the land. Their colony was to take its name from the "memorial year," or the 250-year anniversary of the landing of the Pilgrims. Railroad officials had other ideas about the name. The CBUP wanted to develop a town at the fifty-mile post and, as part of the deal, began surveying lots and announced that it would build a post office. The railroad also changed the Sherman Station name to Sother in honor of Thomas M. Sother, who was a prominent secretary of the CBUP. Any new town would bear that name.[36] Murray promptly dispatched plans for the proposed town of Sother to his fellow directors in London. The directors gave the prospectus full consideration but never raised any suggestion of co-operating with the religious settlement. Instead they would watch and see how the Congregationalists fared.

Murray remained in Kansas through the end of the year and, though he made little more progress with the colony than Smith had before him, he was confident that the colonists had turned the corner. Before leaving the settlement, Murray appointed Charles Mc-Carthy to succeed him as the company's American agent. McCarthy was an interesting choice. He had accompanied Smith as part of the original pioneering group and remained one of the company's most stalwart laborers. Like Fuller before him, McCarthy had a large family that took precedence over company affairs. Nevertheless, he accepted the position knowing full well the challenges attached to it. As for Murray, he had no intention of heading directly for London. Ever since the colony was founded, Josiah Warren had maintained an interest in its progress. Through Ambrose Caston Cuddon, he regularly peppered the company with questions and advice, some of which were printed in the New World. In response to Warren's numerous queries, Radford assured him that Murray would "be able, in an oral communication, to impart more information to you concerning our views and aspirations." While Murray would not come immediately, Radford told Warren that "Mr. Murray is at present at our Colony, and will, on his return journey, endeavour to make a call upon you."[37] Therefore, when Murray left Kansas, he headed for Chicago to view firsthand the devastation of the Great Fire of 1871, then to Massachusetts to make a courtesy call on the elderly Warren.

In November, as Murray was wrapping up his affairs in Kansas, Radford presented the annual accounting of the company's financial well-being. The meeting opened with the regular appeal for workers to rally around the colony in Kansas. Through combined efforts the experiment "should set an example to the world, by putting into practice just principles relating to land, labour, and capital." The shareholders had heard this plea before. What they wanted to learn above all else was: "Is the company solvent?" Radford proceeded to sketch out his estimate of the value of their assets. Some of the land on the 640-acre colony section had been improved through plowing, fencing, or homebuilding. This, he said, made the entire colony worth at least £1,000, "and this in less than three years, and started by a few working men." Radford then produced a balance sheet, calculated from April 1869 to April 1871, finding that the company books were in the black with a total of over £600 in assets, "after making provisions for paying all liabilities." Radford's accounting made a number of assumptions, not least of which was the resale value of the land. Plus, the company had made only minimal payments on the property and remained heavily in debt. However, none of that was relevant to Radford. A successful colony operating on O'Brien's principles was his objective, and achieving such a dream was going to be challenging. As he told his listeners: "Difficulties they had met with and conquered, and if perfect freedom was worth having it was worth struggling for."[38]

By the end of 1871 the Workingmen's Cooperative Colony had made very little progress. Charles Murray thought he had stabilized on-site operations, while John Radford believed that the company was well on the way to solvency. However, for the situation in Kansas to tangibly improve, the directors would have to find a new and substantial source of funding while rethinking their policy of allotting the land. The colonists in Kansas were painfully aware of the need for money. Their utopia was not panning out, and they understood how quickly everything would collapse without stable leadership and steady monetary support.

4

Moral Intoxication

Frederick Wilson

We doubt if there be a single recorded instance in the whole history
of civilized society of any king, ruler, statesman, legislator, prophet,
philosopher, orator, or other public man, seeking honestly, and with
probabilities of success, the reign of justice, humanity, and fraternity
for his fellow-countrymen, that was not overwhelmed with calumny,
overpowered by faction, and ultimately either put to death or forced
to fly for his life and bury himself in poverty and obscurity to escape
the malice of the oppressors of his country.

—JAMES BRONTERRE O'BRIEN, ca. 1850

Settlers arriving in Kansas during the early 1870s envisioned that
rain would follow the plow. The reward for their agricultural labors
would come through the transformation of the Great Plains country into a temperate, forested environment more akin to that with
which they were accustomed. The mere presence of yeoman farmers blessed the entire region because even land untouched by the
plow benefited from the rain that agricultural activity coaxed from
the sky.[1] In 1872, travel writer John H. Tice toured the countryside
along the Central Branch, Union Pacific (CBUP) line. For Tice the empirical evidence that rain followed the plow was manifest in everything he saw. Traveling west from Atchison, Tice observed that the
"country is diversified by hill and dale; the hills rising out to moderate height, and where not occupied by farms, have a dense growth of
young oak, hickory, walnut, and other trees indigenous to the West."

How the trees got started puzzled the local inhabitants, wrote Tice, "for when the settlers first came these hills were covered with prairie grass with no sign of any other growth." The presence of young trees bewildered Tice as well, and he confessed his inability to account for how the seeds arrived. For their growth, however, he gave full credit to American agricultural practices and confidently proclaimed: "it is an occurrence that happens everywhere; not only in Kansas, but in the West, wherever fire is kept out of the prairies contiguous to timber, a young forest growth immediately springs up."[2]

Tice took a few notes at the flag stop of Sother and observed "beautiful and rich agricultural country," but took no notice of the Workingmen's Cooperative Colony. Nevertheless, the shareholders of the Mutual Land, Emigration, and Cooperative Colonization Company agreed with Tice's assessment and shared the common misconception that bringing forth a garden from the grassy plains required little more than their presence. They continued to focus their attention on the dream of building a cooperative community modeled on the social and economic philosophy of Bronterre O'Brien, but failed to adjust to environmental realities. After nearly three years in Kansas and suffering repeated setbacks on their communal farm in the form of prairie fires, poor harvests, and settler attrition, the company directors fostered an uncompromising O'Brienite rigor and held fast to the belief that all difficulties had been overcome. They were confident that company president Charles Murray would return from Kansas with solid evidence that the colony was on the verge of prosperity.

After a residency of fifteen months in the United States, mostly on the Kansas colony, in January 1872 Murray returned to the company's Denmark Street headquarters in London. The company shareholders were anxious to learn what he had to say about the colony and eagerly anticipated his forthcoming presentations. During the week prior to Murray's first speech, Radford prepared the shareholders by reminding them that the choice of Kansas was fortuitous. It was particularly so because the state government "appeared to understand that the education of her children was of vital importance." Educational opportunities remained a point of concern for the O'Brienites, and Radford said that in Kansas "the authorities were instituting an extensive system of education, and the school age was from five to twenty-one years of age."[3] On the evening of January 27, the shareholders filled the Eclectic Hall to hear the first of Murray's talks. Murray, who had earned a reputation as an energetic and fiery speaker, delivered a bland and uninspiring address. He said nothing to contradict John Radford's November financial assessment but added little to persuade listeners of his sincere belief in the colony's future. Murray "described the Company's estates as being well adapted for their colony, in respect of soil, climate, and position, and quoted the opinions of neighboring settlers (well qualified to judge), to show that the estates had doubled in value since purchased, proving the Company to be in a sound commercial position."[4]

Murray's next talk was scheduled for the end of February. During the intervening weeks Radford and James Murray worked to rise above Charles Murray's tepid testimonial. In an early February shareholder gathering, Radford sang the praises of America and pointed to that country's remarkable progress as a sign of its enlightened ways. James Murray joined the discussion and admitted that the company had encountered many unforeseen difficulties in building a colony in Kansas "but congratulated the members on the energetic manner in which they had overcome them." Murray added that his belief in O'Brien's philosophy remained unshaken and hoped that other societies would learn to emulate those principles, for in Great Britain, he said, there was no hope "of effecting any radical, political, or social changes." Therefore, he appealed to those desirous of a fresh start in life and wanting to establish "a new order of society to go out to the Far West, where surrounded by favourable circumstances, they would be able to attain that object."[5] The company shareholders already enjoyed such advantages through their colony land in Kansas. All it took was a rigorous commitment to O'Brien's principles as enshrined in the Articles of Association and the courage to work cooperatively together.

On February 20 the company organized a celebratory soiree to give Charles Murray a proper welcome home gathering and once again to hear him speak on the Kansas colony. On this occasion Murray lived up to his billing in what newspapers described as an "enlivening spectacle" where participants could enjoy both "pleasure and instruction." For the instruction, Murray testified that the land required nothing more than the labor of their fructifying hands. He declared that "the laws and constitutions of the Western States, as well as the climate, soil, and surroundings, offered every encouragement to associations of working men in England to build up for themselves in that favoured land independent homes." Settlers in Kansas were "surrounded by every advantage of civilisation, and with a security for continued progress." Such rewards "required only to be known to the advanced and energetic portion of British workmen, to cause them to organise in thousands to secure such advantages while land is still to be obtained." These benefits were available to all through the "practicability and advantages of cooperative emigration and colonisation." After the instructional lecture that revealed none of the hardships taking place in Kansas, Murray served up a dollop of pleasure through an exhibit of artifacts from the colony. Murray displayed samples of wheat, Indian corn, potatoes, and buckwheat that the colonists in Kansas had grown. The shareholders were gratified to see the produce as well as "a small parcel of the actual soil" taken from the Kansas cooperative. However, Murray also trotted out relics he had picked up in the aftermath of the Great Chicago Fire, and ogling the conflagration's scorched residue "proved not the least interesting object during the evening."[6]

In March Radford reaffirmed the company's commitment to O'Brien's theories of land nationalization and restated the directors' strategy of allowing shareholders in Kansas to lease individual parcels no larger than ten acres. Dividing the land into ten-acre allotments was a guideline that Edward Grainger Smith had established in 1869, but the directors made it formal policy based upon British studies of how much land was required for a farmer to survive in the English countryside. Fully accepting the thesis that rain follows the plow, they embraced the ten-acre principle without making any allowances for the different economic and ecological conditions existing in Kansas and the Great Plains. Radford continued to assert that any shareholder could lease as much land as he or she could cultivate. To this statement, however, he added the caveat that "with the quantity of land now held by the company it was not advisable to make the allotments larger than ten acres." Alfred A. Walton, a former president of the National Reform League (NRL), stood behind Radford's arguments and contended that larger allotments of land were unnecessary. After all, said Walton, the company's ultimate objective had to be cooperative rather than individual farming. He admonished the shareholders to remember the principles and objects of the company. O'Brien taught that evil was the product "from the monopoly of land by a comparative few to the exclusion of the many." Walton said that "if the members would have faith in one another, and adhere to their principles, success would crown their efforts."[7]

For faith and adherence to principles, the shareholders held up the Latter-day Saints as an example worthy of emulation. In April James Murray invited Thomas Moore, a carpenter and relative newcomer to the group, to deliver his inaugural public address on the "Benefits of Organised Colonisation, as Illustrated by the Rise and Progress of the Mormons." Moore likened the difficulties the Mormons encountered in Utah Territory to what the company was experiencing in Kansas. The Latter-day Saints, he said, packed up from Nauvoo, Illinois, moved through an unknown region, and settled in the valley of the Great Salt Lake. Through perseverance and dedication they made the desert bloom. Moore believed that the "result of their unity and labour was evidenced by the immense extent of the country they had colonized, and the prosperous position they had achieved." He looked longingly at the land, villages, and mills the Mormons had developed in Utah and "urged that their success was proof that we could do likewise, especially as we had not [as] many of the difficulties to contend with that they had."[8]

To further build the case for the emigration of advanced reformers from England to the colony, Radford brought forward the example of his old colleague John Days. Days continued his service in the California State Legislature and in 1871 had introduced a resolution before the assembly calling for nationalizing the land of the United States along terms similar to what the O'Brienites were undertaking in Kansas. The bill, which contained two major points, was vintage O'Brien. It called for the "repeal of all laws allowing the sale of the public domain, the lands to be given to actual settlers in such quantities as they can cultivate." It also stipulated a "restoration to the public domain of all lands now reserved for railroad purposes, not actual patented, compensation in money being made for inchoate rights to railroad companies when necessary." Radford, who was brother-in-law to Days, received news of the bill in April 1872, after the legislature had already voted it down. Nevertheless, he mined a nugget from Days's speech to illustrate what the company was working to accomplish with emigration to America.[9] Quoted Radford:

> Land monopoly and its concomitant luxury, has been the cause of the decline of every one of the great cities and nations of ancient date. Where are those cities now? Alas! After having become the prey of land sharks, they live only in the history of the past. Will America benefit by the lessons of the history of Europe? Will she so form the land laws that the horrors quoted will be strangers to our noble country? That she has not done so we will see, that she may do so will depend upon the growing intelligence of the people upon this question, and their choice of representatives to carry out this will.[10]

Questions of land nationalization and the possibilities of British reformers altering the course of American politics remained an interesting topic of discussion for the directors in London. For the colonists in Kansas it was a different reality, as difficulties continued to plague the colony. Residents in the vicinity of the colony had thought highly of Charles Murray and respected the work he had done for the settlement. Because of the goodwill Murray had generated, Charles McCarthy, the newly appointed colony agent, made certain that the primary county newspapers in Seneca were informed when the company president arrived safely back in England and of the February reception over which Murray had presided.[11] For McCarthy, relating news of Murray's travels turned out to be the highlight of his tenure as superintendent. In early May a series of prairie fires swept across the southern part of Nemaha County, the second of which scorched the cooperative. The blaze had ignited along the railroad tracks and likely originated with an errant locomotive spark. The prevailing winds blew the searing flames northeast directly into the colony. Suddenly McCarthy had to organize a team to battle the worst firestorm the colonists had yet experienced. They failed to control the conflagration and lost the fences that George Cox had labored so hard on two winters earlier. Worse yet, the previous year a high wind had blown an inexpertly constructed colony house to the ground. The structure had not yet been rebuilt, and the piled-up lumber only added more fuel to the raging wildfire. The colonists managed to save the main dormitory building, but lost their stables, all the contents of the stables, and their haystacks.[12]

William Beeby, a housepainter, arrived with another small group of settlers just in time for the firestorm. Beeby, who was a close friend of Radford's, remained unruffled, purchased the lease to Edward Rooney's allotment, and began work. For others, however, it was no longer possible to retain a cool composure. The thought of losing another season to rebuilding all that had been lost proved too much for several of the older colonists. Rooney, who had been on the colony grounds since August 1869, packed up in June and left for Salt Lake City. John Stowell, who worked off the colony grounds to help support the settlement, in 1872 married a local woman named Laura Jennings and began establishing his own household. The loss of McCarthy, however, proved far more detrimental. He had been one of the original pioneers and had persevered on the colony since the very first day. With the exception of Edward Grainger Smith, no one had suffered through as many hardships on the colony as

McCarthy. However, like John Fuller before him, McCarthy had a wife and small children and had to secure some form of reliable income. One month after the fire, he moved his family to Chicago, where he found employment as a laborer in a wholesale house.[13]

With McCarthy's departure there was no experienced on-site superintendent to guide the company's cooperative program or lead the colonists. A number of settlers remained on the land and continued a desultory existence on their individual allotments, but after the fire few made an effort to work the collective farm. The company directors in London could not have been altogether ignorant of this predicament but said nothing. Their silence on the matter indicated that they likely comprehended the difficulty. Instead of expressing concern for the devastating setbacks in Kansas, the directors seemed far more interested in considering the proposals of a London eccentric named Frederick J. Wilson. Wilson had been flitting about London's labor societies since the opening of the First International and possibly even earlier. He was an unconventional thinker whose ideas and writings tended to focus on reforming the intellect, albeit in a convoluted style that won him few converts. By 1872 the roughly thirty-seven-year-old Wilson had become interested in communal projects and recast himself as a self-styled master in the art of conceptualizing cooperative villages. He had no practical experience, but nonetheless announced his plans to publish a penny-monthly periodical in which he would "explain a complete system of Cooperative Education, and the arrangements for social enjoyment of existence in a cooperative village." It was to be a vehicle, writes Logie Barrow, "for Wilson to fantasise his architectural symbolism." While it is not known whether Wilson sought out the company directors or they contacted him, in May 1872 he appeared at the Eclectic Hall and presented his conceptual drawings for a model cooperative town.[14]

The Mutual Land, Emigration, and Cooperative Colonization Company and its colony completely beguiled Wilson. Although he had no prior familiarity with O'Brien's philosophy, Wilson saw a struggling company that had already established a cooperative on the plains of Kansas. All it lacked was operating capital and stable on-site leadership to properly develop the land and keep the program going. Wilson believed he could provide both while simultaneously putting his own concept of constructing a cooperative village to the test. During the summer of 1872, Wilson cultivated the favor of the company directors and invited James Murray to write a pair of promotional articles for the *Comprehensionist*, Wilson's new "Journal of Ideas, Thinkers Manual, and Willingwell Gazette." Murray opened in June with a grievance stating how he and his colleagues had "for many years felt the absence of hope that any means can be practically opened for the working-man to materially benefit his condition in England." There was no hope because "the land that really belongs to the State, and which should be held by the State for the benefit of the people at large, is claimed as a personal ownership by the few." The monies landlords demanded for rents and leases represented a scandal, he said. Such a system raised the price of commodities beyond what poor people could pay and allowed the rich to profit from the public purse.[15]

Among the perils of perpetuating a system of private ownership by a few privileged individuals, wrote Murray in his second article, published in July, was that people would not take an interest in their homes or community. Therefore, "home-ties are not formed, the tree the man may plant he will never sit under; so all improvement is discouraged, and the money is spent in transitory pleasures, as dress, amusements, gambling, and bodily gratifications." Because the landowners also controlled the votes in Parliament, such a state of affairs would inevitably continue in perpetuity. England had become a country where it was impossible for workers to improve their condition. The solution, said Murray, was to do as he and his colleagues had done. They looked westward toward the setting sun and determined to build homes for themselves on their cooperative in Kansas. Murray continued his argument by expressing the importance of *continuous mutual* cooperation in emigration and settlement through *mutual colonization*. Anything less was doomed to failure because, as he stated, experience had shown that without mutual cooperation, land had been allotted into individual freeholds. This "procedure has invariably proved fatal to further progress, because thereby letting in the spirit of blind selfishness it has ended in: Landlords who live upon the labour of others and the landless who have to support the landlord and his allies." All land, forests, quarries, fisheries, and mines must be kept as joint property with the returns used for the commonweal. Finally, Murray agreed that individuality was important to any community, but he impressed upon his readers the equally essential point that "the utmost facilities be provided for cooperation in all things; by crediting the colonizers with the capital to cultivate and stock farms, orchards, and gardens, &c., or erect and furnish workshops, mills, and factories."

Plans based upon mutual cooperation, said Murray, were "applicable to the founding of a village or an empire." There was plenty of land available in favorable parts of the world. All that was required was enough foresight to design a settlement plan that left "a comparatively small cost to each allotter; garden and orchard plots can be planted with fruit and forest trees, so as to be in bearing condition by the time that many of the allotters could get out." The first settlers would build new homes that would be ready and waiting for later arrivals so friends and fellow townspeople could live side-by-side. If an industrious people settled under such conditions, Murray wrote, they would never know or fear poverty again. Paying for such a venture was easy as well, he said. The "greater portion of the capital necessary to develop such a colony will be obtained from the land itself — the first capital subscribed being comparable to the first bucket of water put into a new pump, which thereby put in working order — returns ever afterward an unlimited amount." This sort of plan would ensure that an investor making an advance could be repaid in kind or an equivalent value in labor.

Murray's idyllic description was entirely conjectural, but he assured his readers that such a fantastic place already existed. It was the Mutual Land, Emigration, and Cooperative Colonization Company's cooperative colony in Kansas, "which has been organized in the form herein sketched, and having in view all the advantages advocated, besides others equally important and interesting." Just two months after a fire devastated the Kansas colony, Murray wrote that the families living in "the beautiful state of Kansas, U.S., on a line of railroad, and within a fortnight's journey of Liverpool," were enchanted with the land of their adoption. They "desire nothing so much as that their poor, but industrious, fellow countrymen be made acquainted with the advantages which are open to them." He described the colony grounds as having several dwellings and fifty acres broken up and under cultivation, all of which was enclosed by four miles of fencing. Murray highlighted the location of the company's Denmark Street headquarters and urged everyone to join in the cause for their social emancipation.[16]

James Murray was one of the more influential company directors and had access to all news arriving from Kansas. While it was possible that Murray had written the article before reports of the destructive spring wildfire reached London, his glowing portrayal of the company's cooperative program was nonetheless disingenuous. The reality was that the *Comprehensionist* was an obscure journal with a minuscule circulation. Rather than appealing for working-class investors to buy individual shares, it is likely that Murray's article was targeting an audience of one, namely Frederick Wilson. Wilson had money to invest, and Murray's Land-of-Milk-and-Honey spiel was like catnip to him. At the conclusion of Murray's essay, Wilson added a postscript stating that he had personally purchased twenty £1 shares in the company "in the belief that the system adopted by the Society is the best yet proposed for the benefit of the poor." Although new to the company, Wilson claimed the ability to "testify to the great personal sacrifices the original members have made in time, comfort, and money, in practically working out a success, whilst others have done nothing but talking." Wilson's outlay made him one of the largest shareholders in the company, and he was a suddenly influential subscriber who was convinced that the Kansas colony was already a rousing success.[17]

Wilson was a quixotic dreamer and had no realistic conception of the labor and sacrifice required to transform raw prairie land into a cooperative village. However, he was not shy about wielding the influence that accompanied his investment, and the expectations he brought to the company were not necessarily a boon to the colony. Murray's depiction of a stable, pastoral cooperative left Wilson utterly persuaded that the industrious colonists in Kansas were already self-reliant and prosperous. In August he came to the Eclectic Hall and put forward a motion for the company directors to consider launching a second workingmen's cooperative colony in the American West.[18] As enamored as they were with Wilson's financial wherewithal, the directors had enough experience to realize that their new colleague's proposal went well beyond the company's present means. Nevertheless, Wilson remained upbeat and was confident that his innovations could turn the company into a significant operation. His energy and monetary resources helped reignite a temporary spark of life for the dying Kansas colony, but Wilson was no O'Brienite. His ascendancy marked the final downward spiral for the entire project.

In October, after another meager harvest in Kansas, Charles Murray stood before the shareholders to describe the progress the company had achieved during the previous twelve months. He submitted a balance sheet showing the company books to be in order while declaring other undefined company assets as similarly favorable. The company directors had used most of their funds to make land payments and purchase provisions for the colonists in Kansas. They continued to rely on voluntary contributions from the increasingly reluctant shareholders to cover their operational overhead in London. Murray urged the membership to remain faithful and assured them that their patience would be rewarded. He said that "by persistency and energy, the time would soon draw nigh, when the position of the company would be such as to redound to the credit of the shareholder, and be an example it would be well for other societies to follow."[19] At best the company was scratching out a hand-to-mouth existence. Colonists in Kansas farmed individual allotments but made no progress as a collective. Despite the problems, the shareholders gave Murray and the directors a vote of confidence and reelected them for another year's service. The only change involved the corresponding secretary. Radford, who remained a director, handed the secretarial duties back to John Rogers.

At the end of 1872 the workingmen's cooperative in Kansas remained entirely dependent upon financial support from London. The directors could not secure a bank loan for land in the United States, which meant that shareholders were responsible for property taxes and installment payments made to the railroad. The company directors had carried much of the burden but could not do it alone. Murray and his colleagues had to reassure the individual shareholders in London that they had not made a mistake by investing in the company. Their favorite method was through guest speakers offering expert opinion, and in March 1873 Alexander Dupree came to the Eclectic Hall to talk about his travels in America and his intimate knowledge of other communistic societies. Dupree, whose chief qualification appeared to have been a two-year tour of the United States that took him from New York to Kansas, spoke to the group about Robert Owen's New Harmony settlement, the Shaker communities, and the "Free Lovers" of John Humphrey Noyes's Oneida Colony. He "testified to the wealth that abounded in these communities, through the united energy and perseverance of its people." Dupree performed as required and urged the assembly "to persevere in the work they had begun." He affirmed that "in the end they would attain a position equal to any of the model villages in the United States, unfettered as they were by any of the peculiar notions of theology."[20]

With a rekindled vigor, the shareholders were willing to support the venture at least one more year. Colonist William Beeby, who had moved to Kansas a year earlier, had become the company's de facto superintendent since McCarthy's departure. In March he wrote to Radford with an enthusiastic description of renewed work that he was implementing on the colony. Beeby embraced agriculture as a vocation and saw the colony's true potential for future development. He informed Radford how it was his sincere hope "that more members would soon follow and unite, in order to hasten the day when the colony would be pointed to as an example of the working of advanced social and political principles." Following Beeby's advice, the directors organized another small emigration party and selected William Wessel, a thirty-one-year-old agriculturalist, as leader. An observer who witnessed Wessel's departure noted that a noble man had left England for good. He "went to America last Tuesday, to the Kansas Working Men's Estate that a few of them have bought by their hard earned savings, in the hope of having a home where the true principles of existences can be carried out."[21]

As Wessel's group traveled toward Kansas, a debate ensued within the Eclectic Hall over the true fiscal state of the company and its viability for the future. It was a critical moment for the company directors, and they did their best to provide a logical explanation of why the colony continued to struggle. One observer remarked that sending Wessel to the cooperative was needed in order to "throw life and heart into this depressed society." He pointed out that the directors had "saved and borrowed, and been cheated and deceived; and have gone through great hardships to gain their object." Once the remaining installments were paid, "so as to put the title deeds from the railway company into the bank," the colony would be free from debt and ready to progress as had been long anticipated. With an "advanced pioneer" like Wessel "to give courage to the few living on the property, the society can once more look up and take hope of success, for it is prairie land, that can give a full harvest this year, if it is cultivated, so it is the best hope for the people."[22]

Reaching back for the anti-capitalist, anti-middle-class rhetoric that the NRL had always used to great effect, in July Charles Murray fired off a warning that so long as labor was considered a commodity, the producing classes would be at the mercy of the capitalist. He cautioned his listeners that the same economic processes that had degraded English workers and left their families to suffer were also taking place in America. Murray testified to this state of affairs from his personal experience in Kansas and proclaimed that only the unity and intelligence of the people could hold these forces in check. As to what people should do, Murray believed that trade unions offered a poor alternative, since strikes undertaken for bread and butter issues did nothing to improve the overall social condition of the people. Moreover, union leaders took money collected from dues and deposited it in banks, which "enabled the capitalist class to use it against the working class." The only solution, concluded Murray, was cooperative emigration. Workers as a collective had to purchase and colonize lands in distant regions, "which, when done, would effectively place them out of the power of the capitalists."[23]

Radford followed Murray's lead and reminded the shareholders that nationalizing land, credits, and currency had been central to their agenda since O'Brien had founded the NRL. In the twenty-five years since the final petition for the People's Charter, they had led the charge in pushing for peaceful reform at home; however, having failed in that, they had worked to prove the soundness of their mentor's principles in a model community. While the directors had not foreseen all the difficulties inherent in establishing a cooperative colony in Kansas, Radford believed that they had thus far met and overcome all challenges through the tenacity of the shareholders. From this point forward, he said, subscribers to the company had only to uphold their faith in "the same course of action that had hitherto been adopted, and success would be certain." James Murray, who began referring to their program as the "Science of Cooperative Colonization," insisted that a complete plan of action started with the land but had to include a "supply of capital and its repayment, the organisation of production and distribution, and the social and moral arrangement of the community." If these vital points existed in harmony with each other, Murray was certain a brighter future than had yet befallen their lot awaited the colonists. The company was necessary as a feeder for planned future cooperative colonies in America, and with confidence in its principles it "might yet eclipse all its predecessors in the usefulness and magnitude of its operations." What was needed at the moment, he concluded, was a large increase in membership and capital.[24]

The proclamations coming out of the Eclectic Hall swept away an unsigned correspondent, whose statements revealed him to be

Frederick Wilson. He remarked that the company represented "the only instance I know of in which the true principles of land ownership" had been carried out. They had fought an annual battle to make their installment payments but, the writer hoped, before the next Christmas Day the company would secure their colony and continue the grand work. "Surely this society will not stop at a square mile and a quarter of land, but will make a little England by buying a county of the country." They have "opened the road for all — let those come who like." Kansas was fine "prairie land that only requires ploughing to get a crop the first year, which will be a jump from starvation to plenty." All anyone had to do was to "subscribe his pound and go out to live upon his own land a free man." While Wilson was oversimplifying the company's land plan, he confessed that after nearly a year as a shareholder he was so taken with the Kansas colony that "I have put more than a hundred pounds into the society, and hope to go on putting as much as I can on the top of it, until freedom has a footing and is able to hold out a hand of welcome to all who will adhere to the principles of its organization."[25]

Wilson's enthusiasm notwithstanding, the workingmen's colony in Kansas faced an uncertain future as the settlement continued to bleed red ink. The directors had difficulty in collecting the annual installment payment on the land, which was coming due in August, and had to issue yet another appeal to the shareholders to bail out the still unprofitable cooperative farm. It is likely that the company's ongoing plea for money, and their immediate need for £80, was why Wilson's initial outlay of £20 had increased to £100 and more. Wilson may have been confident that success was ensured, but the reality in Kansas was that without stable on-site leadership, the company's cooperative program was unsustainable.[26] The directors were at the point where they had to produce some real, demonstrable progress in Kansas or see everything collapse — and not just the Mutual Land, Emigration, and Cooperative Colonization Company either. O'Brien's old National Reform League was at risk, too. The directors were desperate, which opened the door for Wilson to take over and remold the company in his own image.

In Wilson's mind the only difficulty with building a cooperative in Kansas was enduring the passage out of England and having
enough food until the first crop was harvested, "for there," he believed, "you have simply to put in the spade or the plough and reap
a rich harvest." Because success was all but guaranteed, Wilson saw
the railroad as the true obstacle to progress. Once the CBUP realized
how lucrative the Kansas cooperative was bound to become, it would
demand increasingly higher prices for additional land. Railroads,
he said, "are not guided by philanthropy, but self-interest; and the
only chance, therefore, for a continuous stream will be an emigration fund, or the formation of cooperative companies similar to the
Kansas." Wilson alluded to Wessel's recent move west and said that
after leaving England only last March, he now had "five acres planted
to wheat from the labour of the spring."[27] The idea rattling around
in Wilson's head was not only to bolster the cooperative settlement
in Kansas with more immigrants but to establish more colonies before railroad companies and land speculators got wise to their plan.

In September, at the request of the company directors, Wilson
diagramed his scheme for reorganizing the colony. His outline was
simple and retained the idea of individual shareholders leasing ten-
acre allotments, but he emphasized the importance of developing
the land as a collective. Therefore, Wilson proposed building a small
cooperative village on the property while designating a portion of
land for the group farm. He allowed that shareholders who desired
to farm their allotments should trade their produce in the village
market. Other shareholders who desired to work in various trades
could take their allotments in smaller blocks and trade their services for agricultural produce. Alfred Walton, an architect and surveyor, examined Wilson's recommendations and pronounced them
sound, which left the directors to approve and officially adopt the
plan. Charles Murray and John Radford acquiesced to Wilson's growing influence in the company and actively promoted the "plan for
our future village." The rallies publicizing the plan created something of a stir, and at least on one occasion the police felt compelled
to break up a gathering at Lower Marsh.[28]

Wilson was exuberant and considered his presentation the highlight "to a sort of jubilee meeting of the Kansas Co-operative Society." He had been fully briefed on the tribulations the colonists had suffered through and understood that when Edward Grainger Smith passed away in 1870, "the estate in consequence got into disorder." Because a number of shareholders became disheartened, "the whole responsibility of the success of the company devolved on the few, who have endured great privations in obtaining money to send another agent out, and keep up the payments." However, all that was in the past, he said. The directors had done the good work of keeping the company afloat during the hard times, and through perseverance their objects were finally getting out to the public. Wilson proclaimed that "the silver lining of the cloud of darkness was manifest in the coming sunshine, and the nervous anxiety of prospective confiscation by the railway company was translated into the certainty of continued and successful prosperity." The recent land payment was made "honourably, punctually, and with the compliments of Major Downes [sic], the secretary of the western railways, as to their conduct." The reason the company had trouble up to this point, said Wilson, was that people had to learn the idea of cooperation and think of each other "as shareholders in a commonwealth, instead of independent landowners, so that the welfare of the whole should be recognised." The Kansas cooperative "was and is so novel, that it was only the advanced social thinkers who could appreciate the attempt." Only advanced social thinkers could comprehend the advantages that could be gained when armed with the collective courage to charge "directly in the teeth of the speculative capitalist." The company had triumphed, he believed, and the "society is in such good spirits that it may be described as in a state of moral intoxication."[29]

Wilson's optimism was premature. He believed that the colonists in Kansas had 160 acres under cultivation, which if true would have doubled anything they had accomplished in the past and with fewer workers available. Nevertheless, while Beeby and Wessel were capable and may indeed have gotten production up on the colony, agricultural prices were on the way down. The New York banking establishment of Jay Cooke and Company had invested heavily in the transcontinental railroads and in 1873 was having difficulty marketing millions of dollars in Northern Pacific bonds. When the nation's money supply contracted, the firm was forced into bankruptcy. The collapse of one of the country's leading financial institutions created a chain reaction, and the ensuing panic on Wall Street shattered the nation's economy and ushered in a depression. The immediate impact for Kansas agriculture was a precipitous drop in grain prices just as farmers were bringing in the fall harvest. For the colonists, the Panic of 1873 could not have come at a worse time. Produce from the increased acreage sold for little, and by the end of the year the colonists remained dependent upon largesse from London. Moreover, the economic depression ensured that making the colony self-sufficient would be even more challenging than before.

As 1873 drew to a close, it was clear that the company had become Frederick Wilson's enterprise. Directors like John Radford and Charles Murray understood that their lifelong devotion to O'Brien had become subordinate to Wilson's program. In November Murray tendered his resignation as company president, although he retained a position as one of the company directors. Wilson assumed the presidency, and the colony's financial concerns were now his to administer. He took leadership over an organization that consistently depleted every cent of income on installment payments and essential supplies for the colonists. That the colony had never been able to sustain a self-sufficient cooperative and barely survived its hand-to-mouth existence seemed to make little impression on Wilson. He immediately announced "Plans for the Future Development of the Colony" and pushed the shareholders to endorse a resolution: "That [the] efforts of the organisation be directed towards establishing a colony to consist of 5,000 families."[30]

If Wilson held unattainable ambitions for the Kansas colony, he had perfectly sound logic in selecting the new on-site agent. "Mr. Radford," wrote Wilson, "is the man who is looked up to as the steady promoter to work out" the salvation of the cooperative. No one in the company had devoted themselves so completely to the project as had John Radford. Just as O'Brien had done during the days of the Charter, Radford had sacrificed everything for the cause. He and his family lived on the edge of poverty and gave anything extra to the company as he selflessly persevered in his work as a director, promoter, and fundraiser for the Kansas project. However, for someone who had politically matured under O'Brien and had struggled to support the colony since the day it was founded, Wilson's plan of building a village for five thousand families must have seemed beyond the pale. Nevertheless, Radford was ready to go and assume stewardship over the colony. The company made arrangements in December "for a party to go out next spring, to join the families already on the colony," and Radford would be the leader. Excepting Murray's temporary tenure as on-site agent, Radford would be the first permanent company superintendent in Kansas since Edward Smith who had known O'Brien and was completely devoted to O'Brien's principles.

While Radford made no comment on the company's revised plan of settlement, Wilson's unbridled enthusiasm swept him along. Radford accepted his new position with the assurance that the new president would pay the bills and give the colonists every opportunity to succeed. Wilson understood the expectations the others laid upon him, but his comprehension was muted by his ongoing fantasy of what Kansas offered. The colony was ideal. It possessed "the climate of climates, having only two months winter; land ready for the plough, and a short mile from the railway station." The shareholders, he said, "have spent all their money in paying for the land, which from all accounts, is a paradise, all the hot-house fruits of England growing in the open air." Here the company was, on the brink of success and lacking only the last bit of money needed to send enough colonists over to make the land productive. "Well, they shall have it," proclaimed Wilson. "I will personally guarantee their bills, and if that does not succeed borrow right and left, for the payment is sure." He intended to make the colony work on his terms and again said that the company would "buy land until they have five thousand families living in mutual relation."[31]

Wilson's high spirits and Radford's imminent departure notwithstanding, early in 1874 the Kansas colony became the recipient of some horrific publicity that exposed and laid bare all of its struggles and hardships. Charles Bradlaugh, the editor of the *National Reformer*, had long admired Bronterre O'Brien and the principles for which he stood. Bradlaugh had led fundraising efforts for the dying reformer's Testimonial Fund in 1862 and, although not a member of the NRL, was supportive of O'Brien's disciples. From the beginning he had provided them with regular column space in his periodical to promote their activities in London and Kansas. In September 1873 Bradlaugh began an extended speaking tour of the United States and by January 1874 had arrived in Kansas. He had several speaking engagements lined up in the state including a scheduled talk in Atchison, after which he planned to visit the Workingmen's Cooperative Colony. As bad luck would have it, Bradlaugh slipped on the ice in Kansas City and found himself confined to bed for a period.[32] He had to postpone or cancel part of his tour, although he still found time to travel west to interview George Grant and inspect the newly founded Victoria Colony in Ellis County. Nevertheless, after giving so much support to the O'Brienites, Bradlaugh did not want to miss the opportunity to examine what they had accomplished. Therefore, while Bradlaugh headed for Victoria, he sent a traveling companion (identified only as Mr. Rogers) to Nemaha County to tour the O'Brienite colony and report back on what he observed.

Bradlaugh was shocked when he received Rogers's description of the colony. The pitiable condition of the colonists and "the difficulty which a man unskilled in any trade had in earning a livelihood" was so saddening that he publicly upbraided the company directors and their policies. Bradlaugh was particularly incensed over the ongoing colony rule of restricting shareholder leases to ten acres of land, a point of contention on which he believed the directors were "utterly mistaken." From his own observations, Bradlaugh believed that it was "impossible for a man alone in Kansas to exist on less than sixty acres of land, and he will be far better with 160." The directors had based their ten-acre policy on what they believed worked in England, but Bradlaugh contended that even "in a settled country, this would not be one-fourth the land that is required, and in a district like East Kansas, it is simply absurd." He pointed out that with greater care and a sensible course of action that took advantage of diverse sources of income, the directors might make immigration to the colony a blessing. However, "to send penniless people to earn their livelihood on the land alone; especially in so small a quantity, is horrible cruelty."[33]

Charles Murray had lived on the colony for a full year, yet Bradlaugh immediately recognized what Murray and the other directors had failed to see: "to merely grow grain or Indian corn is practically useless." Bradlaugh understood the economics of distance and argued that the "cost of shipment to Chicago, St. Louis, or to Colorado, the only markets for sale of produce, is too heavy to leave a profit sufficient to maintain the settler." There was still plenty of fertile land available in both Kansas and Nebraska, he said, and if the company really wanted to follow Wilson's advice and expand its cooperative ventures, then livestock was the way to proceed. Bradlaugh believed that small cooperatives of between eight and ten settlers on a 640-acre section growing corn for livestock could make such a system work. He said that if the colonists raised pigs, "they will eat the corn, and the pork finds a ready and profitable market. During the winter, the settler may also get a quantity of cattle." From his temporary perch in western Kansas, Bradlaugh recommended that the colonists allow Texas longhorns to "winter on shares" and take a proportion of the stock as payment for allowing them to graze the land until spring.[34] Bradlaugh was unaware of the Kansas quarantine law, and the Workingmen's Cooperative Colony was too far east of the quarantine line to take advantage of the Texas cattle trade.[35] Nevertheless, his advice concerning how many cooperative settlers could support each other on a single section of land merited further consideration, particularly in light of Wilson's plans for villages of thousands.

Bradlaugh remained well disposed toward the company directors and soon softened his tone. In a follow-up article he allowed that the O'Brienites in London and Kansas were honest in intent and had selected a suitable piece of land for settlement. Rather than being callous and uncaring of the colonists, Bradlaugh believed that the directors' chief error was "in not having been hitherto sufficiently posted as to the conditions necessary to secure a comfortable livelihood for the persons they send out." The sufferings of those already on the colony should have induced the directors to rethink their plans and take a bit more care in the welfare of the settlers. If properly managed, Bradlaugh contended, a workingmen's cooperative in the Great Plains could provide benefits for everyone involved. However, he warned, with improper oversight, as had been the case for the Workingmen's Cooperative Colony up to this point, "it can be nothing but failure if those who come out expect to exist on the produce" from a single allotment of ten acres of land.[36]

James Murray spoke on behalf of the company directors and challenged Bradlaugh's dyspeptic assessment as untrue. Murray felt compelled to defend the policy of ten-acre allotments and reiterated the fact that the company's Articles of Association contained no hard rule limiting shareholder leases to ten acres. Every colonist started out with an allotment of ten acres and a village plot for house and garden, he said. A shareholder could lease as much ground as he wanted with the caveat that he had to put it under cultivation. "The object of this condition," Murray insisted, was "to prevent selfish men getting hold of tracts of land — not for cultivation, but for the purpose of becoming landlords, a system which has cursed Great Britain, and will, if not stopped, equally curse America in its development."[37] Murray and his fellow directors never had any intention of imposing needless suffering on their colleagues in Kansas, but their ideological commitment to equity in landholding caused them to disregard warnings that agricultural conditions and produce markets on the Great Plains were different than those they knew in England. None of the directors gave any indication that they were willing to consider Bradlaugh's suggestions.

Money continued to be the predominant concern among the directors, and under Wilson's leadership they entered into active discussions about how to secure the remaining land payments before said expenditures actually came due. Of more immediate concern was the local land tax owed on the company's Kansas property. The directors were raising funds to send Radford and his family to the colony, and John R. Molineux, chair of the Land and Mortgage Committee, reported that over the previous two years the committee had collected over £400, all of which had been spent in support of the colony. There was enough on hand to send £20 as a portion of the land taxes due, and Wilson wrote to the Nemaha County land tax commissioners asking them to remit the balance to him. Wilson understood that with a "well-tried member" like Radford taking over supervision in Kansas, the colony had a chance. If, however, money woes continued to plague the company, then there was nothing Radford or anyone else could do to salvage the experiment. Therefore, as the directors were announcing plans for a benefit tea party and soiree in Radford's honor, Wilson began taking steps to secure the colony's financial future.[38]

Of all the company directors, none had worked harder than Radford to keep the dream of an O'Brienite colony alive. Radford's colleagues recognized the sacrifices he had made over the years, and as he was making preparations for his family's journey to Kansas, they issued a testimonial on his behalf. "For nearly a quarter of a century," they said, "he has labored as a devoted and untiring advocate of every progressive movement, and been one of the few whose subscription towards every good object could be confidently reckoned upon." Radford's devotion to O'Brien's principles and his generosity in time and money helped keep the project going but left him in difficult financial straits. "Too often it is the fate of those who sacrifice their personal interests for humanity's sake to reap a reward of ingratitude and selfish indifference. To the honour of our party, this is not always the case." As a mark of the directors' appreciation for Radford's work, they issued an appeal "to all advanced thinkers to aid them with a subscription towards a pecuniary testimonial to Mr. Radford, as a slight acknowledgement of the subscribers' appreciation of his worth as a reformer, a citizen, and a fellow labourer in the vineyard of truth, justice, and progress." Such a testimonial could never compensate Radford for all that he had sacrificed, but the directors hoped that it would at least be enough to get his family started on the cooperative in Kansas.[39]

On the eve of Radford's departure, Frederick Wilson stood before the shareholders and proclaimed "that all their difficulties, as regards the remaining land payments and land-tax installments, were now settled." No bank had ever been willing to mortgage a financially strapped working-class cooperative like the Mutual Land, Emigration, and Cooperative Colonization Company, but Wilson was another story. Wilson had the personal assets to offer as collateral, and on the night of Radford's farewell gathering Wilson announced that he had obtained a £700 mortgage from the firm of Marbourg and Lee. The bank gave Wilson a three-year grace period before the commencement of payments, after which the redemption was "at the rate of £50 a year, a mere nothing, considering they had to raise considerably more than that in their distress." Finding themselves released from the anxiety of constantly scrambling for immediate subscriptions, "they could now breathe freely, and exert all their powers for the development of the colony." On paper the colony in Kansas was still the company's property, but in actuality Wilson had become the owner. He alone was responsible for repaying the loan, and he became the sole director with a vested interest in the colony's success.[40]

Early in 1874 Wilson remained unconcerned about past difficulties in Kansas and confidently predicted that once all financial burdens had been lifted, "there would more likely be 500 new members a year; for who would not join the Company who wished to go to America?" With the exception of the colony's inaugural year in Kansas, workers had not subscribed to the company in overwhelming numbers because, as Wilson reasoned, "people do not like joining a society in difficulties; but now that the difficulties are removed, and the egg is satisfactorily hatched, the chick will peck up applicants for admission to membership." He gave a nod to Bradlaugh's criticism of the company's policy of allocating land in ten-acre leases and rationalized: "You may say a man and his family cannot live on ten acres; true, but they have some 250 acres for a cooperative farm at which he can employ his time." Once the colony became profitable and repaid the loan, "the company will buy land, not only in America but in England, and so make their principles a practical example for the public, which hitherto has had to be contented with paper proposals."[41]

For Radford, dedicated O'Brienite that he was, Wilson's bombast was perfectly fine, so long as Wilson paid the bills and did not alter the company's basic program. Wilson, in his customary overstatement, proclaimed Radford's departure for Kansas to be "the most interesting event that has happened since the Creation of the world." John Radford and his family, however, saw the decision to emigrate as a more solemn resolution. The move to Kansas represented an act of affirmation. Radford was not a particularly religious man, but his devotion to O'Brien and belief in O'Brien's core principles represented a worldview that was bordering on the spiritual. More than anything else he wanted to demonstrate the truth of what he believed. If that could best be done from Kansas, then so be it. In his parting statement, Radford acknowledged the testimonial the directors had made on his behalf and expressed "his belief that the Company was now on the high road to a glorious future." Even Wilson was moved to comment that "I never listened to a speech of such heartfelt eloquence, tempered with moderation of common sense." Maria Radford, Radford's second wife, joined her husband on the platform and together "with an octave of little Radfords" they sang "A Happy Farewell to the Land of England." As the meeting ended, the entire crowd joined in with the song: "To the West, to the West, to the Land of the Free."[42]

At the end of March, Radford, whose fortieth birthday coincided with his departure, and John Molineux, age twenty-six, along with their wives and children boarded the train at London's Euston Station to start their journey for Kansas. The party of fourteen traveled to Liverpool and booked passage aboard the steamship *Baltic* of the White Star Line. The company directors appealed to the White Star management to give Radford free passage to America and "explained to them that the agent was the key to a large passage of emigration; if he did not go none could go. If he went and prepared a foothold for the future an uninterrupted stream of emigrants would flow to the land that belongs to them." White Star officials were unimpressed, which led Wilson to lament: "It appears that they have yet to learn that the shillings of the millions are more worth cultivating than the pounds of the few and far between." Radford's party paid for tickets in steerage and left for the United States. As they steamed across the Atlantic, Wilson loudly proclaimed that the "Kansas Company are now elated with new life and vigor."[43]

Almost as soon as Radford had left, Wilson began proposing new rules for the company and working of the colony land. He was maneuvering to restrict shareholder voting rights, but the information was not something Wilson wanted to make public just yet. From the beginning the company directors had been transparent about their goals and principles and, even in the teeth of contradictory evidence, openly maintained their sclerotic commitment to how they organized allotments in Kansas. As Wilson assumed greater control over the organization, however, the company began to take on aspects of a secret society. While Radford was boarding his ship in Liverpool, author Charles Maurice Davies, who was in the process of composing a survey of London's dissident organizations, wrote to James Murray asking for more information regarding colony. Receiving nothing in response to his query, Davies resolved "not to be done in by the coyness of the Kansas secretary." Posing as a worker interested in taking out a subscription, Davies arranged to attend an advertised Sunday lecture at the Eclectic Hall where he proposed "to beard that retiring gentleman in his den." Despite his lighthearted rebuke, Davies had a sincere interest in giving an honest accounting of the company operations. He had delivered compassionate portrayals of other working-class associations and wanted to do the same with the Mutual Land, Emigration, and Cooperative Colonization Company. While Davies's initial criticism was made in frustration, Murray's reluctance to engage in any meaningful correspondence cued the experienced Davies that he would find an association embroiled in internal difficulties.[44]

The shareholders' meeting of April 1874 fulfilled Davies's jaded expectations. Although company rhetoric continued espousing an anticipated surge of new subscribers, Davies's mere presence made it obvious that the small assemblage of roughly ten men and three women had become unaccustomed to newcomers at their gatherings. Davies remarked that one person, "a red-headed, bright-eyed young man, with a nosegay in his button-hole, scrutinized me severely when I came in, as indeed did all the assembled except the second secretary, who was an austere-looking gentleman in reverend black." While the topic under discussion "was a Mr. Radford, who it appeared had just set sail with his wife and family for the Colony," the attendees excluded Davies and prevented him from participating in a "conversation about people and things utterly unknown to all except the initiated." Other than Joseph Molineux, whose brother John was traveling to Kansas with Radford, none of the members would suffer themselves to speak with Davies. While Davies attempted to extract some information from Molineux, he had little luck. Molineux was not being obtuse. Because he had no sway with Wilson and no position of authority, he simply "could not command the publications of the Association" that Davies wanted to examine. Therefore, after "about an hour listening to this not very edifying conversation, and watching men and boys paying their pence to the officials — I presume subscriptions to this mystic Association," he left in disappointment. Davies said: "I was prepared to sympathize greatly with the objects of the Association, but I confess I cannot understand why, if the scheme is *bona fide* intended for the public good, the Association should be converted by its officials into a secret society."[45]

Davies fully understood that the Kansas colony had been "wallowing in all but insurmountable difficulties, with a strain on the pockets of the promoters that literally deprived them of butter for their daily bread." He allowed that the company may have begun with good intentions and reproduced the favorable review of Radford's departure that Wilson had written for the *Royal Leamington, Warwickshire, & Centre of England Chronicle* so his readers could draw their own inferences. Nevertheless, said Davies, if the company directors wanted to reach new subscribers and stabilize their operations in both London and Kansas, they would have to be more civil to people with honest inquiries and stop treating them in a Dickensian "circumlocutory backstairs kind of manner."[46] Davies's cynical impression of the company was a reflection on Wilson's takeover. While Charles Murray, John Radford, and other early leaders had been students of O'Brien and freely associated with the working-class people they hoped to recruit, Wilson came from a position of privilege and expected others to gravitate toward him. He was confident in his own ideas and preferred a style of micromanagement where the directors rubberstamped his new proposals with a minimum of debate. Wilson became the dominating presence at company headquarters in London and the governing voice of authority within the organization.

As overbearing as Wilson had become in London, in Kansas he remained a distant figure with little influence. In Kansas it was John Radford who now held the responsibility of bringing an elusive self-sufficiency to the cooperative colony. Radford's party disembarked at Castle Garden on April 15, and by the end of the month they had arrived safely in Kansas. Charles McCarthy, who still held the official title of colony superintendent, briefly returned from his home in Chicago to meet Radford. He came to Kansas to relinquish control of the colony books but also to purchase some horses for a few unnamed clients back east. McCarthy and William Wessel helped the Radford and Molineux families get settled comfortably in the communal dormitory. Wessel, along with William Beeby, had been running the colony in McCarthy's absence, and all three remained with Radford as he settled in to help draw up a "plan of work to occupy the ensuing season." The Radford and Molineux families each accepted a ten-acre allotment, and under Radford's stewardship the new arrivals prepared to labor with the established colonists in a cooperative effort to bring the common land under cultivation.[47]

Radford enjoyed some early success and seemed to be living up to expectations. In June he wrote back to his London colleagues to express how delighted everyone was with the colony. The imagery he relayed of Maria Radford and the children fishing on the banks of the Nemaha River and catching enough fish in the morning for the evening meal captured everyone's attention. "Fancy a family living in the heart of an unhealthy part of London last February, who had no possibility, apparently, of ever getting away from England, fishing on their own property in May!" The lesson to be taken away from this story was the incredible feats people could accomplish "if they would only combine for practical objects." Radford had made the Kansas colony work, and it "has gone and done what other people only talk about, without any intention of doing."[48] What was missing from Radford's correspondence was any mention of the cooperative farm and progress being made in sowing a crop for fall harvest.

The letters describing Kansas as a paradise-in-waiting continued in July, which indicates that some of the stories related may have come from Wilson's imagination rather than Radford's actual words, particularly since they appeared only in the paper where Wilson was a correspondent. In July's letter it was said that Radford engaged in the unlikely activity of contemplating the "thousands of miles of beautiful cleared land, that only wanted the plough to turn it up and yield an abundant harvest, laying idle, and thousands starving at home." At the time there were five families living on the colony, and Radford's hands would have been full organizing labor and coordinating work schedules. According to Wilson, however, Radford was standing at the door of the dormitory where "he could see miles away the waving grass, and yet it was useless." For this state of affairs Radford's alleged letter castigated the state of Kansas. "The Kansas Government ought to be ashamed of itself. What have they to do? Advance the passage, and tools, and food to the settlers as a capital, and let them farm out their liabilities and their freedom. Why not? It would pay well, and the benefit to the country of Kansas would be splendid."[49]

The truth of the colony was that Radford was working diligently toward making the settlement self-sufficient. He had reacquired a small number of cows and horses and gotten the colonists to work at putting significant acreage under cultivation. Everyone, he wrote, was "working together in the best of spirits."[50] Molineux followed Radford's lead and remarked on "the progress of work on the colony." He also wanted to make it clear that there was "unanimity of action among the agent and members" in Kansas, which was a great source of satisfaction to the shareholders in London. The colony seemingly had turned the corner, and the sacrifices the group had made over the previous five years finally seemed to be paying off. Molineux's letter was published in mid-August, which meant that he dispatched it in late July. It was the last good news to come out of Kansas.

Hardship was the one constant on the Workingmen's Cooperative Colony, and in August the worst ecological disaster the colonists had yet faced ensured that simple survival would remain their primary focus. The grasshopper plague of 1874 swept in from the northwest and struck Nemaha County on the last day of July. Ravenous locusts consumed everything in their path and laid the countryside to waste. The devastation was so severe that one regional commentator remarked: "The corn fields resemble well poled bean patches, while the apple trees have been stripped of their leaves, and in many orchards this year's growth of wood destroyed." Another correspondent looked directly at the land in the locality of the cooperative colony and stated that the "grasshoppers have made havoc with everything in the vegetable line, and in consequence many hopes have been destroyed; many plans frustrated, and more or less suffering will inevitably follow." The situation was grim, and harmony between neighbors disintegrated as fast as the grasshoppers could eat. The journalist observed the beginnings of "a general scramble after grass in this vicinity, and some clashing and war of words." Oddly enough, in the midst of the adversity a new colonist, George Dutch, arrived, and Radford, ever the optimist, informed the local press that he was "taking hold of work in good earnest, and the prospects of the Company are improving."[51]

Despite Radford's hopeful forecast, the colony had suffered a mortal blow. The environmental devastation of 1874 ensured that any hope for self-sufficiency would have to be delayed yet another year. In London the full implications of building a cooperative colony on the Kansas plains finally started to dawn on Wilson. Due to the financial aid he had given the company, in late July Wilson voluntarily resigned his position as company president. The mortgage remained in his name, and he had a financial stake in the colony far greater than that of any other shareholder. He retained a dominant position among the directors, and his resignation involved little more than a surrender of the chairman title to James Murray. While the directors gave Wilson a unanimous vote of thanks "for his having so generously done that which will place the undertaking beyond failure," they also understood that they were going to have to "do all that lay in their power to develop the resources of the Colony" if they were to continue sending immigrants to Kansas. Since 1869 they had been struggling to make cooperation their primary goal; however, the colony's annual property taxes were due in August, and the grasshopper devastation did nothing to elevate anyone's spirits. A sense of desperation set in. Alfred A. Walton, a longtime NRL member and colleague of O'Brien's, turned the company's principles upside down when he emphasized the "necessity of first making the undertaking commercially successful" before they could "put advanced principles of the society into practical application on the colony."[52]

In Kansas, Walton's admonition to concentrate on commercial affairs must have seemed a cruel joke. Farmers throughout Nemaha County were suffering, and in April 1875 J. A. DeForest, a local dignitary from the neighboring town of Wetmore, urged Governor Thomas A. Osborn to speed the distribution of state relief. DeForest noted that the "destitute are beginning to get uneasy as their supply of food is very short." Not everyone had exercised the best judgment, and "in expectation of receiving the aid proposed they in some instances have used means for seed or feed for teams and are now left with very little for their families." The Kansas State Central Relief Committee responded to the appeals for aid with a donation of twenty thousand pounds of flour for Nemaha County. The southern tiers of county townships received more than half the assistance. Harrison Township, the location of the Workingmen's Cooperative Colony, received 2,500 pounds of flour, which was more than any other township. Radford remained silent on how much aid went to the English settlers, but other than scattered individual farms, theirs and the Memorial Colony at Sother, which struggled as badly as the English, were the only settlements in the sparsely populated region. The colony suffered along with everyone else, and by March 1875 only the Radford and Molineux families remained in residence on the cooperative.[53] Although Radford doggedly pressed on and remained absolutely committed to O'Brien's ideals and the colony's success, the dream was over. The shareholders in London had lost all patience, and no more hopeful colonists would follow George Dutch, the last settler to come from England as a member of the colony.

5

Hold Up the Lamp of Hope

John Radford

Workers of the farm, railroad and factory unite, stand together in
the battle of life and at the ballot box, to strip these modern tyrants
of the power to either destroy industrial self-protecting union or
prevent the complete freedom of political action at the ballot box.

—JOHN RADFORD, 1893

As the new year of 1875 dawned on the Workingmen's Cooperative
Colony in Kansas, only two people held on to the vain hope that
it could yet recover. One, Frederick Wilson, was leading the directors of the Mutual Land, Emigration, and Cooperative Colonization
Company in London and had gambled a significant amount of his
own money on the project. He had a vested interest in success, and
a bankruptcy would cost him dearly. The other, John Radford, was
the colony superintendent in Kansas and remained faithful to the
original dream of an O'Brienite cooperative. He refused to concede
that Bronterre O'Brien's ideas had not made the collective farm a
success. The fault had to lie with unprincipled colonists, irregular
financial support, or natural disasters beyond the company's control, but not in O'Brien's philosophy. Radford remained dogged in
his determination to make the cooperative accomplish something,
but in this resolution he was alone. Without additional colonists to
labor on the common land, there was little he could do beyond sift
through the wreckage. Radford and Wilson oversaw the final dis-

mantling of the colony, but the O'Brienites in London and Kansas adapted to the new reality and persevered in their faith.

The tragedy of the Kansas cooperative reverberated beyond the Great Plains, and its impact on the O'Brienites in London was more than financial. When members of the National Reform League (NRL) founded the Mutual Land, Emigration, and Cooperative Colonization Company in 1868, they did so with the understanding that it would mean the eventual demise of O'Brien's NRL. If the colony was a resounding success, NRL members would have moved to Kansas to participate in their more perfect society. On the other hand, because it was so intimately entwined within the NRL, the colony's failure had the potential to drag the older organization down with it. Of the shareholders who agreed to become colonists in Kansas, most were young and never had been personally acquainted with O'Brien. It had been their task to build the colony infrastructure and start the cooperative village. The older shareholders, individuals who had known and worked with O'Brien, remained in London and, with few exceptions, elected not to emigrate. They did not relocate to Kansas in part because the on-site colonists never built the planned village, but also because it had been their intent from the beginning for the colony to stand as an example that they could wield while continuing O'Brien's struggle in Britain. Regardless, fault for the colony's poor development lay at the feet of the board of directors rather than with the members in Kansas. All values, all structure, all knowledge should have emanated from the company headquarters, but the company directors never developed a method to reinforce their authority in Kansas. The directors took for granted that the colonists would follow O'Brien's philosophy, and they provided the settlers with inconsistent direction and leadership. As Wilson moved into the Eclectic Hall and solidified his control over the emigration company, older members began to move on to other projects. Whether it was from a personal dislike of Wilson or simply because they recognized that the end had come, in 1874 the members of the NRL ceased operations. Just one year short of its twenty-fifth anniversary, the National Reform League, the last surviving Chartist society in London, shuttered its doors.

The NRL may have terminated activities, but the O'Brienites did not. In an ironic turn of events, in 1874 Martin Boon, who had opposed the emigration scheme from the beginning, emigrated to South Africa and continued as an O'Brienite reform activist in his adopted home. Of the older O'Brienites who had supported the Kansas project, most became active in the Manhood Suffrage League (MSL) and utilized that forum to continue the fight for their mentor's Chartist principles. In 1874, William Morgan, a close friend of Charles Murray, founded the MSL as the Democratic and Trades Alliance. In 1875 the organization adopted the MSL moniker and began meeting at Queen's Head in Little Pulteney Street. The tavern became a center for O'Brienism, as historian Stan Shipley wrote: "All the companionship, political enthusiasm, and scholarship, were transferred from the Eclectic Hall to the 'Queen's Head.'" The intent behind the MSL was to be keenly political and force the trade unions beyond simple bread and butter issues. The league became one of the most prominent of London's forward-thinking metropolitan clubs and served as a precursor to Great Britain's first socialist political party. Charles and James Murray became founding members of the MSL, as did former NRL members John Rogers, William Townshend, George Milner, George Harris, and Robert Gammage. These old Chartists gave the new league agenda a strong O'Brienite interpretation from which it never flinched. Rogers served as the club's first chairman, while men like Charles Murray and Townshend became two of the group's strongest leaders.[1] James Murray continued on at the Eclectic Hall with Wilson through 1875, but after 1874 Charles Murray was no longer actively involved in what had by this point become Wilson's colony in Kansas.

By January 1875, Wilson's assurance had transformed into an overweening hubris. In reviewing Joseph Arch's program of cooperative emigration, Wilson castigated Arch for considering Canada over other parts of North America, particularly Kansas. In 1872 Arch had been a founding member of Britain's National Agricultural Labourers' Union and had, since a tour of Canada in 1873, assisted thousands of British farm workers in finding new homes in Canada and Australia. Wilson claimed Arch was making a mistake because, from Wilson's perspective, Radford had already proven beyond a doubt that cooperative farming worked in Kansas. In Kansas, wrote Wilson, "the land is clear, the climate fine, and the neighbors [are] friendly, and profit is got at once out of the cleared-by-nature land." Despite the ruinous experience of the previous five years and the reality that only the Radford and Molineux families remained on the cooperative, Wilson continued building castles in the air. For him, the Kansas colony was all "a toy affair." It remained his ambition that the company would soon "go in for 36 square miles, and then for 360 square miles," and so on. For the moment, however, the workingmen's colony in Kansas was what Wilson had, and he said: "As a little rill will represent a broad stream of emigration, the Cooperative Colonization Company only demand a pound to be paid into the company, and after six months, if a man can pay his passage, we can put him in a village plot." The cost for a shareholder to lease such a plot was a mere £1 per year, and with it, he feigned, came schools and work opportunities. If a shareholder "is a mechanic he can earn his own living at once, and if an agriculturalist there is the cooperative farm for him to work upon."[2]

Wilson was not ignorant of the ongoing setbacks plaguing what remained of the Kansas colony, and his buoyant assertions masked his own unease as he attempted to salvage something of his investment. The final correspondence he posted to the *Royal Leamington, Warwickshire, & Centre of England Chronicle* reflected his growing concerns. In early April he again scolded Joseph Arch and denigrated Arch's good work as a foil to highlight the benefits of Kansas. However, by the close of the month he was clearly despondent. Wilson wrote: "Nothing is alive in London, but the east wind; nothing is heard but coughing; and nothing is seen except fog, mist, damp, and umbrellas. Let us go to Kansas."[3] No new shareholders came forward, and instead of becoming a great stream of emigrants, the little rill had all but dried up. By May 1875 Wilson had come to the realization that significant changes had to be made if anything was to be saved.

From the beginning the Mutual Land, Emigration, and Cooperative Colonization Company had been a democratic organization. An elected body of directors made administrative decisions, but when new proposals or elections for director positions were brought before the entire membership, each shareholder, regardless of shares held, received one vote. Ownership of a single share, even a partially paid share, entitled a shareholder to emigrate to Kansas, provided the shareholder was willing to finance his or her own passage to the United States. This type of system was too messy for a man like Wilson, particularly since he had invested hundreds of pounds in comparison to the single pound many shareholders had put forward. He therefore sought to streamline the decision-making process in order to implement his own ideas more quickly and efficiently. In May he amended the company's Articles of Association to restrict shareholder voting rights. Wilson's changes stipulated that only those shareholders holding three fully paid shares for more than six months had the right to vote or participate in company business. Furthermore, only those shareholders with ten fully paid shares could qualify for a ten-acre allotment in Kansas.[4] Wilson's reasoning behind the rule change was twofold. First, by prepaying for ten shares, an immigrant headed for Kansas would have put down close to the equivalent value, if not more, of the market price for his or her ten-acre allotment. Second, since the new restrictions disqualified a large number of shareholders from voting, Wilson was free to ram forward almost any change he wanted.

Wilson may have had a genuine belief that his amendments would spark a renewed interest in the company; however, the opposite proved to be true. Workers who at one time may have demonstrated curiosity in the Kansas colony had lost all confidence. The few inquiries the company had been receiving dried up completely. In the earliest days of the project, Radford and the Murray brothers had delivered fervent discourses akin to revivalist preachers stirring up a congregation. By November 1875 inquiries in the emigration scheme had become so flaccid that the best the company directors could accomplish was issue a forlorn announcement: "It was decided last Sunday that these meetings should be made more popular." Wilson delivered a series of scolding lectures on "A Preliminary State of Dissatisfaction," by which he meant "dissatisfaction with every institution, philosophy, or business." No one, he said, had the right to complain unless able to suggest a remedy. His answer was the cooperative in Kansas, which had been established, he said, "to be a harbour of refuge for all [who] were dissatisfied with things as they were."[5] By December even Wilson seemed to have realized that no one was going to emigrate to Kansas so long as the image surrounding the colony was one of failure. He therefore began touting a new Willingwell Association, which called for home colonization loosely based upon O'Brien's old plan of land nationalization. Unlike O'Brien, Wilson was an erratic and simplistic thinker who never grasped the class issues that underlay all of O'Brien's philosophy. In his typically garrulous style, Wilson described Willingwell in an abstract fashion: "The top of the organisation was colour; the base of the organisation was for members of a village, who approved of their principles, to form themselves into branch societies, and to work the intention as far as possible within the branch." By promulgating his incoherent ideas, Wilson presumed that workers would be inspired to seek out more information.[6]

As presumptive leader of the remaining shareholders in London, Wilson had not forgotten his colleagues in Kansas and still clung to a thread of hope that the colony could yet survive. It had been a rough year for the cooperative. The grasshoppers that overran the colony in 1874 left it prostrate and decimated the work Radford had done. Famine had swept the region early in 1875, and a second wave of grasshoppers in the spring ensured another desperate year. By March only the Radford and Molineux families continued working the company land. They were struggling simply to survive. John Molineux had managed to retain ownership of a horse through the difficult months, which helped the two men try once again to farm some of the ground. Unfortunately, catastrophe followed on the heels of calamity as hard times defined the day-to-day existence on the colony. By the end of 1875 the horse had died. The company directors vowed "to have subscriptions enough to supply a breaking team to the land next spring," but given the stagnant recruiting efforts in London it was a hollow promise. Although the chance of attracting new subscribers was essentially nonexistent, as late as December 1875 the company directors continued promoting the colony based on the naïve idea that "the grass only required turning over to become corn land." While they found news of Radford having killed a feral pig for food to be amusing in comparison to another story about the Prince of Wales hunting one for sport, it helped them realize that they had to do a better job in relieving "the first settlers as much as possible on their arrival." Wilson, however, was more concerned with "the payments that a colony should make to the company" than with pigs. As the few remaining group members in London finished out the year, they raised a toast "to celebrate the hope of the future, that was closing the door of past misfortune."[7]

While any semblance of a cooperative in Kansas had ended in the wake of the grasshoppers, the colony persisted in name so long as Wilson continued sustaining it from London and Radford remained on the land and committed to its development. Despite Wilson's hopes and Radford's determination, the elements would not cooperate. In February 1876 another prairie fire started along the railroad tracks. The flames swept up from the southwest and burned the colony's meager stores of hay. Wildfire had been the bane of the settlement throughout its existence, but coupled with the famine of the previous season, the struggles became too much even for Radford. With a wife and seven children in need of food, the company's colony superintendent turned to his engraving skills and began designing metal jewelry for sale in Atchison and other nearby towns. Unlike previous supervisors, Radford stuck with his ten-acre allotment and refused to abandon the colony. Nevertheless, because his family was of primary concern, he announced plans to establish a permanent jewelry business in the local area.[8] Radford had little choice in the matter. There were a number of former colonists living in the vicinity, but none would join him on the colony, as the desire to work a collective farm or prove O'Brien's principles had evaporated. Radford's personal commitment to O'Brien's ideals never wavered, but resurrecting a dead cooperative was a task that proved too much for his abilities.

By the summer Wilson had come to the belated realization that the colony truly had failed. Repayment of the mortgage was due to begin in 1877, but of more immediate concern was the annual property tax. With no new subscribers coming on board and old shareholders leaving, it became impossible for Wilson and the directors to solicit funds for a chronically unprofitable cooperative. Wilson had finally reached his tipping point and was no longer willing to shovel his own money into the project. Therefore, at a late July meeting held in the Eclectic Hall, Wilson took the floor and "proposed that — in consideration of their inability to develop the Colony, and as the liabilities would increase — the Company divide the 600 acres among the members." As the leading shareholder and individual personally responsible for paying off the mortgage, Wilson was not planning on giving away his investment or bearing the full burden of repayment. Instead his proposition was for the shareholders to take land in "proportion to their subscriptions, and charge the acreage with the share of the mortgage and expenses, which, at £1,000, would be about £2 the acre."[9] He allowed the directors to take a month adjournment to consider the proposal before bringing it to a vote.

Having modified the company's Articles of Association a year earlier, Wilson had no trepidations concerning which direction the vote would go. During the interim he used the Eclectic Hall to tout a new "Freehold Land and Tenement League." The league was another instance of Wilson's idiosyncrasies, and like the short-lived Willingwell Association, it operated on an inchoate formula with predictably unspectacular results. By the end of August the shareholders of the Mutual Land, Emigration, and Cooperative Colonization Company reconvened and agreed to Wilson's proposal. In consideration of his accountability for the loan, the directors conceded that Wilson had the right to place the mortgage entirely in his name. They also agreed "that members of the Company should take up land in proportion to their subscriptions, paying 30s an acre, village allotment of half an acre, and two and a half acres of woodland — £8." Payment of interest, to begin at three percent, would commence in 1877 when recompense for the initial loan came due. On September 13 the directors confirmed the formal transfer of title, and Wilson's ownership became legal. The directors did place one stipulation on Wilson: "that any member of the company may select any portion of the land he likes" up to a maximum of thirty acres. The purchaser could leave "the capital unpaid as long as he pleases, at an interest rate of three percent, in 1877, and increasing at the rate of one half percent per annum, until it reaches the permanency of six percent." Wilson agreed to the conditions, and on November 8, 1876, the title passed entirely into his name.[10]

In restricting the division of the land into thirty-acre parcels, the directors were attempting to be fair with everyone who had purchased shares. It was their assumption that a scramble might ensue for the property. No dispute emerged because a thirty-acre allotment was still too small for an individual settler to make a living in Kansas. The colonists who wanted to make a living as farmers had already claimed or purchased nearby homesteads, while others who wanted to earn a living as tradesmen had relocated to Seneca, Wetmore, or other nearby towns. Few of the remaining shareholders in London retained any interest in buying the acreage themselves. The colony land remained the domain of the Radford and Molineux families, who became Wilson's tenants. George Dutch was also on the estate, having recently returned to attempt work on his ten-acre allotment. It was an ignominious end to the colony, and even as the directors were transferring title to Wilson in London, the settlers in Kansas had to band together one final time to fight yet another fire that threatened their homes. Inexperience continued to plague the colonists even as their experiment was breaking apart, and this time the blaze was of their own making. Dutch had gone out to harvest his potato crop. In order to ease his labors, he elected to clear away the surrounding weeds by burning them. A local correspondent scoffed: "The fire proved a little lively for him, and had it not been for the immediate assistance of the other members they probably would have lost their houses."[11]

The buildings survived the flames, but combating the wildfire was the last collective action the colonists ever took. John Molineux began erecting a house on his ten-acre allotment in March 1876 and by April 1877 was ready to move in. He became one of the more aggressive of the former shareholders in purchasing colony land. Nothing changed hands on Section 25 in 1877, which undoubtedly discomfited Wilson, who was late in meeting the annual property tax that year. This led Wilson to lift the thirty-acre restriction on land sales to shareholders, after which the property changed hands fairly quickly. Molineux obtained the entire northwest quarter section of the old colony ground and became one of the most steadfast farmers in the region. Although he had not been a regular resident of the colony since his 1872 marriage, John Stowell became the only member of the original pioneering band to maintain a presence on the land when he purchased a northeast forty-acre parcel. Stowell was a resident of Wetmore, and in 1877 he built a new house and started a lumber business in the town. Dutch took eighty acres for a farm, while Radford purchased a forty-acre plot. The remaining 320 acres remained Wilson's responsibility until 1883, when the final transfer to London shareholder William Fish was completed. Fish also obtained the entire forty-acre wooded parcel in Section 19. Only one other shareholder, William Worcester, obtained a small section of the old colony ground, which he purchased in 1885 from Fish. The communal dormitory became Fish's property. Fish's family briefly lived in the structure after immigrating to Kansas, but by 1887 the building either had been torn down or had fallen over.[12] The Mutual Land, Emigration, and Cooperative Colonization Company continued as a paper organization until January 1884 when, after three unanswered letters of inquiry, the Registrar of Joint Stock Companies declared it an inoperative association and dissolved its charter.[13]

The religious settlers of the Memorial Colony fared no better than the socialist residents of the Workingmen's Cooperative Colony. The Congregationalists likewise gave up after the grasshopper plague. In 1877 travel writer Reuben Smith passed through the region and observed that the fifty-mile post at Sother remained nothing more than a flag stop. It was "located in very productive country," he said, "but no village improvements have been made here yet."[14] In a final stroke of irony, as both colonies were ending operations, a land speculator named George C. Stahl invested in the area and began platting a new town that he named Goff. Founded in 1877, Goff was less than one mile southwest of the O'Brienite cooperative. Unlike the socialist utopia, the religious colony, and the proposed, but never built, railroad town of Sother, the commercial village of Goff proved successful. A number of former colonists, including William Wessel and Benjamin Beeby, moved to Goff and made it their permanent home.[15]

Radford's forty-acre farm was located very close to Goff on the extreme southwest corner of the old colony grounds. Like the Molineux family, the Radfords resolved to stay and prove that the land could be productive. Nevertheless, while Molineux became a prosperous farmer, Radford suffered indignity and frustration. In August 1877, while Radford was working in front of his house, a nearby settler's feral boar wandered into the yard. The boar became provoked, attacked Radford, and proceeded to maul him. William Radford quickly fetched a dog in an attempt to drive the beast away; however, the boar overpowered the dog, then attacked and mauled the boy. Maria Radford drove off the animal with a club, but not before the enraged boar had time to severely wound the two men. The incident left Radford and his eldest son unable to work. The family had given everything they owned to the colony effort and had nothing saved to see them through difficult times. They subsequently became a public charity case. The local press notified the populace that the Radfords were in desperate need. Since "the unfortunate affair," they "are left without the help of the larger members of the family. Those of our citizens who want to 'do good' can find no worthier subjects just now than this unfortunate family." Radford managed to retain ownership of his land, but he realized that under the circumstances he could not continue as a farmer. Shortly after the mauling, Radford began expanding his handmade jewelry business and moved his family to Wetmore.[16]

Regardless of the colony's failure or the disbanding of the company headquarters in London, the O'Brienites continued to play a significant role in Kansas. Throughout the five years of the colony's existence, the company successfully transplanted to Kansas a collection of British workers who were steeped in methods of radical political agitation. While it is not possible to precisely tally the number of immigrants who came to Kansas through the company, earlier estimates of fifty shareholders, many with families, were fairly accurate.[17] A few of the settlers moved away, but a significant number remained in the region. Colonist John Stowell offered a maudlin assessment as to why some persevered.

> It mattered not to the early Kansas settler that the grasshopper ate up his corn, wheat, and in fact, all green vegetation, or that it was blasted by hot winds or dried up for want of rain; yet he loved the country and even if he was compelled to leave his homestead for a few years because of the failure of crops, he would pine for "home" and would return. There was something exhilarating in the sunshine; the air was pure and resembled that of the ocean; and last but not least, he felt a freedom which is inexplicable and incomprehensible to those who have not experienced the pleasurable sensation.[18]

Through classes at the Eclectic Hall these men and women had been indoctrinated in the six points of the People's Charter as well as Bronterre O'Brien's seven fundamental propositions of the NRL. They were fully versed in social utopian ideas through direct communication with Robert Owen, Étienne Cabet, and Josiah Warren. By way of the London section of the International Working Men's Association, which had met in the Eclectic Hall, they had an intimate familiarity with Karl Marx's scientific socialism. Without exception, whenever one of the O'Brienites appeared in a political context, it was on the side of radical reform and labor. Whether as individuals they were able to conform to local mores or not, none were ambivalent in their hostility toward capitalist exploitation of labor. The same courage that brought the O'Brienites to Kansas gave them the nerve to stand up for social, political, and economic reform, and their presence added a dimension of complexity to the area.

Of the O'Brienites in the United States, John Days had set the early standard as a reformer in his adopted home. Back in 1872, John Radford had drawn attention to Days's work as an advocate for land nationalization in the California State Legislature. For Radford, Days's actions served as an example worthy of emulation, but what Days did behind the scenes came back to inspire his brother-in-law in a different way. In 1871 Days had introduced, as he said, "a set of resolutions in favour of the land of the United States being held for the people thereof." In crafting his legislative proposal, Days came across a pamphlet by Henry George entitled *Our Land and Land Policy*. Days's proposed bill quoted George's pamphlet at length. The legislation failed, but afterward Days sought out George in San Francisco. Days wrote: "I first met Henry George personally in the month of May, 1872, and I loaned him all the writings of Bronterre O'Brien, together with Gammage's history of Chartism. He returned them within so short a time that he could not have had time to read them carefully, let alone study them. He told me that when he wrote the pamphlet he had never read or seen any work on the land question."[19]

Days moved to San Francisco after losing his seat in the legislature and by August 1872 had become president of a lyceum in the city. This was a Sunday afternoon discussion group not unlike what Days would have remembered from his early years in the NRL's Eclectic Hall. Days knew that in *Our Land and Land Policy* George made a statement in support of private property in land; therefore, he invited George to spend an afternoon debating the land question. In his presentation before the group, George affirmed that he stood in favor of private property. Days questioned him on this with the observation that the arguments George crafted contradicted his blanket statements on property. According to Days, it was a transformative event. "From that day to the day of his death, Mr. George openly opposed by word as well as argument private property in land."[20] While Days may have believed he was responsible for a paradigm shift in George's thinking, what he actually accomplished was to alert George that some of his language was obscure and that he needed to revise his writing for purposes of clarity.

Henry George maintained a collegial relationship with Days and consulted with the old O'Brienite as George began writing his seminal work, *Progress and Poverty*. George began work on the book in September 1877, and late in that year Days was among a select group of men with whom George would meet to discuss the economic portions of *Our Land and Land Policy* that he was in the process of revising for the book. By 1878 these conversations led Days and the other men with whom George was consulting to form the Land Reform League of California. The league, devoted to abolishing land monopoly, was the first association in the United States organized to disseminate Henry George's ideas. Days remained close to George throughout the writing of *Progress and Poverty*. He was one of the colleagues whom George sought out for advice and trusted for criticism and counsel.[21] While Days was by no means the most prominent of George's advisors, his presence ensured an O'Brienite influence on the final manuscript and led to a few intemperate allegations that George may have lifted all his ideas directly from O'Brien.[22] Henry George's masterpiece, *Progress and Poverty*, was published in 1879, and by late 1880 it began to garner a large audience of readers.

It is not clear exactly when John Radford learned of *Progress and Poverty* or whether he remained in contact with his former brother-in-law. The Radford family had moved to Wetmore shortly after the incident with the boar. Radford opened a jewelry business in the town and, for a brief time, lived a nondescript existence while concentrating on making a stable home for his family. It was during this interlude in Radford's life that he was introduced to a young mail carrier, John T. Bristow. Wetmore was a small community and had never before had a newspaper, but when a weekly opened for business in 1882, it printed an open letter from Henry George containing an excerpt from *Progress and Poverty*. Radford subsequently reemerged to offer his critique of George's thesis.

Radford took issue with the excerpted portion of the book and pointed out how George lamented the growth of corruption and the decay of republican spirit. In paraphrasing George, Radford wrote that he "warns us of the time when from out of our great cities will spring a new race of barbarians, whose torch and sword will shatter society and bequeath to another age the task of re-building on a purer and firmer basis."[23] Since 1868 Radford had thrown everything of himself into the proposition that the United States was somehow better than Europe and immune to the corruption of aristocratic regimes. O'Brien had seen the situation with greater clarity, and in contemplating America he had written: "In truth, universal suffrage is no guarantee at all for liberty, unless it be accompanied, on the part of the working classes, with a knowledge of their social rights and a consequent determination to use political power for their establishment."[24] O'Brien had understood that without workers first being educated in basic economics and a full understanding of their social rights, they were easily subject to manipulation and demagoguery. Nevertheless, O'Brien had also taught his followers the necessity of using political means to achieve social ends. If trade union activities were combined with political agitation, Radford could not fathom America's cities declining into barbarism.

The selection Radford found troubling came toward the end of *Progress and Poverty*. There George issued a dire warning of how easily modern civilization could decline into tyranny. In musing over how the appearance of a democratic form of government could remain in place while the actual substance of freedom was lost, George wrote: "Extremes meet, and a government of universal suffrage and theoretical equality may, under conditions which impel the change, most readily become a despotism. For there despotism advances in the name and with the might of the people." George continued by describing how, during times of economic depression, people tormented by poverty would gladly "sell their votes to the highest bidder or follow the lead of the most blatant demagogue." In George's view, technological progress was no bulwark against the rising tide of ignorance. "Whence shall come the new barbarians?" he wrote. "Go through the squalid quarters of great cities, and you may see, even now, their gathering hordes! How shall learning perish? Men will cease to read, and books will kindle fires and be turned into cartridges!"[25]

George's analysis of the danger inherent in an undereducated and ill-informed workforce gaining universal suffrage mirrored O'Brien's earlier scrutiny. Radford was not in disagreement over such a point and clearly understood that it had been a long and bitter struggle "from the dark and bloody past to the arena where light and liberty are entering the souls of men." He also realized that it would yet be "a weary struggle from political freedom to intellectual development and an empire of social justice in all the relations of life." For Radford, however, the pertinent question was: "Can we march from 'good to better and do battle with the wrong' under our form of government where every man is a citizen, and every citizen a voter?" After comparing Jeffersonian democracy with the system of rotten boroughs that provided representatives for Britain's House of Commons, Radford declared: "Let us not decry our glorious Republic. Where is the country that can absorb several thousand strangers a day without a social disruption? What nation spends so much in dotting its territory with school houses and so little in forts and arsenals?" George's statement that the new barbarians could emerge from America's industrial cities struck Radford as ludicrous. He countered with the argument: "The brave man should not rapine because paradise is not within reach. Monopoly one side, and debasement the other may be regretted. The forces of conscience and intellect must be used to purify the reason." The fact that common men such as Abraham Lincoln and James A. Garfield could rise, "fill the kingly chair, hallowed by the shades of Washington and Jefferson, proves the dignity of worth, the power of the people." Calling on his own O'Brienite schooling, Radford wrote that the power of a united workforce could overcome the influence of demagogues. This ability "leaves far in the shade the efforts of some trafficking politicians who may rule to spoil for a day — the morrow comes, when the ballot box is arbitrator."[26]

George observed that technological progress had created "not merely the steam engine and the printing press, but petroleum, nitroglycerine, and dynamite."[27] Mankind's ability to create marvels of progress was accompanied every step of the way by advancements in developing materials of incomprehensible destructive power. Radford countered George's argument with a statement of faith that it simply was not possible to destroy everything. Radford wrote: "There is no ocean deep enough to bury in oblivion the telegraph, no volcano hot enough to resmelt the steam engine, no dynamite powerful enough to destroy the railroad and printing press. Neither does the power nor craft exist that can secure to the rich, the learned, and the powerful, the monopoly of all the blessing, science, which is but a child as yet, is daily opening up to the world."[28]

Radford felt obliged to remind his readers that George, one year earlier, had traveled to the United Kingdom and, having gotten involved with the Irish land question, found himself "seized by the vassals of that monarchy and cast into prison." Rather than being prosecuted, wrote Radford, the "light of a free America shone on his dungeon bars — the door is opened — the people welcome him across Ireland. British thinkers and workers alike applaud him — he returns safe to his western home, a living example of the American Republic." For Radford, the United States offered a "nobler order of life" than what he had known in England. In America, he stated, mankind "shall 'stand erect in self respect' and true freedom — shall march rejoicing, never to be again conquered."[29]

Henry George's visit to the United Kingdom did create a stir, and it was one that did not escape the notice of Radford's former O'Brienite colleagues in the Manhood Suffrage League. Historian Martin Crick wrote that the O'Brienites continued using "learning as a weapon in the class struggle, and the MSL provided them with a stage from which to air their views." By 1880 Charles Murray had become the organizing agent for the Social and Political Education League and coordinated over two hundred lectures a year for audiences numbering in the hundreds. The lecture series served as a front for the MSL.[30] In late 1881 Henry Mayers Hyndman came as part of the lecture series to address the MSL with a discussion of George's *Progress and Poverty*.[31] Born in 1842, Hyndman was a radical journalist who in 1881 published *England for All*, a book that popularized the ideas contained within Marx's *Das Kapital*. As a devotee of Marx, Hyndman found it impossible "to read through *Progress and Poverty* without detecting its gross economic mistakes." He nonetheless generated discussions of George's book because, as Hyndman wrote, "George will teach more by inculcating error than other men can impart by complete exposition of the truth." An elderly Marx found Hyndman's logic absurd and held that the danger of disseminating erroneous beliefs was too great. Regardless, Hyndman remained convinced that "George's temporary success with his agitatory fallacies greatly facilitated the promulgation of Marx's own theories in Great Britain," because George's easily read book had inspired workers to seriously contemplate social, political, and economic questions again.[32]

Henry George was not responsible for reintroducing socialism to England. It was already firmly established within working-class political clubs, of which the MSL was one of the more prominent examples. In the words of Shipley: "It was in the discussion of the theories of Bronterre O'Brien, Robert Owen and, more occasionally, Karl Marx, in the metropolitan clubs of the seventies, which produced an atmosphere in which an avowedly socialist movement could emerge."[33] Hyndman recognized the opportunity and believed that with renewed sympathies toward reform the time was right to unify the numerous radical clubs for the development of a true socialist party in Great Britain. In this he was joined by the members of the MSL, including the O'Brienites. On June 7, 1881, both Charles and James Murray were on hand for the first meeting of Britain's Social Democratic Federation (SDF).[34] Charles Murray's lecture series, organized through the auspices of the Social and Political Education League, now became a propaganda arm of the SDF, while James Murray served on the SDF Executive Committee. Modern socialism and socialist candidates for political office arrived in Great Britain with the formation of the SDF, but in many respects the O'Brienites in the MSL and earlier in the NRL had laid the foundations upon which the party was built.

Charles Murray nursed a lifelong hatred of the middle classes that remained undiminished in the final decade of his life. In the spring of 1882 Murray was on hand at the Patriotic Club in Clerkenwell Green for a fund-raiser benefiting the Red Cross Society of the People's Will. This was a Russian Red Cross Society raising money for "the benefit of the political sufferers in prison, exile, and banishment in Russia and Siberia." It would have been an unremarkable event except for the fact that leading the Russian Red Cross delegation were two men, Prince Peter Kropotkin and Nicholas Chaikovsky. Kropotkin was an anarchist and former member of the IWMA, while Chaikovsky was a nihilist and former member of the Cedarvale Commune. Cedarvale had been a progressive communist community in southeastern Kansas. It was contemporaneous with the O'Brienite Workingmen's Cooperative Colony and operated on many of the same principles. Murray and Chaikovsky had similar experiences in Kansas; however, when the two men met in London, Murray verbally assailed Chaikovsky and Kropotkin as allies of the middle classes, "the worst enemies of the people." If English radicals gave their backing to the Red Cross Society, said Murray, they "would be supporting and encouraging the Nihilist movement in its most aggressive shape."[35] Murray, who never wavered in his defense of O'Brien's methods of peaceful political reform, saw nihilism and anarchism as destructive ideologies that undermined worker solidarity and benefited the middle class.

In Kansas nihilism was not a topic under discussion; rather, temperance was the issue of the day, and the O'Brienites found themselves enmeshed in the controversy. In 1881 Kansas became the first state in the Union to constitutionally prohibit the manufacture and sale of alcohol. While the legislature outlawed saloons, pharmacies could continue the legal sale of alcohol for medicinal purposes.[36] In 1882 Charles McCarthy, one of the original pioneers and a former superintendent of the Workingmen's Cooperative Colony, returned to Wetmore from Chicago. McCarthy had been one of the most steadfast of the original colonists, but he left for Chicago in 1873 in order to support his family. He worked briefly as a warehouseman in Chicago, but soon found employment with the Standard Oil Company.[37] Although he had no pharmaceutical experience, when McCarthy returned to Kansas he took advantage of his Chicago connections to open a pharmacy in Wetmore. Of all the O'Brienites in Kansas, McCarthy strayed furthest from his mentor's teachings. His drugstore was a front that served as an intermediary point to help funnel liquor from Chicago into Kansas. Since it was legal for pharmacies to sell medicinal alcohol, it became common in many parts of Kansas for pharmacists to offer a discreet backroom meeting place where a customer and his companions could imbibe a bracing restorative snort in a convivial social atmosphere. McCarthy's pharmacy was no different. To counter any temperance crusader who might take affront at this technical skirting of the law, he made certain, particularly during elections, to provide generous libations for local politicians and businessmen.

John Stowell, McCarthy's old friend and fellow O'Brienite, took a different course, one that would inevitably bring the two old reformers back together. In 1869 Stowell and McCarthy had stood in unity on the stage of the Eclectic Hall in London as part of the first pioneering group that the company membership chose to settle in Kansas. Like McCarthy, Stowell also came to live in Wetmore, but Stowell sided with the temperance cause and took a strong interest in local political ethics. In 1883, as part of a taxpayers' meeting, Stowell admonished his fellow residents to report any wrongdoing on the part of elected officials. Stowell lectured: "If any person knows of any thing that shows crookedness in any county affairs, they will put the same in writing, have it sworn to, and send to either of the investigating committees." He served as marshal for the city council and, as a temperance candidate, in 1883 won election as Wetmore city treasurer.[38]

As temperance men like Stowell gained elective office in Wetmore, McCarthy's legal troubles began to mount. Local law enforcement officials arrested the druggist in June 1883, and Judge Histed of Seneca fined him one hundred dollars for violation of the prohibition law. McCarthy claimed poverty, and the judge subsequently jailed him until such time as he could raise money to pay the fine. Despite his misfortune, McCarthy had many old friends who remembered him from the colony and new friends who patronized his medicinal establishment. Wetmore's other pharmacist, a man named Rote, began gathering signatures on a petition appealing to Governor George W. Glick to pardon McCarthy and remit his fine.[39] The petition did not sit well with Wetmore's temperance men. As the formal request was circulating, H. C. DeForest informed Glick that his office would soon receive "a petition for the pardon of Chas. McCarthy for selling intoxicants in violation of the law. I do not believe Mr. McCarthy is a proper person for executive clemency or that either of the reasons given in the petition are true." The petition claimed that McCarthy deserved amnesty because of his innocence and inability to pay. DeForest alleged that McCarthy had "openly and defiantly violated" the law and owned, in his wife's name, property in Chicago valued at between six and eight thousand dollars. Leaving him incarcerated was better, groused DeForest, "than to have him turned loose to make his living by selling a commodity in violation of law that is worth less than nothing thereby making paupers and criminals."[40]

Governor Glick responded with the announcement that he would "not under any circumstances be a nullifier of law, and parties must depend on either not getting arrested or winning their cases in court." McCarthy bowed to the inevitable. He appealed to those in debt to his business and obtained his release by the end of July. McCarthy left for Atchison but soon returned to Wetmore to ply his trade. The fight was not over. In 1885 Stowell, J. W. Perry, and several other temperance men signed an indictment against McCarthy, and by September the pharmacist again found himself imprisoned for violating the prohibition law. This was too much for McCarthy, who shot back from the Seneca jail against what he viewed as the hypocrisy of his accusers. McCarthy took the stance that the prohibition law was a restriction on personal freedom. Plus he argued that he had used his business for the good and assisted reform candidates, whom he considered friends, to gain elective office. During the 1883 election, McCarthy had generously provided liquid refreshment to voters pledging to cast their ballots for Stowell. Given the two men's long friendship, Stowell's charges against McCarthy stung. McCarthy countered that Stowell was "considered one of the foremost men of the temperance movement, but he cannot deny . . . that when he ran for the office of Treasurer of Wetmore township he paid me for drink in order to further his election." He leveled a similar accusation against Perry and fumed that "these model reformers are not the men to come forward" and admit that they bought liquor because "they are afraid the purpose they got it for should be known."[41]

The heat was on the temperance men, and Perry confessed that he drank beer at McCarthy's pharmacy. Stowell expressed sadness at his old comrade's disgrace and alleged that during his candidacy he never spoke to McCarthy. Soon afterward, however, he was compelled to divulge that McCarthy had called on his office to congratulate him on his victory and to request compensation for a small monetary sum expended in Stowell's interest. Stowell remarked that he did not find the request strange, particularly "after the close friendship that had existed between us for over fourteen years." Stowell had to admit that he paid the few dollars McCarthy claimed was out of pocket and "considered this more honorable than to dispute an act done with good motives. In this I simply paid him his demands, but whether for cigars or other purposes he did not say and I never knew. I did not ask him to aid my election in any way." Stowell was fully aware of McCarthy's business interests in Wetmore, and his claim of paying the pharmacist without knowing the details of where the money went may have been a case of selective ignorance. Nevertheless, in true political fashion, Stowell turned the issue on its head and declared that "accursed liquor" rather than electioneering was the true problem. Had it not been for the influence of alcohol, grieved Stowell, "my old friend McCarthy would never have tried by any word he could utter or any act he could do, to injure my humble reputation. As an old and mutual friend remarked yesterday, 'He would rather have suffered his hand to have been cut off.'" Stowell was proud of the work he had done for temperance reform and wrote that he did not contend against alcohol peddlers for his own benefit but "for the rising generation and for our common country's good against the liquor traffic and its many evil influences." Espousing the same expectations as he had learned as an O'Brienite in the Eclectic Hall, Stowell asserted that through "precept and example," temperance reformers could "increase our numbers and extend our influence until we have a party numerous and united and which can enforce the laws of Kansas."[42]

McCarthy felt betrayed. After serving out his sentence, he retreated to Chicago as an outcast. Although some of his children remained in the area as permanent residents, McCarthy's bootlegging days were over. Stowell, on the other hand, rose to become one of Nemaha County's leading dignitaries. By 1886 Stowell had sold his lumber yard and purchased the *Nemaha County Spectator*.[43] His reform interests remained firmly O'Brienite, and as one of Wetmore's leading newspaper editors, Stowell found a voice that expanded well beyond the temperance crusade. His activism became readily apparent as labor disputes on Jay Gould's railroad empire in 1885 and 1886 propelled both Stowell and John Radford headlong into the political arena.

Known across America as the "Wizard of Wall Street," Gould was a railroad speculator whose predatory dealings foreshadowed modern business practices. Unlike industrialists who invested for long-term development, Gould had little interest in operating his railroads for the public good. Instead he used his railroad investments to manipulate the stock market and exploit other people's work for his own short-term gain. Gould personified the grasping capitalist parasite that the O'Brienites despised. Already infamous for bleeding the Erie Railroad dry, his attempt in 1869 to corner the gold market, and the resultant Black Friday stock market crash, by 1879 Gould had focused his attention on the West and obtained a controlling interest in the Missouri Pacific Railroad. In that same year he added the Central Branch, Union Pacific to his growing railroad empire.[44] Although unconcerned about anyone who resided in the CBUP territory, Gould's actions against labor on his Kansas holdings caught the attention of the Kansas O'Brienites and made him the unwitting target of their ire.

Concomitant with Gould's commercial expansion in the West was an explosive growth of membership in the Knights of Labor. This was an industrial union that formed against the backdrop of European socialism and the Paris Commune. The Commune, in the words of historian Leon Fink, "represented the ultimate reunification of the workers' movement with the state and institutional centers of economic power." Labor intellectuals understood that the "withering away of the state," which they saw happening in the Commune, meant an elimination of the "bureaucratic apparatus" that allowed the middle class to govern over the working class. The O'Brienites in London had embraced this concept and supported the Commune to the detriment of their own colony in Kansas. The founders of the Knights of Labor adopted similar ideals, and in the union's Declaration of Principles the group members declared that "it is the purpose of the Order to establish a new and true standard of individual and national greatness." This new standard was to be based upon the organization of all workers into a single solidarity; the use of peaceful means to develop a cooperative system that would replace the wage system of labor; and united power at the ballot box to obtain the necessary legislation. As with the O'Brienites, the Knights envisioned a new order of society where "moral and industrial standards of worth" would replace wealth as the measure of human dignity.[45]

The Knights of Labor had become established in Kansas as early as 1874 with local assemblies based on geography rather than occupation. Convinced that legislative solutions could redress labor grievances, the union worked closely with the Kansas Republican Party and helped found a state Bureau of Labor. The organization leaders desired to maintain cordial relations with elected officials and sought peaceful and intelligent methods for settling industrial disputes. For that reason the Knights' preferred method of wielding power was through boycotts rather than strikes.[46] However, the union's genial relationship with Kansas lawmakers ended in 1885 as Jay Gould decided to flex his corporate muscle over workers in his railroad empire. In that year shopmen on two of Gould's railroads, the Wabash line and the Missouri, Kansas, and Texas, refused to accept wage reductions. In retaliation, Gould instituted a lockout against the shopmen on the Wabash line, but union members across Gould's holdings acted in solidarity to shut down his railroads and break the lockout. Kansas governor John A. Martin arbitrated the settlement between Gould and his workers, and the successful end to the labor dispute sparked a dramatic growth in membership for the Knights.[47]

With the triumph over Gould in 1885, union officials in Kansas became more independent and began to distance themselves from the Republican Party. At the same time, however, many of the new rank-and-file members felt flush with power and wanted to push for all they could get from Gould. Gould and H. M. Hoxie, vice president for Gould's railroads, determined that the time had come to break the union. Against the counsel of the Knights' national leadership, in February 1886 workers on Gould's Texas Pacific line, a rail line that Gould had put into receivership, called a strike in protest of the dismissal of a union foreman and other grievances. This marked the beginning of the Great Southwest Strike, and sympathetic railroad workers on Gould lines in Texas, Kansas, Missouri, Arkansas, and Illinois joined the work stoppage. Gould and Hoxie were well aware that the Knights' leadership was unprepared for a protracted walkout and refused any good faith negotiations under the pretense that they had no authority to intervene with a company in receivership. In spite of this, members of the Knights striking on Gould's other lines were summarily fired, and the only response they had left was to seize control of railroad equipment in order to prevent scabs from continuing railroad operations. Violence between union members and railroad agents took place in Atchison, Kansas City, and Parsons, and by the beginning of April the state militia placed Parsons under martial law. With no hope for an arbitrated settlement, a failure of the national union leadership to control the situation from the beginning, and loss of public support, the strike failed. Gould broke the union on May 4, 1886, the same disastrous day as the Haymarket Affair in Chicago.[48]

Because the old Central Branch railway had become part of Gould's Missouri Pacific network, the strike impacted everyone living along the line. The O'Brienites followed the strike's progress and were sympathetic to railroad employees. As individuals they remained relatively quiet during the entire conflict, but the final outcome was something they could not ignore. Radford, the strongest activist of the Kansas O'Brienites, had suffered a personal tragedy in the years preceding the railroad strikes. Maria Radford had died in 1883, and Radford's Wetmore jewelry business had failed that same year. In 1885, the year the Knights won a temporary victory over Gould, Radford was living in a Wetmore boarding house. He soon retreated to his forty acres on the old colony grounds and tried to live as a farmer, but Radford's talent was not in agriculture. In 1886 he supplemented his income by traveling with his sons to county schoolhouses to present a magic lantern show while selling puzzle key rings and other handmade trinkets he designed "to tickle the fancies of the farmer's wife or daughter." Radford seemed destined to live out a nondescript existence, but Jay Gould's breaking of the Knights of Labor shocked the old O'Brienite into casting his lot with American labor. He joined the Knights and, following through with his belief that union activities had to be combined with political agitation, turned his attention to politics. In 1887 he became an itinerant stump speaker for the Union Labor Party in northeastern Kansas. This move dismayed his old friend Stowell, who in September commented that Radford had "fallen among political Philistines."[49]

Stowell's comment was in reaction to the Union Labor Party and not Radford's labor ideals. He believed that reform was better achieved through the Republican Party. Stowell shared Radford's advocacy toward workers, which he demonstrated through his own response to Gould. After breaking the union, Gould heartlessly cut worker wages, which left many section men — men who performed nine months of seasonal labor per year — in dire straits. Gould's actions struck Stowell as unnecessarily cruel, so in March 1888 Stowell took the side of the railroad employees in an open letter to the reviled industrialist. Stowell was nobody's fool. Rather than heap scorn or threaten violence upon the man who had slashed wages, he utilized the old Chartist tactic of precept and example. Stowell stroked Gould's ego by praising his exceptional sense of humanity. Continuing in the same vein, he assured Gould that in "all kindness and Christian humility it is our most earnest wish that you receive the prayers of all the people of the United States." Taking this tack almost to the point of absurdity, Stowell remarked: "No doubt you think it an impossibility, but my dear sir, it is admitted by the world that you are, if not the best man, one of the best men that the world ever saw. You have performed mericles [sic]: so did Jesus. You are the best man to-day, as Christ was in His day. He was persecuted: so are you. He died, as you will. He sits near the Throne as we hope you will be permitted to do." Immediately after appealing to Gould's vanity with comparisons to Christ, Stowell warned him that the only way to receive the prayers of the people and ensure his entry into heaven would be to "give your SECTION MEN on the Central Branch of your Missouri Pacific Railroad a dollar and a half per day instead of one dollar and fifteen cents." Stowell judiciously informed Gould that his reputation as "an honorable business man" was secure and that he was prepared to offer any further information that would help the railroad tycoon in understanding his workers' plight.[50]

In addition to publishing the letter, Stowell had the foresight to mail a copy directly to Gould. Remarkably, the letter succeeded in capturing Gould's attention. Sidney Dillon, Gould's personal secretary, telegraphed back: "Yours received. Mr. Gould has just reached the United States in his yacht, but will not be home for a few days. Write full particulars."[51] Stowell was ecstatic and eagerly responded with an explanation that worker complaints stemmed more from cuts in working hours than from the meager pay. In 1887, with more than three months lost in layoffs and other cutbacks, Central Branch section men averaged $254.15 for a year's labor. After subtracting the twenty-five cents per month that Gould deducted for support of the railroad hospital in Sedalia, Missouri, Stowell explained that section men received a mere $251.90 for the year. Stowell wrote: "Divide this amount by 312, the number of working days in the year, and you have an average wage of less than 80 cents per day." To Stowell such a miniscule amount was untenable. He appealed to Gould, and "to the world at large, and ask if you think that eighty cents per day is enough to keep a man and his family?" Stowell wanted to be clear that workers were not protesting the amount of pay earned per day, but instead protested "against the present system which is now imperative upon this road, and that is only giving them work from spring until fall, compelling them to be without employment through the long and tortuous winter."[52]

Stowell's unique approach intrigued Gould to the point where he took the uncharacteristic step of responding. In his correspondence to Stowell, the industrialist admitted: "I would not have answered your letter at all if it had been put in the usual way but owing to the straight forward manner in which you wrote, I feel like writing you personally." While forced to admit that wages he paid to section men on his railroad seemed small, Gould quickly dismissed the topic with the vague promise that he would do his "best to obtain an advance for them." Having made that small concession to the workers, Gould used the remainder of his communiqué to wallow in self-pity and offer excuses as to why his suffering was worse than that of his underpaid employees. Just days after his personal secretary telegraphed that Gould had been out for a leisurely cruise on his private yacht, the railroad tycoon had the temerity to write: "No doubt you think, as the majority of people do, that

I have a soft, easy time and that I am seeing an amount of pleasure not usually enjoyed by man. But, my friend, let me here tell you that my life is not all sunshine." Gould's underhanded business practices left him with countless enemies, and he wanted Stowell to understand "that nearly every man's hand is against me. I have to be ever on the alert for there are manipulators on the market that are ready to ruin me both in wealth and reputation." Portraying a streak of paranoia, Gould lamented over "the number of hours I lay awake thinking of the various projects and enterprises in which I am interested. It matters not how pure my motives may be they are invariably misconstrued." Gould confessed that he found it impossible to tear himself away from the "whirlpool of excitement and speculation" and disclosed that for him the "fact of having is not as pleasurable as the expectation of having." Like the proverbial rich man who lies awake at night fretting over how to extract the last nickel from a poor man's pocket, Gould rationalized that he had no choice but to cut wages. The entrepreneur complained that "strong competition will and has reduced dividends, and perhaps necessitate the reduction of wages to justify the operation of the roads."[53] With so much of his letter focusing on his personal angst, Gould betrayed where his true sympathies lay. He made no dispensation for his workers.

Stowell's effort at moral persuasion was revealing in the response it provoked from Gould but futile in the desired goal of helping the section workers. The youngest and most straitlaced of the Kansas O'Brienites, Stowell had never benefited from O'Brien's personal tutelage, and he attempted to make use of methods that O'Brien had shown to be ineffective. Moral persuasion backed by the collective strength of an entire nation's workforce was acceptable, but an individual appeal to middle-class morality was bound to fail for the simple reason that ethical concerns were an inconvenience to middle-class businessmen like Gould. O'Brien wrote that superior moral "qualities are only drawbacks and impediments in the way of success in business. Hence no clever profitmonger ever thinks of encumbering himself with them."[54]

One year after his correspondence with Gould, Stowell sold his newspaper and, after apprenticing with a local attorney in Seneca, enrolled in law school at the University of Kansas. After earning a bachelor of laws degree in 1891, Stowell moved to the town of Seneca and became a legal advocate for workers and a local Populist Party organizer.[55] He learned through experience what O'Brien had taught in 1850 during the founding of the National Reform League; namely, that there had to be a "diffusion, amongst the people at large, of sound political and social knowledge." O'Brien wrote: "Real *political* they believe to be inseparable from real *social* power, and the converse. To make the people appreciate universal suffrage, we must teach them what they lose by the want of it, and what they may fairly expect from a wise and legitimate use of it."[56]

O'Brien's message was prescient for Kansas of the 1890s. Better than any other Kansas O'Brienite, John Radford understood O'Brien's admonition to teach the people what they had to gain, or lose, by exercising their right of suffrage in an organized manner. Radford had joined the Knights of Labor and by 1887 was traveling around the region delivering orations on behalf of the Union Labor Party, a forerunner to the Populist Party. In January 1888 he gave up his small farm on the old colony grounds and moved with his boys to the town of Horton in neighboring Brown County. Radford never really fit in with the bucolic life of his adopted home near the old colony. He decided to relocate to a town where he believed people had a greater appreciation for his elocutionary ability and did not look down on him, as a local paper remarked: a "familiar, though eccentric, character." Although he rented seven acres in the small village of Kennekuk over the Atchison County line and intended to raise vegetables to supplement his income, that plan never materialized, as his speaking schedule did not allow much time for agriculture. Instead he took a home in West Horton with two of his sons, John Maximilian and James. Radford rapidly became a local reform leader and by 1890, as the new People's Party was emerging as a statewide force, he became conspicuous within the organization for his nonagricultural background. At a September 1890 Populist convention in Hiawatha, an observer noted that "some of the most sensible looking men to be found in the county" were present. These reform leaders were "mostly farmers, excepting the Horton delegation, which was headed by a Mr. John Radford, who is very much a Knight of Labor. Mr. Weaver, of Hiawatha, is about such a man as Brother Radford, only he can't talk so much."[57]

The political situation in Kansas was roiling with change and not unlike that in England during the Chartist uprising. Since the late 1860s there had been a precipitous decline in the market price for farm produce; for instance, historian Scott McNall's research indicates that in 1866 a bushel of corn sold for sixty-six cents, whereas by 1889 that same bushel sold for as little as ten cents. With less disposable income, farmers were unable to pay exorbitant railroad rates for shipping grain, let alone usurious interest rates on mortgages. Subsequently, small farms failed to survive, and numerous families suffered through the ignominy of a foreclosure. As with industrial workers, appeals for elected officials to assist agricultural laborers by setting minimum prices, capping interest rates, or regulating railroads seemed to fall on deaf ears. As it became progressively more apparent that the leading political parties were indifferent, if not hostile, to the needs of farmers in Kansas, many decided that the time had come to form a new political faction — one that was less beholden to corporate interests.[58]

Conditions for farmers and workingmen were not unique to Kansas, and with a similar state of affairs prevailing in many parts of the country, new organizations known as Farmers' Alliances began to form. In many ways analogous to industrial labor unions, the alliances coalesced into two major regional associations: the National Farmers' Alliance (Northern Alliance) and the National Farmers' Alliance and Industrial Union (Southern Alliance). Local Kansas affiliates initially were connected to the Northern Alliance; however, by the time the two state alliances consolidated in the summer of 1889, the Southern Alliance was dominant in the region. A national convention in St. Louis met that same year. While it failed to merge the two national alliances, the St. Louis Convention did adopt a unified set of reform demands that established common goals and set the stage for meaningful political reform.[59]

In Kansas the Populist, or People's, Party formed in Topeka in June 1890 and issued a call for an August statewide convention. John Radford, dedicated to reform as he had been his entire life, was present at the creation. In response to the call for a state convention, in July local reform leaders in Brown County convened in Hiawatha to elect delegates for the August gathering in Topeka. Reaffirming the principles of the St. Louis platform of 1889, the assembled representatives called for an abolition of national banks; the free and unlimited coinage of silver; new laws against trusts and combines that speculated in agricultural produce; prohibitions against foreign ownership of land in the United States; the development of a system of barges on the Missouri and Mississippi Rivers to compete with the railroads; government control of transportation; and direct election of U.S. senators. While the remnants of the Knights of Labor worked closely with the Populists, in Brown County the delegates wanted to be clear that the meeting was a "people's convention, not a Knights of Labor convention or an alliance convention, but a convention of the people." The group subsequently resolved that "we hold to national rather than party supremacy; the good of the whole nation rather than a section of our country and, if there must be class legislation, then we favor the toiling millions rather than the non-laboring thousands." Radford served as a member of the credentials committee for the meeting and was elected as an alternate delegate to the state convention in Topeka. He delivered one of the speeches in response to the convention resolutions, to which a resident journalist gushed: "John Radford of Horton is an eloquent speaker."[60]

During the Populist organizational meetings in June, Mary Elizabeth Lease of Wichita emerged as one of the nascent party's most persuasive speakers. In the words of historian Brooke Speer Orr: "Mary Lease's evangelist-style speeches stirred listeners' emotions and roused their anger over the seemingly ubiquitous 'money power' in America." For this reason, party officials asked Lease to undertake a lecture tour of the state in order to build up support for the Populist agenda. Lease agreed and delivered at least 160 speeches in the months leading up to the 1890 elections.[61] A visit to Brown County was included on Lease's circuit, and in early September the great Populist orator spoke in Hiawatha and Horton. Lease's appeal was immense, and a local newspaper remarked: "Never, in the history of Brown county, was there a larger crowd out to hear a political speaker than last Thursday at the fair ground when Mrs. Mary Lease of Wichita, stepped on the improvised platform on the race tracks before the grand stand." Lease captivated the audience from the beginning as she "arranged the two old parties before the bar of justice and with a master effort." As she delivered her plea of support for the People's Party the crowd became so enthusiastic that a local reporter jibed: "We noticed old time republicans and democrats blistering their hands by vigorous plaudits."[62]

Radford was present for Lease's lectures. While the day belonged to Lease, party organizers in Brown County were anxious to maintain the momentum that Lease's speeches had created. Therefore Populist officials sent out a slate of local speakers, of which Radford was prominently featured, to canvas the county in the weeks remaining before the election. In October, after Lease had moved westward and was speaking in the town of Wetmore near the old colony grounds, Radford remained in Brown County to promote the Populist cause before local crowds. Radford was a practiced orator and devoted campaigner on behalf of the People's Party candidate for governor, John F. Willits. His lengthy orations were well received and inspired listeners "to stay longer to listen to the live issues of the day."[63]

Radford's O'Brienite principles fit in neatly with the predominant themes of the 1890 Populist campaign in Kansas. O'Brien had been among a handful of Chartists to clearly articulate the link between politics and economics, and it was a doctrine his followers had been expressing ever since. However, what had been avant-garde thinking in O'Brien's day was accepted dogma for the Populists. For example, in north-central Kansas, congressional candidate

John Davis campaigned on the theme that the system of wage slavery "rests on sixty millions of people. It makes paupers which society must feed; and it has created thousands of millionaire slave masters." John Grant Otis, a communitarian socialist who had moved to Kansas from Vermont, adopted an aggressive stance that would have sounded familiar to any Chartist from O'Brien's era. Wrote Otis: "When the American people shall introduce co-operation into the field of PRODUCTION as well as into the field of DISTRIBUTION, and shall organize for 'work' as we organize for 'war'!; then will we behold PROSPERITY such as the world has never witnessed."[64] The platform of the 1890 Populist campaign in Kansas could have been written in London's Eclectic Hall, which made Radford and other O'Brienites in Kansas natural advocates for the cause.

In the 1890 elections the Populists won four of Kansas's seven congressional seats and took control of the lower house of the state legislature. It was a stunning victory that emboldened members of the People's Party to press even harder for the next campaign. Radford remained an important voice for the Knights of Labor in regional Populist meetings and was popularly known as "the silver tongued orator of Horton."[65] However, in the spring and summer of 1891 Radford's political activities went on hiatus as his son and namesake, John Maximilian Radford, fell ill with what was vaguely diagnosed as trouble with his spine. Physicians were unable to treat the condition, which quickly deteriorated. The younger Radford died on May 25, 1891, from what doctors initially pronounced as a diseased spleen but what was finally revealed to be bowel cancer. The young man, whose middle name was a tribute to O'Brien's hero, Maximilian Robespierre, was twenty-five. Members of the Knights of Labor conducted the funeral service in a grove behind the Radford home and acted as pallbearers as they carried the body to its final interment in the Horton cemetery.[66]

Radford, who was fifty-seven at the time of his son's death, returned to the fray after the funeral. His role among the Populists was analogous to the responsibilities he earlier had fulfilled within the Mutual Land, Emigration, and Cooperative Colonization

Company. He held no political office but remained an important regional organizer for the People's Party and represented West Horton on the County Central Committee.[67] In 1891 the *Journal of the Knights of Labor* published an American edition of O'Brien's book *The Rise, Progress, and Phases of Human Slavery*, and as O'Brien's views found wider distribution among American radicals, Radford's voice grew louder. In the 1892 campaign he brought the febrile intellectual energy of his O'Brienite views into the arena for the elections. A prominent member of the local Weaver Club supporting James B. Weaver's bid for the presidency, Radford threw himself headlong into the campaign for the entire Populist ticket. In response to speculation that a possible fusion with a local Democratic candidate, D. G. Olinger of Hiawatha, would lead to a dispersion of the People's Party, Radford scoffed: "If such a piece of weakness or trade stirs the palsied pulses of the western worshipers of Carnegie, Protection of Capital, Frick and the Pinkertons, they are welcome to it." For Radford it was patently obvious that Populist "voters will swell the grand chorus of National rejoicing in November."[68] Radford was a tireless campaigner and through the Weaver Club gave lively speeches on behalf of Weaver and Populist gubernatorial candidate Lorenzo Lewelling. In November Radford and other Populists were justified in claiming victory. Weaver won the state's electoral votes, while Lewelling captured the governor's office. The only question that remained was the issue of the state legislature and how much control the Populists actually could claim.

For Radford the installation of the "first People's Party government on earth" represented more than a triumphant moment for Kansas Populism; a government truly of the people signified an affirmation of everything that the O'Brienites had been struggling to attain since the push for the People's Charter in Britain. He traveled to Topeka on January 9, 1893, for the celebratory inauguration of Governor Lewelling; however, rather than allow himself to be swept up in the festive atmosphere, Radford knew from his tutelage under O'Brien that electing individuals who genuinely represented the interests of agricultural and industrial workers constituted only the first step. The difficult work of legislating social and economic reform still lay ahead. O'Brien taught his students that once a system of private property had become entrenched in "a country, which God made for all its inhabitants, and for all generations born upon it, to be brought up, or otherwise monopolized or usurped by any particular section of any one generation (be that section large or small), and that moment your community is divided into tyrants and slaves." No government, regardless of its form, based upon such a corrupt foundation, could be reformed so long as land continued to be held as private property.[69]

Radford agreed with O'Brien's sentiments and, after listening to Lewelling's inaugural address, observed that the new governor made no statement "more cogent than the declaration, 'that if it is unlawful for the poor to take the property of the rich, it should be just as emphatically acknowledged that 'tis unlawful for the rich to take the property of the poor.'" Having more than a little experience with this issue, Radford replied: "The solution of this property question will open the gateway to an earthy Eden. It has been the problem of the ages. It lies unresolved at our feet."

Farmers and industrial workers possessed precious little tangible property, which Radford believed a gross injustice because it was the labor of agricultural and factory workers that produced and sustained property. As a direct result of their bodily toils, mental efforts, and learned skills, the wealth of the working class was defined as their labor. Said Radford: "It is that which has produced railroads and equipped them, yet owns not a yard of road bed nor an old scrap pile. It builds cities, then rents houses to live in. Erects machinery which doubles our muscular power every seven years, yet stands outside the factory door begging to be hired. It has cleared the western wilderness and made the desert bloom with homes, for which rents are now paid to those who never saw them."

Radford held high hopes for Lewelling's commitment to reform and quoted the portions of his address that meshed with his O'Brienite sentiments: "The producers labor in the field, mine and factory, while the millionaire appropriates their earnings, and rides through life in a gilded carriage attended by servants." Lewelling effectively harnessed the seething anger of the moment, and Radford proudly congratulated the governor for his understanding of issues that mattered to workers. "Kansas," Radford quoted Lewelling, "has stepped to the front to check oppressions, protect and advance the interests of all its citizens, demand the rights of laborer and producer, and change the system by which the west has produced the material to feed and clothe the world, and yet is herself left simply a vassal to organized wealth."

Radford's optimism for Lewelling's new administration was tempered by decades of service in the frontline trenches of reform. He knew the difference between empty rhetoric and the actual practice of legislating and enforcing reform. He thus made it clear that only the passage of time would tell if Lewelling and the Populists truly understood the task before them.

> The enunciative of these historic truths form a grand contrast to the patriot-like talk of most public men. To secure these checks and produce such changes, new laws are needed which if defended by eternal vigilance and an enlightened public conscience would be a blazing light to show the pathway to a new and better time, when want shall not stretch its withered hand for charity, but when justice, liberty, and equality shall prevail. If Kansas can with united councils take some steps on the road indicated, then in the history of the movement for the abolition of the wages slavery she will have earned the same standard of honor, which she has always deserved for repelling the western inroad of chattel slavery. Will she do it? Will love of country stand above party? The fingers of time will tell.[70]

While members of the People's Party applauded Radford's words, those who did not embrace the Populist message found his discussion of Lewelling's inaugural speech to be alarming. Opponents of Populism in turn accused Radford of being a bomb-throwing anarchist. For an individual who had studied Chartist philosophy with Bronterre O'Brien, participated in the London section of the International Working Men's Association, marched in support of the Paris Commune, and come to Kansas as part of an experiment in social utopianism, such a provincial misreading of socialist ideals clearly offended his sensibilities. Radford mocked that "the state is just now deluged with a flood of big word blowers. Whoever utters or commands a new thought becomes, in their eyes, a teacher of anarchy, communism, socialism, agrarianism, and incendiarism. All these terms are sometimes used in one essay, as if they were all synonymous." What Radford gleaned from such ad hominem attacks was that the opponents of reform had no commonsense platform of their own except as "apologists of the present rule and ruin system." Radford, however, had an argument: "If it is the mission of Kansas to check oppression, turn back the hands of plutocratic misrule, hold up the lamp of hope and point out the channel which shall redeem her from vassalages to organized wealth, she must earn her guerdon for leadership by the wisdom of her laws and her power to put them in practice; her counselors' power vanish where they began, at the ballot box. Change of party must bring change of decrees. 'By their fruits ye shall be judged.'"[71]

He realized better than most that for a change in governing parties to have any meaning, a radical reform in the system of industrial production and distribution was essential. Before this time, said Radford, the nation had failed to secure its agricultural, mineral, and manufactured wealth for the benefit of those most responsible for its production. After detailing a portion of Lewelling's agenda for reform, Radford said that "if this generation can lead the next, be it not only a few steps toward the new and better future, where equality shall prevail. Then all the triumphs of arts, science, and culture will be eclipsed."

Toward the end of February 1893, John Radford again departed for Topeka. He felt that his knowledge and years of experience would be of benefit to the new administration, and it was his hope that Governor Lewelling would see fit to award him a patronage appointment in compensation for the time and money he had given to the campaign the previous fall. However, he also went to the state capital in order to witness the political train wreck that was undermining the lower house of the state legislature.[72] While the Populists had won the governor's office, four congressional seats, and the state Senate, they had failed to win decisive control over the state House of Representatives. The election results gave the Republicans a slight edge, but using charges of election fraud, the Populists claimed to own the majority of seats. The Republican House, led by George L. Douglass, and the Populist House, led by John M. Dunsmore, both declared themselves to be the legitimate assembly and met separately in the Representative Hall until mid-February. After each side had attempted to unseat the other, the Republicans decided to settle the issue with violence. With the sheriff, a large number of deputies, and most of the state militia on their side, the Republicans smashed down the door to the Representative Hall and forced the Populist representatives out. The governor intervened and agreed to let the Republican-dominated state Supreme Court decide the issue. There was no bloodshed in the legislative war of 1893, but the Republicans won the conflict. On February 28 the court decided in favor of the Republicans, and the Populists occupying the disputed seats were compelled to vacate.[73]

The Republican victory in the legislative war meant that there would be little cooperation between the Populist Senate and the Republican House. Reform was stalled, and the dispute ultimately proved politically damaging to the Populist cause. The great promise of the People's Party remained unfulfilled, but for rank-and-file members like John Radford, it signaled only a minor setback that would be rectified in the next election. Radford was witness to the Supreme Court's remarks on its decision, for which he expressed no small degree of disdain for the majority opinion. He was also present for the closing ceremonies of the short-lived Populist House of Representatives and saw nothing but "the resolve of unconquered heroes." He reported that the "fiat members were consoled by the thought that they were only left to rest by the wayside. They had fought the good fight" and "had stood the ordeal like old guards." Always looking to the future, Radford proclaimed: "Two years will soon pass. The people of the state will rally to help us put you again in the front ranks. Together we will march on to the day of final victory."[74]

For John Radford, however, it was the end. He had been an outspoken opponent of fusion with the Democratic Party, and Lewelling's administration actively pursued a fusionist agenda. Radford was thwarted in his desire for a gubernatorial appointment and for a brief time reconciled himself, as the Horton press remarked, "as outside door-keeper" of the state house "without pay as usual."[75] Instead of returning to his old home in Horton, Radford took up residence in Topeka and resumed his trade of engraver. He found employment with J. C. Darling on the corner of Kansas Avenue and Eighth Street in the city and specialized in engraving gold and silver jewelry and in manufacturing badges and emblem pins.[76] Radford celebrated his sixtieth birthday in March 1894, and continued as an active member of the Shawnee County Populist Party. In April he joined other radicals in voicing support for Coxey's Army. He resided at 810 Kansas Avenue through the beginning of 1897, after which he no longer appeared in Topeka directories. Radford moved to Leavenworth and briefly took up residence with his daughter Elizabeth Royan (Ryan). He continued working in Leavenworth as an engraver and badge manufacturer until 1903, when his health deteriorated to the point where he could no longer practice his craft. In 1903 he moved to live with his daughter Mary Johnson in Kansas City, Kansas.

In March 1906 Benjamin Beeby, the son of colonist William Beeby, was returning from Guthrie, Oklahoma, and stopped in Kansas City on his way home to the town of Goff near the old colony grounds. During his layover he took the time to pay a social call on his father's old friend John Radford. Rather than the energetic Radford of years gone by, Beeby found a sickly old man who was "quite feeble and bereft of the sight of one eye."[77] It was the last contact anyone outside of Radford's own family had with the old O'Brienite. John Radford died on April 26, 1906, exactly thirty-seven years after launching Edward Smith and the first band of colonists off from London's Victoria Docks. He was appropriately mourned as one of the pioneers of Nemaha County and a promoter of the "English Colony" near Goff.[78] Unlike his mentor Bronterre O'Brien, whose gravesite in Abney Park was adorned with an impressive monument, Radford was buried quietly and anonymously in an unmarked grave in Kansas City's Woodlawn Cemetery.

Conclusion

The O'Brienites

When evaluating the O'Brienites and the Workingmen's Cooperative Colony in Kansas as a social movement, the entire process of group development must be considered. From mobilization under O'Brien and the National Reform League during the Chartist era, through the institutional development of the Kansas colony, to the final dispersal of O'Brien's ideas in Britain and the United States, the O'Brienites represented more than a small company of British radicals who failed at an isolated experiment in the American West. The Workingmen's Cooperative Colony was a unique O'Brienite experiment that had deep roots in British Chartism and branches that extended into modern British socialism and Kansas Populism.

In 1837, during the most intellectually productive phase of his career, Bronterre O'Brien set out his plan for land nationalization, which was lauded as the "true theory." O'Brien believed that dominion over the soil belonged to the nation alone. It was therefore a common birthright of all citizens to benefit from the mineral and agricultural wealth of the land. Liberal political economy, however, had defined the land as a commodity that could be bought and sold as private property, thus enriching the aristocratic and middle-class minority of the population while the majority of working-class people remained landless and destitute. O'Brien considered such a practice to be immoral and unjust because, as he said, it "bestows on a few worthless individuals what is the inheritance of the whole, and which goes on every year augmenting the possessions of those individuals, without any acts of their own to merit it; while the inheritance of the majority is rendered more and more precarious."[1]

O'Brien identified, as Thomas Spence had done before him, "the need to devolve economic and political powers attendant on private ownership."[2] In his account of Spenconia, Spence explained that land ownership, which was economic power, and control of government were intimately connected.[3] Although O'Brien, like Spence, understood that the people had first to gain control of government and use the force of the state to redistribute land, it had become a question of the wealthy middle class against the impoverished working class. The unequal distribution of wealth was the cause of working-class miseries, and for O'Brien the only rational way to alleviate the problem was to nationalize landholdings and redistribute parcels by way of a lease among the workers. "For instance," he said, "how many thousands are there of mere shopkeepers, who would much rather be cultivators of the soil, or otherwise usefully employed, if they knew how or could be so?"[4] Nevertheless, O'Brien well understood that disparity of wealth in a country could be overcome only through equal representation in government. "It is not the *quantity* of capital in a country that is of so much importance, but the *nature* of it, and the mode of its distribution." O'Brien continued by reiterating his belief that the only way to overcome monopolization of wealth and to effect a fair and equitable distribution of resources was through an educated workforce collectively exercising the right of universal suffrage.[5]

Concomitant to O'Brien's idea on land nationalization was the theory of currency reform, a concept he initially inherited from William Cobbett. What Karl Marx derided as "currency quackery" was O'Brien's belief that middle-class capitalists tyrannized and robbed the people by using gold and silver, both speculative commodities, as the basis of currency. He considered the practice of linking the value of a nation's legal tender to the fluctuating price of precious metals to be a form of economic cannibalism that impoverished workers in the midst of the wealth that they had produced. O'Brien wrote of the middle classes: "With their fictitious paper-capital, they contrive to wheedle the farmer out of his produce, which they re-distribute again (at large profits) in their respective localities."[6] Instead of a gold standard, he believed that "the National Currency should be based on real, consumable wealth, or on the *bona fide* credit of the State, and not upon the variable and uncertain amount of scarce metals."[7] For O'Brien, real and consumable wealth meant a monetary system based upon a corn or labor standard. A farmer or craftsman producing trade goods valued at a given amount (the sum to be determined by "disinterested officers") would receive symbolic notes at a labor exchange that could then be deposited or used to buy consumables of equivalent worth. With prices fixed to the value of labor, and all trade conducted at state-run labor exchanges, freeloading middlemen would be eliminated and capitalistic speculation in currency would end.

After the third attempt to push the People's Charter through Parliament failed in 1848, Chartism as a national movement fell into decline. Many former Chartists began to drift toward Marxism, but O'Brien took another path. He understood how dangerous revolutionary rhetoric was, and when he learned the disastrous results of John Alexander's effort to join Étienne Cabet's Texas Icarian settlement, O'Brien turned his attention to educating the working classes in matters of social reform. He recognized how easily ordinary workers could be politically manipulated when they remained oblivious of their basic rights. "It ever was so, it ever will be so, with a people ignorant of the social rights: they will never risk life or limb in defence of their *political* till they comprehend their *social* rights." Therefore, when founding the National Reform League (NRL) in 1850, he stressed that a program of education coupled with progressive reform was necessary in order "to protect society from violent revolutionary changes."[8]

O'Brien's emphasis on peaceable methods to enact meaningful reform caused him to lose favor among mainstream Chartists, but the power of his ideas attracted a devoted coterie of followers. For O'Brien and those who believed in him, the NRL's program, like the People's Charter before it, represented a means to an end. Through education, demonstrations, and united action at the ballot box, members of the NRL believed that the working classes could attain political realignment. Once the middle classes had been stripped of their exclusive control over government, then the people could work toward necessary social reforms, "or a reformation of society through the operation of just and humane laws." O'Brien continued to support fundamental political reform through the six points of the People's Charter, but the Charter "unaccompanied by the social reforms we demand, might possibly prove a danger for all classes." To the Charter he added the seven propositions of the NRL "in order to work out the complete emancipation of the whole people, politically, socially, morally, and intellectually."[9]

Members of the NRL intended that the first three propositions be provisional because the intent behind them was to relieve temporary evils. These included a repeal of Britain's Poor Law; government purchase of small parcels of land for relocation of the urban poor; and shifting the burden of repaying the national debt, which O'Brien viewed as a mortgage on property, to the property-owning middle class. O'Brien intended that the last four propositions be "of a permanent kind, to cure permanent evils," and it was these proposals that became sacrosanct for NRL members and the foundation for the Kansas colony. It was in the last four propositions that O'Brien outlined his plan for nationalizing the land and natural resources; a system of national credit that would enable citizens to lease land without being subjected to "the tyranny of wage slavery"; to eliminate the gold standard while making corn or labor, "the bona fide credit of the state," the standard for currency; and to establish labor exchanges where agricultural produce, craft goods, and other exchangeable wares could be traded fairly and equitably. Once these basic reforms were in place, others, such as education and nationalization of public utilities and transportation networks, were to follow. However, O'Brien deemed the seven principles of the NRL as an essential first step. "Without these," he said, "justice cannot be done to humanity; society cannot be placed in the true path of improvement, never again to be turned aside or thrown back."[10]

O'Brien's followers embraced the NRL's seven principles with the certainty of a theologian adhering to sacred tenets. They remained committed proponents of obtaining political representation through the six points of the People's Charter, but proving the infallibility of O'Brien's canon of reform ideas was what drove members of the NRL. Thus using the Eclectic Hall to educate workers with a basic understanding of "the relation of property to labour" became a cornerstone of the NRL. The O'Brienites indoctrinated a new generation of activists with O'Brien's ideas and gave the organization longevity even as other Chartist clubs faded out of existence. While NRL members continued pressing for equal political representation in Parliament, NRL headquarters at the Eclectic Hall became a vibrant institute where workers could take courses in grammar and composition, mathematics, and sciences or listen to lectures on political theory and current affairs. O'Brien, like other intellectual Chartists, saw education as an essential step toward political liberation. He used it to enlighten members of the working class to the point where they could demand to know why "the soil, the money, the privilege, the dignity, the power of the State, should be shut up in the hands of a few, and those few so unworthy of the honour, and incapable of the trust."[11]

Although during O'Brien's later years the younger O'Brienites flirted with the idea of communitarianism, they remained fiercely loyal to their mentor and focused their primary energies on education and his political reform program. Upon O'Brien's death in 1864, his followers stood over his grave and took a solemn oath that they would devote their lives to a zealous adherence and propagation of the principles of their revered teacher. From their headquarters at the Eclectic Hall, members of O'Brien's National Reform League remained at the fore of British radical reform movements and even hosted the London Section of the International Working Men's Association. However, they were O'Brienites, not Marxists, and disagreements over Marx's program along with frustration over Parliament's seeming refusal to enact reform legislation of any consequence led them to consider establishing a cooperative community in the United States. The O'Brienites harbored few illusions about America and had no intention of disappearing into the wilderness or establishing a commune simply for the sake of cooperative living. O'Brien had taught them that in "America the workpeople are flying in thousands from the manufacturing states, into the back-woods of the West, in order to escape the grinding and murderous gripe of Mammon."[12] Those who arrived first, he continued, would likely prosper and become landlords. Nevertheless, as the commercial importance of the West increased, the land would be bled dry and wages would ultimately deteriorate for those who came to work for the property owners. The O'Brienites understood the process of settlement but nonetheless wanted to provide evidence that there was a viable and humane alternative to what they believed had proven to be ineffective ballot-box democracy, selfish trade unionism, and Marx's revolutionary rhetoric.

Despite O'Brien's warnings about the true state of America's political economy and opposition to emigration, the allure of the American West fascinated the O'Brienites. They had always found the idea of Jeffersonian agrarianism appealing for its promise of political equality, and they inherited O'Brien's belief that in "America there is less danger than anywhere else of the people losing their political rights." O'Brien wrote: "This is owing partly to the greater equality in property which subsists there, but chiefly to the agitation of *social* questions which has been forced upon the working classes of late years by the continuous arrival of European emigrants competing with them in the labour-market, and alarming them, by their example, as to what might prove their own fate hereafter, should they suffer a powerful territorial and commercial aristocracy to grow up amongst them. Hence the springing up of the 'Free Soil' and 'National Reform' movements in the United States." Nevertheless, O'Brien saw genuine peril in America and argued that the country's "agrarian laws are not a jot better than those of France and England; and her commercial spirit is even more ravenous and unscrupulous."[13] Regardless of O'Brien's warnings, the opening of the West, the construction of transportation links, and the Free Soil rhetoric that created the Homestead Act impressed upon the O'Brienites that an opportunity to prove their mentor's principles by way of example was available. It created a new and compelling stimulus to arguments for emigration.

When the O'Brienites made the decision to plant a colony in the United States and formed the Mutual Land, Emigration, and Cooperative Colonization Company, they did so primarily "for the further development of all those Social, Political, and Moral rights inculcated by many of our great Reformers living, and dead, but more especially the teachings of the late Bronterre O'Brien, upon whose principles our proposed Colony will to a great extent be founded."[14] After establishing the Workingmen's Cooperative Colony in Kansas, Edward Grainger Smith became its first superintendent. The intent was for the company directors in London to act in the role of the state by maintaining ownership of the colony land for the good of all subscribers while leasing out small parcels to individual shareholders. Rents paid on the individual leases were the only form of taxation, with the anticipation that the collective revenue would be sufficient to maintain the company while extending credit to members too poor to emigrate on their own. Labor was designated as the medium of exchange on the colony estate, while in London the directors opened a cooperative store to help fund the colony and provide credit for emigrants.

Exactly one year after establishing a presence in Kansas, while Smith was still alive and expectations remained lofty, Henry Clinton came to the Eclectic Hall with a blueprint for constructing an associated village on the colony grounds. Although never built, the plan was remarkable in two aspects. First, it reflected the O'Brienite belief in gender equality. When discussing the "grand problem which has yet to be solved — namely, how the *quantity* of repulsive work, and the discomfort in general, everywhere throughout the world, may, to the utmost possible degree, be *minimized*," Clinton included women's domestic labor. Thus the O'Brienites sought the utopian goal of freeing women "from avoidable repulsive employment — that is to say, from unnecessary cooking and house-drudgery."[15]

The second noteworthy aspect of Clinton's design was in its anticipation of architectural plans for cooperative labor commonwealths such as California's Llano del Rio and descriptions of pneumatic tube systems such as those described in Edward Bellamy's utopian novel *Looking Backward*. Alice Constance Austin, a devotee of feminist author Charlotte Perkins Gilman, drew up the architectural blueprint for Llano del Rio in 1915, and like the Workingmen's Cooperative Colony in Kansas, her grand design emphasized gender equality. Although never realized, Austin's proposal for a circular city, called a Civic Center, with a radial street pattern was modeled on Ebenezer Howard's 1898 diagram for a Garden City.[16] Howard's description of a model city surrounded by green belts, which inspired the Garden City movement of the twentieth century, was undeniably related to the O'Brienites' plans for an associated village.

Although Howard did not credit the O'Brienites, he was extremely well read, and he traveled in similar circles. Born in England in 1850, Howard traveled to Nebraska in 1871 and briefly attempted farming just north of the Workingmen's Cooperative Colony. After a short stint in Chicago, in 1876 Howard returned to London. A man who thought carefully about social issues, Howard admired Bellamy's *Looking Backward* and Henry George's *Progress and Poverty*. In 1882 he became obliquely involved with Henry Hyndman and the O'Brienites in Britain's Social Democratic Federation (SDF). In that year the SDF republished Thomas Spence's 1775 pamphlet on land reform. In his tract, Spence argued that every parish should become a corporation and use its collective power to reclaim its lost rights to land. Rents then collected could be used for public purposes rather than private profit. Spence's ideas had influenced O'Brien, and they intrigued Howard. To Spence's thoughts Howard fused John Stuart Mill's descriptions of planned colonization. It was on this point that he differed from the directors of the Mutual Land, Emigration, and Cooperative Colonization Company. Howard understood what they failed to grasp: namely, that unemployed London laborers required factory jobs and could not be expected to succeed as small leaseholders of land.[17]

A direct line of thought can be traced from Spence in 1775 to Alice Constance Austin and Llano del Rio in 1915, and the line passes through Bronterre O'Brien and the O'Brienites. Howard was introduced to Spence's pamphlet through Hyndman and the SDF and, as Mark Bevir writes, "O'Brienism was the language of the members of the SDF."[18] Spence's ideas came to the SDF through the efforts of the O'Brienites in the NRL and the Land and Labour League, both of which had promoted Spence during the 1860s and 1870s. The NRL, of course, touted these concepts because O'Brien had read Spence, had known older followers of Spence, and, in part, modeled his own true theory of land reform on Spence's ideas.[19] O'Brien made it clear in 1838 that the "SPENCEAN doctrine is not only preached, but details for its practical working are brought prominently to public view."[20]

The O'Brienites were uncompromising to the point of intransigence. Once an idea became part of their canon, it was difficult to dislodge. Therefore, even after Smith died in 1870 and company president Charles Murray had a personal look at the colony, nothing changed. The directors continued to insist that rents paid on individual ten-acre allotments would support the entire enterprise. The operation hobbled forward because the directors refused to admit that they could not prove O'Brien's ideas in a model community. However, with no plan for employment on the cooperative other than what the workers themselves could create on their leased acreage, it became impossible to maintain a stable population of indoctrinated settlers. Colonists forced off the cooperative in search of employment often did not return and, while new shareholders arrived as replacements, the colony population remained transient. Radford chastised departing workers for placing individual money concerns over collective affairs, but without a steady and reliable superintendent to keep settlers focused on the cooperative goal, there was little anyone could do. Regrettably, their grand utopian village was never built.

Radford's appointment as colony superintendent in 1874 represented an instance of putting the right man in charge at the wrong time. Radford maintained an unswerving devotion to O'Brien and

O'Brien's agrarian philosophy, but by the time he arrived the colony was already in its final death throes. Frederick Wilson's infusion of cash during the previous year had kept the colony from collapsing, but he had done nothing to make life on the plains tolerable for the colonists. The experiment could not be revived, and Wilson oversaw the final sale of the former Workingmen's Cooperative Colony in Kansas.

The O'Brienites who settled on the colony in Kansas and those who remained behind in London went their separate ways after Wilson disposed of the colony lands. The London O'Brienites represented an older generation of reformers. Many had been working together since 1848 and remained united following the dissolution of the NRL. After 1874, once the NRL ceased operations, William Morgan led the O'Brienites in forming the Manhood Suffrage League (MSL). It was O'Brien's disciples who kept the socialist ideal alive during the 1870s and, as Bevir writes, many young reformers in London "learnt their radicalism from the O'Brienites before going on to join the Marxist groups of the 1880s." The British anarchist Frank Kitz, who had served as secretary of the MSL, in later years remarked that it was members of the MSL who "were the chief actors in bringing about the revival of socialism." Once the MSL joined with Hyndman in forming the SDF in 1881, Hyndman boasted that "Charles Murray and all the old '48 men are heartily with us."[21] The O'Brienites consistently maintained their belief that social revolution could happen peacefully through equal political representation and land nationalization. The same belief that led to their communal experiment in Kansas caused them to resist Marxist calls for collective ownership of the means of production. It was O'Brienite backing of Hyndman that guided the SDF to demand reforms that, they believed, would create a truly democratic state and end middle-class exploitation.

The O'Brienites who relocated to the United States represented a younger generation of reformers. Without the active network of socialist clubs that existed in metropolitan London, and without the common bond of the 1848 uprising holding them together, they drifted apart after the colony disbanded. Some moved away, but a surprising number of them remained near the old colony and settled in the small towns of Corning, Goff, Sabetha, Seneca, and Wetmore. Most of the former colonists had been ordinary laborers in London and had joined the company primarily for the opportunity for some land in the American West. Since they had not been reform leaders in England, they remained common workers in Kansas. However, when the Populist Party became active after 1890, the names of those still in the area invariably appeared as local members. They may not have been firebrands like "the old '48 men," but they were not about to support middle-class capitalist ideals either. A few, however, did rise to make the O'Brienite voice heard: John Days, who advised Henry George in the writing of *Progress and Poverty*; John Stowell, who challenged Jay Gould's railroad policies; and John Radford, who became a regional Populist leader. Even John Fuller, who gave an annual lecture to local high school students on the topic "Wealth Is Not Worth," became a Populist Party organizer within the town of Seneca.

Of all the O'Brienites in Kansas, it was Radford who remained the most devoted to O'Brien's principles. Had he never left London, Radford undoubtedly would have joined his colleagues and been a leader within the ranks of the SDF. In 1880s Kansas, however, his radical beliefs made him an eccentric and, ultimately, an outcast in his adopted home of Wetmore. It was not until after Gould broke the Great Southwest Strike and the Knights of Labor in 1886 that Radford relocated to neighboring Brown County, Kansas, to start anew. Radford joined the Knights and became an itinerant stump speaker for the Union Labor Party. His renewed activism led him to become a recognized countywide political organizer when the Populist Party formed. Like his old colleagues in the SDF, Radford believed that social revolution in America could happen peacefully through equal political representation and land nationalization. He readily joined the Populists in the hope that once elected, Populist officials would step forward and do more than simply "enunciate historic truths" by vigorously enacting new legislation that would restructure society and abolish wage slavery. Radford wrote that these laws "if defended by eternal vigilance and an enlightened public conscience would be a blazing light to show the pathway to a new and better time, when want shall not stretch its withered hand for charity, but when justice, liberty and equality shall prevail."[22]

Like his mentor O'Brien, Radford understood that political equality represented only the first step toward their shared vision of a new and better world. Despite his early optimism, Radford's Populist moment in Kansas was brief. After the legislative war of 1893 confirmed Republican Party control of the state House of Representatives, any hope for vigorous reform legislation was stalled. The Populist Lorenzo Lewelling, a one-term governor, pursued fusion with the Democratic Party and never recognized Radford with a political appointment. Radford subsequently returned to his old profession of engraving. He died in 1906, leaving no students to carry on the O'Brienite tradition.

What can be said of the O'Brienite legacy? The influence of the group in British politics is undeniable. William Morris, author of the utopian novel *News from Nowhere*, joined the SDF in 1883 but distrusted Hyndman's dictatorial leadership. Despite his autocratic style, Hyndman had the support of the O'Brienites because, like them, he was a supporter of state socialism and believed in working through the parliamentary system to attain nationalization. Unlike the O'Brienites, however, Hyndman was not a champion of internationalism, and this is where the conflict with Morris and other intellectuals emerged. Unable to dislodge Hyndman from his post, in late 1885 Morris, along with Eleanor Marx and others, separated from the SDF to form the Socialist League. Rather than work through the parliamentary system, which was designed to compromise and postpone radical change, Morris and his followers subscribed to a more orthodox version of Marxism. They wanted to educate workers and prepare them for the popular revolution that would spring up from the grass roots. Unfortunately for Morris, most of the anarchists within the SDF followed him into the Socialist League, and in 1890 their activities led to another schism that crippled the organization. Many of the orthodox Marxists, including Morris, reconciled and rejoined the SDF.[23]

In 1893, in West Yorkshire, a branch of what had been the Socialist League formed a new Independent Labour Party. Although the SDF under Hyndman remained aloof, the new party benefited from Fabian Society influence and considerable support from the trade unions. By 1900 this regional organization coalesced into what is recognized today as Britain's modern Labour Party.[24] Most of the old O'Brienites were dead by this point. Charles Murray had died in 1889, and his younger brother James followed him to the grave a few years later. While it is important not to overstate the O'Brienite case because those who had followed O'Brien were no longer around to impact events, it is nonetheless true that their diligent work at keeping the socialist ideal alive and educating workers during the many decades since 1848 helped lay the foundation for the SDF and other parties that followed in its wake.

In Kansas and the West, the O'Brienite legacy is more intangible. Although the O'Brienites in Kansas never gained individual influence beyond the regional level, O'Brien's *The Rise, Progress, and Phases of Human Slavery* was cited in the 1891 *Farmers' Alliance History and Agricultural Digest* and perhaps served as a reference for a few Populist Party proposals.[25] The famed Omaha Platform, for example, advocated an end to the gold standard while simultaneously calling for implementation of the subtreasury plan. While the Populist demand to eliminate the gold standard was linked to the free silver issue, the subtreasury plan was a variation on the older concept of labor exchanges. Like O'Brien's proposals, the subtreasury plan sought, as Lawrence Goodwyn writes, "to mobilize the monetary authority of the nation and put it to work in behalf of a sector of its poorest citizens through the creation of a currency designed to benefit everyone in the 'producing classes,' including urban workers."[26] Charles Macune, author of the subtreasury plan, envisioned government-run warehouses, or "subtreasuries," where a farmer could deposit his crops and receive symbolic notes, or subtreasury certificates. These certificates would be legal tender, government-issued greenbacks that were deemed acceptable for all public and private debts. The subtreasury warehouses minimized overhead costs involved with handling, storage, and insurance while eliminating the middlemen who profited at the expense of the farmer.

O'Brien would have approved of Macune's subtreasury plan because it addressed a specific critique that O'Brien had leveled against the United States. Regarding money, O'Brien believed that the United States was worse than either France or England. "We allude to her preference of metallic money to symbolic money; which is the result of the fraudulent paper-systems she has so often smarted under. There is no subject upon which the American working-classes are so lamentably at fault as the subject of money. They fancy that an honest paper system is impossible, because they have so often been cheated by the worthless rags of fraudulent usurers; and in this suicidal delusion the bullionists and usurers take good care to confirm them." He considered credit to be "the most potent of all levelers of modern production."[27] Therefore, Macune's proposed government credit for farm produce to sustain small landholders paralleled many of O'Brien's own thoughts on the subject. For O'Brien, agriculture was the most profitable occupation and the basis of all other professions. "Agricultural prosperity can alone yield the means of re-production and prosperity to all the rest." He continued that "the surplus of agricultural product is the *real capital* which sets the artisans and handcraftsmen to work."[28] With agricultural produce serving as real capital, O'Brien argued, "all commerce must be gradually reduced to equitable exchange on the principle of equal values for equal values, measured by a labour or corn standard."[29]

Unlike Marx, O'Brien did not advocate for collective ownership of industry and agriculture. He believed in nationalizing the land, but, as he said in 1837, it was the responsibility of the state to oversee the national domain and lease parcels of land to individual citizens. A person leasing the soil could do as he or she wanted with the acreage taken, but should a lessee make improvements or discover mineral wealth, then the rent paid to the state would increase accordingly. As O'Brien wrote: "If a new mine be discovered, or a town built, why should not the public reap the advantage of the high rental accruing in consequence, instead of leaving it to a few rapacious individuals, who are thereby enabled to make slaves of all around them?"[30]

Following O'Brien's theory, every citizen of the nation would become a part proprietor of the soil, or owners of the means of agricultural production. He differed from Marx in this aspect because Marx excluded small landholders from the working class and believed that collectivization of agriculture was the only solution to the economic problems created in a capitalist system of farming. O'Brien, who had developed his agrarian views through studies of Spence, Cobbett, and Henry Hunt, did not tie agriculture directly to the bourgeois middle class. In fact, O'Brien's thoughts on land tenure were more congruent with the ideas of later American socialists than were Marx's. In Oklahoma, for example, socialists included in their program the "demand that land be redistributed into the hands of working farmers." The party platform also argued "that members of the rural working class own the means of agricultural production."[31] The parallels between the Socialist Party of Oklahoma's platform and O'Brien's thoughts on land redistribution were striking. When elaborating on the plan to allow farmers to rent land from the state, the party added a plank calling for a "constant enlargement of the public domain." Furthermore, in the party's "Renters and Farmers Program," Oklahoma socialists openly refuted orthodox Marxism and declared that the Socialist Party's principal mission was "to facilitate the passing of the land from the possession of the landlords into the hands of the actual tillers of the soil."[32]

For O'Brien and his followers, the questions of land nationalization and agriculture were essential to his theory of social reform. They argued that it was the responsibility of the state to gradually resume "its ancient, undoubted, inalienable dominion and sole proprietorship over the lands, mines, turbaries, fisheries, &c." The state would hold all land and natural resources "as trustee in perpetuity for the entire people, and rented out to them in such quantities as the law and local circumstances may determine." This was a necessary reform because "the monopoly of the land in private hands is a palpable invasion of the rights of the excluded parties, rendering them, more or less, the slaves of landlords and capitalists, and tending to circumscribe or annul their other rights and liberties."[33] Like O'Brien, early twentieth-century socialists in Oklahoma believed that "the concentration of land into the hands of a few large landowners — was in actuality the *cause* of rural poverty."[34]

Beyond O'Brien's philosophy, a handful of his followers, like Days, Radford, and Stowell, had a small impact on local and state politics. However, the true significance of the O'Brienites remains the Workingmen's Cooperative Colony. Founded in 1869, the colony was the only explicitly O'Brienite utopian colony ever attempted in the United States. Furthermore, it was among the earliest political pragmatic colonies established after the Civil War. Unlike earlier Owenite, Fourierist, and Icarian cooperative colonies, and unlike the perfectionist religious colonies, political pragmatic communities sought, in the words of Robert Fogarty, "an arena to test and publicize their principles in action." Owenism was a recognized antecedent to the O'Brienite colony. Its founders certainly embraced the cooperative ideal and assumed collective financial responsibility for their community. However, cooperation for its own sake was not their primary objective. Cooperation was a tool to demonstrate that there was a peaceful alternative to the Marxist ideal of violent class warfare. Fogarty writes: "They wanted to show the world and their fellow radicals that socialism could work and that there was a method by which practical socialism could be put to use in direct fashion."[35]

Later political pragmatic colonies, places such as California's Kaweah Cooperative Commonwealth (established in 1885), the Colorado Cooperative Company (established in 1894), Washington's Glennis Cooperative Industrial Company (established in 1894), and the Freedom Colony of Kansas (established in 1897) attempted to prove the practicality of ideas found, respectively, in Laurence Gronlund's

Cooperative Commonwealth, Henry George's *Progress and Poverty*, Edward Bellamy's *Looking Backward*, and G. B. de Bernardi's *Trials and Triumphs of Labor*. None were any more successful than the Workingmen's Cooperative Colony, yet all, and others that were no larger and had a similar life span, are well known. Llano del Rio in California, for example, was founded in 1915. Rather than concentrate solely on agriculture, Llano del Rio attempted to build industry but, like the Workingmen's Cooperative Colony, it remained unprofitable. Workers were forced to seek off-colony employment as day laborers, and environmental problems were a major concern. Disagreements arose between resident colonists and absentee directors, and by 1917 the colony ceased operations. The most significant difference was that many colonists left Llano del Rio in 1917 to try again at New Llano in Louisiana, whereas the O'Brienites returned to their activist roots and reentered the political arena. Nevertheless, the original settlement remains a curiously analogous story, yet Llano del Rio is celebrated among communal historians while the Workingmen's Cooperative Colony has been marginalized.

There are several possible explanations. First, Bronterre O'Brien never wrote a romanticized utopian novel like *Looking Backward*, nor did he put down his philosophy in a straightforward format such as *Progress and Poverty*. O'Brien was a journalist whose writings were confined largely to newspapers. There were his polemical, partially completed biography of Robespierre and a collection of articles posthumously published as *The Rise, Progress, and Phases of Human Slavery*, but there was nothing easily accessible to the average reader. O'Brien was a political agitator who, during his lifetime, railed against cooperative schemes. No one associated his name with utopian colonies. Second, the O'Brienites did not advertise their colony particularly well. Like their mentor, the O'Brienites were recognized as political activists. They did put out a promotional newspaper, the *New World*, in 1870; however, it was a small penny periodical with a circulation confined largely to subscribing members of the company. They also had a regular column in Charles Bradlaugh's *National Reformer* but used the space to report on political activities as much as on colony affairs. Third, once the colony was established, they made no effort to disseminate O'Brien's ideas or recruit new members from the local population in Kansas. The O'Brienites were focused on providing relief for fellow workers in the United Kingdom and assumed that Kansans would follow their example once it became obvious that the grand experiment could provide full employment and at the same time make the Great Plains blossom. As individuals, Radford, Days, and a few others certainly promoted O'Brien's philosophy in the United States, but not within the context of the colony.

No one living in the vicinity of the colony ever heard of Bronterre O'Brien or knew anything of the philosophy that the colony members were trying to put into action. Knowing nothing of who the colonists were or what they believed in, local residents like John T. Bristow, who in 1931 wrote down his childhood recollections of the colony, simply let imaginations run wild. In Bristow's mind's eye, what had been a noble socialist experiment on the Great Plains turned into a fool's errand, the colonists became "rascals" and "misfits," and the wood-frame communal dormitory became a castle — Llewellyn Castle. The Workingmen's Cooperative Colony disappeared from history, replaced by local folklore.

Appendix

Partial list of shareholders and family members of the Mutual Land, Emigration, and Cooperative Colonization Company who emigrated from England

Name	Occupation
John Ambrose	Common Laborer
Mary Ambrose	Wife of John
Thomas Ashton	Agriculturalist
William	
Horace	
William Beeby	Painter/Agriculturalist
Betsy Beeby	Wife of William
Benjamin	
George	
Henry Belshaw	Laborer/Agriculturalist
Elisabeth Belshaw	Wife of Henry
Robert Bielby	Laborer/Agriculturalist
Jane Bielby	Wife of Robert
Elizabeth	
Louisa Ellen	
+ Mary Anne	
Edward Booker	Carpenter
William Byford	Railway Porter

Robert Clark	Architect
John Coney	Carpenter
George Cox	Carpenter
Jane Cox	Wife of George
George P.	
William	
Harriet	
Henry	
Frederick	
Susan	
Sophia Days	Unknown
William Delbridge	Stone Mason
George Dutch	Carman
Mary A. Dutch	Wife of George
Charles	
William Dutch	Horse Keeper
Walter Edgington	Joiner/Agriculturalist
Rebecca Edgington	Wife of Walter
William Edwards	Joiner/Agriculturalist
× John Fuller	Coppersmith
Ann Fuller	Wife of John
Henry	
John Jr.	
William	
Walter	
Martha	
Helena	
+ Herbert	
Joseph Harrison	Farm Laborer
A. D. G. Hazel	Engine Fitter
George Hearn	Undertaker
Robert Hill	Carpenter/Joiner
Sophia	
William Jenkins	Painter/Paper Hanger
× Charles McCarthy	Laborer

Mary McCarthy	Wife of Charles
Charles Jr.	
Thomas	
Eugene	
Justin	
Felix McCarthy	Lithographic Printer
Isaac May	Laborer
John R. Molineux	Painter
Charlotte Molineux	Wife of John
Florence	
Isabel	
+ Alfred	
Josiah Morley	Bricklayer
Sophia Morley	Wife of Josiah
Walter	
John Mourdant	Wood Turner
*× Charles Murray	Boot Closer
Thomas Neil	Engineer
Sarah Plowman	Dealer
× John Radford	Engraver/Metal Worker
Maria Radford	Wife of John
Elizabeth	
Jane	
Mary	
William	
John Maximilian	
James	
Rebecca	
Robert Rogers	Lawyer
Edward (George) Rooney	Warehouseman/Agriculturalist
*= Charles Sargood	Carpenter
*= James Sargood	Carpenter
Thomas Savings	Printer/Agriculturalist
Mary Savings	Wife of Thomas
Alice	

= John Shallis	Tanner
× Edward G. Smith	Carpenter
Elizabeth Smith	Wife of Edward
John Stowell	Warehouseman
John Trent	Plasterer/Agriculturalist
George Walker	Lawyer
Ann Walker	Wife of George
George	
William	
Elizabeth	
Mrs. W. Walker	Unknown
George Weston	Carpenter/Agriculturalist
William Wessell	Agriculturalist/Collector
Martha Wessell	Wife of William
Herbert	

[key]
* Returned to England
= Never settled on the colony
+ Born on the colony
× Served as colony superintendent

After the colony collapsed, three shareholders in the Mutual Land, Emigration, and Cooperative Colonization Company immigrated to Kansas to join family or to purchase former colony lands.

Name
William Fish
James Slark
William Worcester

John T. Bristow mentioned a small number of families who he claimed came to Nemaha County, Kansas, from England as part of the colony. These are unconfirmed by any other source, although a few of the family names do have corresponding listings as shareholders in company records. Several definitely had no connection to the colony.

Name	Remarks
William Conover	From Canada
Gates family	From New York
Helsby family	Unknown
McConwell family	Unknown
Morden family	Possibly John Mourdant
Perry family	Possibly Alfred Perry or William Parry
Mrs. Terbit	Margaret Turbit from Indiana
Weeks family	From Ohio
Minnerva	Possibly Minnie Rogers

Notes

Introduction

1. John T. Bristow, *Memory's Storehouse Unlocked: Pioneer Days in Wetmore and Northeast Kansas* (Wetmore KS: John T. Bristow, 1948), 199.

2. Mark Twain, *Roughing It* (New York: Harper & Brothers, 1913), 1:6–13.

3. Bristow, *Memory's Storehouse Unlocked*, 199–200.

4. George C. Adriance, Seneca, to John T. Bristow, Wetmore, October 20, 1931, quotation in Bristow, *Memory's Storehouse Unlocked*, 193.

5. William G. Cutler, *History of the State of Kansas* (Chicago: A. T. Andreas, 1883), 2:958.

6. Ralph Tennal, *History of Nemaha County, Kansas* (Lawrence: Standard, 1916), 340–41.

7. Tennal, *Nemaha County*, 85, 125, 341.

8. Tennal, *Nemaha County*, 86, 340–41; John Fuller, *Art of Coppersmithing: A Practical Treatise on Working Sheet Copper into All Forms* (Mendham NJ: Astragal Press, 1993), 7.

9. John T. Bristow, "Two Residents of Llewellyn Castle Remain to Tell of English Colony at Wetmore," *Topeka Daily Capital*, November 15, 1931.

10. Bristow, *Memory's Storehouse Unlocked*, 198.

11. Bristow, *Memory's Storehouse Unlocked*, 198.

12. Bristow, *Memory's Storehouse Unlocked*, 198.

13. Bristow, *Memory's Storehouse Unlocked*, 358.

14. Bristow, *Memory's Storehouse Unlocked*, 199.

15. Bristow, *Memory's Storehouse Unlocked*, 192.

16. Bristow, *Memory's Storehouse Unlocked*, 194–95.

17. Bristow, *Memory's Storehouse Unlocked*, 200–201.

18. C. Rex Molineux, "The English Colony at Llewellyn Castle & the Molineux's," Seneca KS, September 18, 1989; C. Rex Molineux, Sabetha, Kansas, to Gary R. Entz, Salt Lake City, April 12, 1997.

19. Andrew Whitehead, "The English Colony at Llewellyn Castle," *Kanhistique* 13 (October 1987): 14.

20. Robert S. Fogarty, "American Communes, 1865–1914," *Journal of American Studies* 9 (August 1975): 152–53.

21. Paul S. Boyer, foreword to *America's Communal Utopias*, ed. Donald E. Pitzer (Chapel Hill: University of North Carolina Press, 1997), ix.

22. Robert S. Fogarty, *All Things New: American Communes and Utopian Movements, 1860–1914* (Chicago: University of Chicago Press, 1990), 18.

23. Fogarty, *All Things New*, 32, 60.

24. Norman Saul, "Cedarvale Communist Community," in *Encyclopedia of the Great Plains*, ed. David J. Wishart (Lincoln: University of Nebraska Press, 2004), 227.

25. Kenneth E. Miller, "Danish Socialism and the Kansas Prairie," *Kansas Historical Quarterly* 38 (Summer 1972): 163.

26. Fogarty, *All Things New*, 104–105.

27. Fogarty, *All Things New*, 102–103.

28. H. Roger Grant, "Portrait of a Workers' Utopia: The Labor Exchange and the Freedom, Kan., Colony," *Kansas Historical Quarterly* 43 (Spring 1977): 62.

29. Blanche M. Taylor, "The English Colonies in Kansas, 1870–1895," *Historical Magazine of the Protestant Episcopal Church* 41 (March 1972): 18; Robert W. Richmond, *Kansas: A Land of Contrasts*, 4th ed. (Wheeling IL: Harlan Davidson, 1999), 168.

30. Daniel C. Fitzgerald, *Faded Dreams: More Ghost Towns of Kansas* (Lawrence: University Press of Kansas, 1994), 40.

31. Taylor, "The English Colonies in Kansas," 24, 31–34; Richmond, *Kansas*, 167–68.

32. William McCord has used the span of forty years as a criterion for utopian success. However, Rosabeth Moss Kanter defined the longevity standard for success-failure theorists when she concluded that a sociological generation of twenty-five years was necessary before certifying a communal society as successful. William McCord, "Building Utopias: Successes and Failures," *International Journal of Comparative Sociology* 33 (September 1992): 152; Rosabeth Moss Kanter, *Commitment and Community: Communes and Utopias in Sociological Perspective* (Cambridge: Harvard University Press, 1972), 244–46; Donald E. Pitzer, "Developmental Communalism: An Alternative Approach to Communal Studies," in *Utopian Thought and Communal Experience*, ed. Dennis Hardy and Lorna Davidson (Enfield: Middlesex Polytechnic, 1989), 69.

33. Kanter, *Commitment and Community*, 243; Doug McAdam, *Political Process and the Development of Black Insurgency, 1930–1970* (Chicago: University of Chicago Press, 1982), 36.

34. William L. Niemi and David J. Plante, "Democratic Movements, Self-Education, and Economic Democracy: Chartists, Populists, and Wobblies," *Radical History Review*, no. 102 (Fall 2008): 186.

35. Ben Maw, "Bronterre O'Brien's Class Analysis: The Formative Phase, 1832–1836," *History of Political Thought* 28 (Summer 2007): 253.

1. The Sorrow of the Land

1. Robert G. Gammage, *History of the Chartist Movement, 1837–1854* (1894; reprint, London: Merlin Press, 1976), 71.

2. David Goodway, *London Chartism, 1838–1848* (Cambridge: Cambridge University Press, 1982), 18.

3. James Bronterre O'Brien, "To the Radical and Social Reformers of Great Britain & Ireland," *Bronterre's National Reformer in Government, Law, Property, Religion, and Mor-*

als, February 4, 1837, 33; *Small Chartist Periodicals* (facsimile ed.), ed. Dorothy Thompson (New York: Garland, 1986).

4. J. F. C. Harrison, *Quest for a New Moral Order: Robert Owen and the Owenites in Britain and America* (New York: Charles Scribner's Sons, 1969), 248.

5. James Bronterre O'Brien, "Breaking Up of the Leeds Trades' Union," *Poor Man's Guardian*, June 21, 1834; Alfred Plummer, *Bronterre: A Political Biography of Bronterre O'Brien, 1804–1864* (Toronto: University of Toronto Press, 1971), 41–42.

6. George D. H. Cole, *The Life of Robert Owen* (Hamden CT: Archon Books, 1966), 234.

7. William Lovett, *Life and Struggles of William Lovett: In his Pursuit of Bread, Knowledge & Freedom, with some short Account of the different Associations he belonged to & of the Opinions he entertained* (London: MacGibbon & Kee, 1967), 37.

8. George Spater, *William Cobbett: The Poor Man's Friend* (Cambridge: Cambridge University Press, 1982), 2:488–89.

9. Cobbett to Hunt, June 15, 1829, in John Belchem, *"Orator" Hunt: Henry Hunt and English Working-Class Radicalism* (Oxford: Clarendon Press, 1985), 195.

10. William Cobbett, *Rural Rides* (London: Penguin, 2001), 382.

11. Belchem, *"Orator" Hunt*, 199–200.

12. Plummer, *Bronterre*, 27.

13. James Bronterre O'Brien, *Bronterre's National Reformer*, January 7, 1837.

14. G. D. H. Cole, *Chartist Portraits* (London: Cassell, 1989), 242.

15. T. M. Parssinen, "Thomas Spence and the Origins of English Land Nationalization," *Journal of the History of Ideas* 34 (January–March 1973): 138.

16. G. I. Gallop, "Introductory Essay: Thomas Spence and the Real Rights of Man," in *Pigs' Meat: Selected Writings of Thomas Spence, Radical and Pioneer Reformer* (Nottingham: Spokesman), 17.

17. Parssinen, "Thomas Spence," 141.

18. Iorwerth Prothero, *Radical Artisans in England and France, 1830–1870* (Cambridge: Cambridge University Press, 1997), 269.

19. E. P. Thompson, *The Making of the English Working Class* (New York: Vintage Books, 1966), 812.

20. David Stack, ed., *Bronterre O'Brien*, vol. 4 of *Lives of Victorian Political Leaders II* (London: Pickering & Chatto, 2007), xii.

21. Plummer, *Bronterre*, 33–35; "Bronterre's Second Letter to the People of England," quoted in Plummer, *Bronterre*, 35–36.

22. Thomas Spence, "A Further Account of Spensonia (1794)," in *Pigs' Meat*, 88.

23. Bronterre O'Brien, "Social Occupations," *Bronterre's National Reformer*, January 7, 1837.

24. Bronterre O'Brien, "Mr. O'Connell and the Lambeth Radical Association," *Bronterre's National Reformer*, February 25, 1837.

25. Quoted in Plummer, *Bronterre*, 177.

26. Spence, "The End of Oppression (1795)," in *Pigs' Meat*, 93.

27. Lovett, *Life and Struggles*, 84; *Bronterre's National Reformer*, February 11, 1837; *London Mercury*, March 5, 1837; Plummer, *Bronterre*, 79.

28. James Bronterre O'Brien, *Bronterre's Life and Character of Maximilian Robespierre* (London: J. Watson, 1838), 470.

29. *London Mercury*, June 8, 1837.

30. Henry Jephson, *The Platform: Its Rise and Progress*, 2 vols. (London: Macmillan, 1892), 211.

31. Plummer, *Bronterre*, 87.

32. Flora Tristan, *Flora Tristan's London Journal, 1840*, translated by Dennis Palmer and Giselle Pincetl (Charleston MA: Charles Rivers Books, 1980), 49.

33. Frank Peel, *The Rising of the Luddites, Chartists, and Plugdrawers*, 2nd ed. (Heckmondwike: Senior and Co., Printers, 1888), 325.

34. Quoted in Plummer, *Bronterre*, 117.

35. James Bronterre O'Brien, *A Dissertation and Elegy on the Life and Death of the Immortal Maximilian Robespierre* (London: G. Holyoake & Co. and E. Truelove, 1859), 5.

36. Gammage, *History of the Chartist Movement*, 198.

37. Donald Read, *Cobden and Bright: A Victorian Political Partnership* (London: Edward Arnold, 1967), 29–30.

38. "The Last of the 'Starved Viper,'" *Northern Star and Leeds General Advertiser*, September 17, 1842, in *Bronterre O'Brien*, ed. Stack, 77.

39. Stack, "Complete Suffrage," in *Bronterre O'Brien*, 131.

40. Iowerth Prothero, "Chartism in London," *Past and Present* 44 (August 1969): 96.

41. *National Reformer and Manx Weekly Review*, January 30, 1847, in *Bronterre O'Brien*, ed. Stack, 131.

42. Quoted in Jamie L. Bronstein, *Land Reform and Working-Class Experience in Britain and the United States, 1800–1862* (Stanford: Stanford University Press, 1999), 107–108.

43. P. M. Ashraf, *The Life and Times of Thomas Spence* (Newcastle upon Tyne: Frank Graham, 1983), 124.

44. *National Reformer and Manx Weekly Review*, January 30, 1847, in *Bronterre O'Brien*, ed. Stack, 176.

45. Stack, introduction to *Bronterre O'Brien*, xix.

46. Stack, introduction to *Bronterre O'Brien*, xix.

47. Bronstein, *Land Reform and Working-Class Experience*, 107.

48. Stan Shipley, *Club Life and Socialism in Mid-Victorian London* (London: Journeyman Press, and the London History Workshop Centre, 1983), 10.

49. "The British Section of Icarian Communists," *Bulletin of the International Institute of Social History* 1 (August 1937): 84–88.

50. Wilbur S. Shepperson, *Emigration and Disenchantment: Portraits of Englishmen Repatriated from the United States* (Norman: University of Oklahoma Press, 1965), 74–75; Ray Boston, *British Chartists in America, 1839–1900* (Manchester: Manchester University Press, 1971), 18.

51. *Reformer*, May 26, 1849, quoted in Wilber S. Shepperson, *Six Who Returned: America Viewed by British Repatriates* (Reno: University of Nevada Press, 1961), 75–76.

52. Robert P. Sutton, *Communal Utopias and the American Experience: Secular Communities, 1824–2000* (Westport CT: Praeger, 2004), 56–57.

53. Madeleine B. Stern, *The Pantarch: A Biography of Stephen Pearl Andrews* (Austin: University of Texas Press, 1968), 34–36.

54. *Reformer*, May 26, 1849, quoted in Shepperson, *Emigration and Disenchantment*, 76.

55. Shepperson, *Six Who Returned*, 76.

56. Malcolm Chase, *Chartism: A New History* (Manchester: Manchester University Press, 2007), 335.

57. Stack, introduction to *Bronterre O'Brien*, xx.

58. Plummer, *Bronterre*, 198.

59. James Bronterre O'Brien, *The Rise, Progress, and Phases of Human Slavery: How It Came into the World, and How It Shall Be Made to Go Out* (London: William Reeves, 1885), 109.

60. O'Brien, *Human Slavery*, 100.

61. J. Bronterre O'Brien, *Propositions of the National Reform League for the Peaceful Regeneration of Society* (London: Working Printers' Co-operative Association, 1850), 1–4, British Library; *Reynolds's Political Instructor*, January 5, 1850; Plummer, *Bronterre*, 199–200; Gammage, *History of the Chartist Movement*, 351.

62. Plummer, *Bronterre*, 204–205.

63. Prothero, *Radical Artisans in England and France*, 122.

64. Plummer, *Bronterre*, 205–206.

65. Jonathan Rose, *The Intellectual Life of the British Working Classes* (New Haven: Yale University Press, 2001), 36–37.

66. Plummer, *Bronterre*, 222.

67. "What Are We Fighting For?" *Reynolds's Newspaper*, August 5, 1855.

68. *Reynolds's Newspaper*, July 22, 1855, quoted in Plummer, *Bronterre*, 230.

69. John Radford, "The Progress of Our Company," *New World* (London), November 1870, FWA Case A g 18, Family Welfare Association Library, Senate House Library, University of London.

70. Radford, "Progress."

71. Karl Marx, "Inaugural Address of the International Working Men's Association," in *The First International and After*, vol. 3, *Karl Marx: Political Writings*, ed. David Fernbach (New York: Vintage Books, 1974), 78.

72. Roger Wunderlich, *Low Living and High Thinking at Modern Times, New York* (Syracuse NY: Syracuse University Press, 1992), 142–43.

73. Wunderlich, *Low Living*, 2–3.

74. Josiah Warren, Thompson's Station, New York, to A. C. Cuddon, London, March 12, 1853, photocopy, Josiah Warren Papers, Labadie Collection, University of Michigan.

75. William Bailie, *Josiah Warren: The First American Anarchist* (Boston: Small, Maynard, 1906), 66.

76. A. C. Cuddon, London, to Josiah Warren, New York, November 7, 1861, photocopy, Josiah Warren Papers.

77. George Harris, *Working Man*, June 15, 1867.

78. Margot Finn, *After Chartism: Class and Nation in English Radical Politics, 1848–1874* (Cambridge: Cambridge University Press, 1993), 193.

79. Charles Murray, *A Letter to Mr. Jacob Holyoake; Containing a Brief Review of That Gentleman's Conduct and Policy as a Reformer, with Special Reference to His Reply to Mr. Linton, and the "Boston Liberator:" His Criticism upon the Stranger of the "Leader" Newspaper, and Defence of the Cobden Policy; with the Writer's Opinion upon Free-Trade Measures, and on the Position and Interests of the Middle and Working Classes; &c. &c. &c.* (London: Samuel Bovingdon, Sherrard Place, Golden Square, 1854), 9, British Library.

80. Murray, *A Letter*, 7.

81. Murray, *A Letter*, 6–9.

82. Cutler, *History of the State of Kansas*, 2:958.

83. Shipley, *Club Life and Socialism*, 14–16.

84. John Breuilly, Gottfried Niedhart, and Anthony Taylor, eds., *The Era of the Reform League: English Labour and Radical Politics, 1857–1872. Documents Selected by Gustav Mayer* (Mannheim, Germany: Palatium Verlag im J & J. Verlag, 1995), 29.

85. Andrew Whitehead and Gary R. Entz, "Radford, John (c.1834–1906): O'Brienite, Cooperative Colonist, and Kansas Populist," in *Dictionary of Labour Biography*, ed. Keith Gildart and David Howell (New York: Palgrave Macmillan, 2005), 12:234.

86. Plummer, *Bronterre*, 240, 249.

87. Stack, introduction to *Bronterre O'Brien*, xx–xxi.

88. Plummer, *Bronterre*, 243–44; "Letter from Victor Hugo to G. E. Harris (December 30, 1864), Labour History Archive, Manchester," in *Bronterre O'Brien*, ed. Stack, 230.

89. "The Funeral of Mr. James Bronterre O'Brien, B.A.," *National Reformer, Secular Advocate and Freethought Journal*, January 8, 1869; "Funeral of Mr. Bronterre O'Brien," *Reynolds's Newspaper*, January 1, 1865.

90. Institute of Marxism-Leninism of the C.C., C.P.S.U., *Documents of the First International: The General Council of the First International, 1868–1870* (Moscow: Progress; reprint, London: Lawrence & Wishart, 1963), 3:491, 504, 512–13, 514, 523, 524; Henry Collins and Chimen Abramsky, *Karl Marx and the British Labour Movement: Years of the First International* (New York: St. Martin's Press, 1965), 73.

91. *International Herald*, June 1, 1877, quoted in Mark Bevir, "The British Social Democratic Federation, 1880–1885: From O'Brienism to Marxism," *University of California Postprints*, paper 2584 (1992): 8.

92. Karl Marx and Frederick Engels, *Letters to Americans, 1848–1895: A Selection* (New York: International, 1953), 89.

93. Stern, *The Pantarch*, 115.

94. Marx and Engels, *Letters to Americans*, 89.

95. Edward Royle, *Radicals, Secularists, and Republicans: Popular Freethought in Britain, 1866–1915* (Manchester: Manchester University Press, 1980), 194.

96. *Working Man*, May 4, 1867.

97. Max Beer, *Fifty Years of International Socialism* (London: George Allen & Unwin, 1935), 134; Shipley, *Club Life and Socialism*, 2, 66.

98. O'Brien, *A Dissertation and Elegy*, 4; Shipley, *Club Life and Socialism*, 10.

99. Walter L. Arnstein, *Britain Yesterday and Today: 1830 to the Present* (Lexington MA: D. C. Heath, 1976), 110–11.

100. Quoted in Finn, *After Chartism*, 240.

101. D. G. Wright, *Popular Radicalism: The Working-Class Experience, 1780–1880* (London: Longman Group, 1988), 176–79.

102. *Working Man*, May 4, August 3, 1867.

2. High Moral Chivalry

1. Genevieve Troka, California State Archives, Sacramento, to Gary R. Entz, McPherson, Kansas, August 21, 2000.

2. Charles Murray, "A Political Reunion," *National Reformer* (London), June 28, 1868.

3. John Radford, "The Progress of Our Company," *New World*, November 1870; Murray, "A Political Reunion."

4. John Radford, "The Progress of Our Company."

5. Oscar O. Winther, "The English in Nebraska, 1857–1880," *Nebraska History* 48 (Autumn 1967): 209–33; Oscar O. Winther, "The English and Kansas, 1865–1890," in *The Frontier Challenge: Responses to the Trans-Mississippi West*, ed. John G. Clark (Lawrence: University Press of Kansas, 1971), 235–42; Brian P. Birch, "Popularizing the Plains: News of Kansas in England, 1860–1880," *Kansas History* 10 (Winter 1987): 262–74.

6. *Reynolds's Newspaper*, December 12, 1869.

7. *Address by the Promoters of the Mutual Land, Emigration, and Colonization Company, to the Working Classes of Great Britain, and to the Parties about to Emigrate* (London: Published at the Offices of the Company, 1868), 12–14, British Library; R. Wake, *The United States as a Field for Emigration: With a Description of Nebraska: Hints to Emigrants & c.* (London: J. Clarke, 1867); Bayard Taylor, *Colorado: A Summer Trip* (New York: G. P. Putnam, 1867), 182.

8. *Address by the Promoters of the Mutual Land, Emigration, and Colonization Company*, 2.

9. *Address by the Promoters of the Mutual Land, Emigration, and Colonization Company*, 3–9.

10. Edward Grainger Smith, London, to David C. Butler, Omaha, October 19, 1868, Governor David C. Butler Papers, Series 1, General Correspondence, Nebraska State Historical Society.

11. James C. Olson and Ronald C. Naugle, *History of Nebraska*, 3rd ed. (Lincoln: University of Nebraska Press, 1997), 147–55.

12. Smith to Butler, December 28, 1868, Butler Papers.

13. In addition to Smith, the members of the executive committee were John Rogers, James Murray, Charles Murray, John Radford, Alfred Fuzzen, James Culley, W. McHeath, Frederick Wade, and James Balls.

14. Bernard C. Steiner, *Life of Reverdy Johnson* (Baltimore: Norman, Remington, 1914), iii–iv, 37, 198.

15. "Proposed Emigration of London Artisans to the United States," *Bee-Hive* (London), January 2, 1869.

16. "The Novel Emigration Scheme to Nebraska," *Bee-Hive*, February 13, 1869.

17. Edward Grainger Smith, "Novel Emigration Scheme to Nebraska," *Bee-Hive*, February 20, 1869.

18. Smith, "Novel Emigration Scheme to Nebraska,"

19. *Bee-Hive*, February 27, 1869.

20. *Bee-Hive*, March 6, 1869.

21. "Cost the Limit of Price," *National Reformer*, March 21, 1869.

22. *National Reformer*, April 11, 1869.

23. *National Reformer*, April 11, 1869.

24. "Memorandum of Association," April 13, 1869, Records of the Mutual Land, Emigration, and Co-operative Colonization Company, Ltd., BT 31/1457/4367, National Archives, Kew, London.

25. *National Reformer*, April 25, 1869.

26. Ion Perdicaris's further engagements got the United States involved in a serious diplomatic incident. See Barbara W. Tuchman, "Perdicaris Alive or Raisuli Dead," *American Heritage* 10 (August 1959): 18–21, 98–101.

27. *National Reformer*, April 25, 1869; *Reynolds's Newspaper*, April 25, 1869; New York Passenger Lists, 1820–1957, May 17, 1869, *Paraguay* [database online]; available from Ancestry.com. Traveling with the band were family members Sophia and Walter Morley; Sophia Hill; and Mary, Charles Jr., Thomas, Eugene, and Justin McCarthy. At just two months of age, Justin was by far the youngest colonist.

28. *Reynolds's Newspaper*, April 25, December 12, 1869.

29. *National Reformer*, May 2, 1869.

30. *National Reformer*, May 9, 1869.

31. *Reynolds's Newspaper*, December 6, 1869. The company directors countered that no one other than the Sargood brothers abandoned the expedition. However, John Coney and William Jenkins never appeared in any record after arriving at Castle Garden. Plus, William Cutler's short biography of John Radford, made from Radford's own statements, indicates that only six of the ten selected shareholders completed the journey. *Reynolds's Newspaper*, December 12, 1869; Cutler, *History of the State of Kansas*, 2:958.

32. *National Reformer*, May 16, 1869.

33. *National Reformer*, May 23, 1869.

34. New York Passenger Lists, 1820–1957, May 17, 1869, *Paraguay* [database online]; available from Ancestry.com.

35. Michael M. Bartels, *Missouri Pacific: River and Prairie Rails: The MoPac in Nebraska* (David City NE: South Platte Press, 1997), 43; Paul Wallace Gates, *Fifty Million Acres: Conflicts over Kansas Land Policy* (Norman: University of Oklahoma Press, 1954), 134–40; George L. Anderson, "Atchison and the Central Branch Country, 1865–1874," *Kansas Historical Quarterly* 28 (Spring 1962): 9–11.

36. *Atchison Daily Champion and Press*, April 7, 1869.

37. Anderson, "Atchison and the Central Branch Country," 11.

38. *Bee-Hive*, July 10, 1869; *National Reformer*, July 11, 1869.

39. *Bee-Hive*, July 10, July 31, 1869.

40. *Bee-Hive*, July 31, 1869.

41. Quoted in Anderson, "Atchison and the Central Branch Country," 11–12.

42. *Bee-Hive*, July 31, 1869; *Daily Atchison Patriot*, June 26, 1869. KHS.

43. *Bee-Hive*, July 31, 1869.

44. *Bee-Hive*, July 31, 1869.

45. In 1869 the colony land was located in Granada Township. In 1870 Granada Township was divided in half, with the western portion—the portion containing the Workingmen's Cooperative Colony—becoming Harrison Township. Cutler, *History of the State of Kansas*, 2:940.

46. Register of Deeds, Nemaha County, Seneca, Kansas, 66538; Book 26, 198, Book 19, 79–80, Nemaha County Courthouse, Seneca.

47. *Bee-Hive*, July 31, 1869.

48. *Bee-Hive*, July 31, 1869.

49. *National Reformer*, July 18, 1869; *Bee-Hive*, July 17, 1869.

50. *National Reformer*, July 18, 1869; *Bee-Hive*, July 17, 1869.

51. John Stowell, "Reminiscences of the English Colony," *Seneca Tribune*, September 3, 1891; *Seneca Weekly Courier*, February 10, 1871, Newspaper Collection, Kansas Historical Society.

52. *Reynolds's Newspaper*, December 6, 1869, February 6, 1870.

53. *Bee-Hive*, July 24, 31, 1869.

54. *Bee-Hive*, July 31, 1869.

55. *Bee-Hive*, August 7, 21, 1869; *National Reformer*, August 22, 1869.

56. *Seneca Tribune*, September 3, 1891.

3. An Honest Social State

1. *National Reformer*, October 17, November 28, 1869.

2. Martin J. Boon, *Home Colonization* (London: Edward Truelove, 1869), 5–6. See also Martin J. Boon, *A Protest against the Present Emigrationists* (London: Land and Labour League, 1869), 1–8, British Library; Shipley, *Club Life and Socialism*, 8; Plummer, *Bronterre*, 267; Collins and Abramsky, *Karl Marx and the British Labour Movement*, 165.

3. *National Reformer*, November 28, 1869; *Seneca Tribune*, September 3, 1891.

4. *Reynolds's Newspaper*, December 12, 1869.

5. *National Reformer*, December 12, 1869.

6. *Reynolds's Newspaper*, December 12, 1869.

7. *Reynolds's Newspaper*, December 19, 1869.

8. *Reynolds's Newspaper*, January 23, 1870.

9. Paul Wallace Gates, *Fifty Million Acres: Conflicts over Kansas Land Policy* (Norman: University of Oklahoma Press, 1954), 171–74.

10. *Reynolds's Newspaper*, January 23, 1870.

11. *Reynolds's Newspaper*, February 6, 1870.

12. *Reynolds's Newspaper*, February 27, June 30, 1870.

13. Bristow, *Memory's Storehouse Unlocked*, 195; Tennal, *Nemaha County*, 124.

14. "Co-operative Emigration to America," *Penny Bee-Hive* (London) February 19, 1870; *National Reformer*, February 13, 20, 1870.

15. *Penny Bee-Hive*, February 19, 1870.

16. *Penny Bee-Hive*, April 23, 1870.

17. Tennal, *Nemaha County*, 85–86; Cutler, *History of the State of Kansas*, 2:948.

18. "Latest News from the Colony," *New World*, November 1870.

19. Henry Clinton, "Associated Homes: An Address to the Shareholders of the Mutual Land, Emigration, and Co-operative Colonisation Society," April 24, 1870, FWA Case A g 18, Family Welfare Association Library, Senate House Library, University of London.

20. Bronterre O'Brien, "note," in *Babeuf's Conspiracy for Equality*, by Philippe Buonarroti, trans. Bronterre O'Brien (London: H. Hetherington, 1836; reprint, New York: Augustus M. Kelley, Bookseller, 1965), 161–163n.

21. Clinton, „Associated Homes."

22. Tennal, *Nemaha County*, 85.

23. "To Correspondents," *New World*, November 1870.

24. *Republican* (London), March 1, 1871; Andrew Whitehead, "The *New World* and the O'Brienite Colony in Kansas," *Bulletin for the Society for the Study of Labour History* 53 (1988): 40–43.

25. "Funeral of the Late Mr. Smith," *New World*, November 1870; Tennal, *Nemaha County*, 85.

26. "Funeral of the Late Mr. Smith."

27. "To Correspondents," *New World*, November 1870.

28. "Arrival of the Chairman in Kansas," *New World*, November 1870; Bristow, *Memory's Storehouse Unlocked*, 196.

29. Bristow, *Memory's Storehouse Unlocked*, 196. Bristow's narrative embellishes the level of colonist reluctance in allowing Murray access to the books.

30. "The Progress of Our Company," *New World*, November 1870.

31. "Prospectus of the Mutual Land, Emigration, and Co-operative Colonisation Company (Limited)," *New World*, November 1870.

32. Finn, *After Chartism*, 273–83.

33. Finn, *After Chartism*, 285–87.

34. Breuilly et al., *Era of the Reform League*, 319; Shipley, *Club Life and Socialism*, 17–18; Royden Harrison, ed., *The English Defence of the Commune (1871)* (London: Merlin Press, 1971), 153.

35. "From Sother," *Seneca Weekly Courier*, March 31, 1871; Tennal, *Nemaha County*, 341.

36. "Sother Correspondence," *Seneca Weekly Courier*, May 19, 1871.

37. "To Correspondents," *New World*, November 1870.

38. *Bee-Hive*, November 11, 1871; *National Reformer*, November 12, 1871.

4. Moral Intoxication

1. Paul D. Travis, "Changing Climate in Kansas: A Late 19th-Century Myth," *Kansas History* 1 (September 1978): 48–58.

2. John H. Tice, *Over the Plains and on the Mountains; or, Kansas and Colorado Agriculturally, Mineralogically, and Aesthetically Described* (St. Louis: Industrial Age Printing Co., 1872), 12–13.

3. *National Reformer*, February 18, 1872.

4. *Bee-Hive*, January 27, February 17, 1872.

5. *National Reformer*, February 25, 1872.

6. *Bee-Hive*, February 24, 1872; *National Reformer*, March 3, 1872; *Seneca Weekly Courier*, April 19, 1872.

7. *National Reformer*, March 10, 1872; *Bee-Hive*, March 16, 1872.

8. *National Reformer*, April 14, 1872.

9. *National Reformer*, April 21, 1872; Congressional Globe and Appendix, 42d Cong., 2d sess., pt. 2 (Washington: Office of the Congressional Globe, 1872), 1303; Genevieve Troka, California State Archives, Sacramento, to Gary R. Entz, McPherson ks, August 21, 2000.

10. *National Reformer*, April 21, 1872.

11. *Seneca Weekly Courier*, March 1, April 19, 1872.

12. "Sother Items," *Seneca Weekly Courier*, May 10, 1872.

13. "Sother Items," *Seneca Weekly Courier*, June 21, 1872.

14. *Labour and Unity: A Monthly Journal for Foresters, Oddfellows, and Kindred Societies* (London), July 1872; *National Reformer*, May 12, 1872; Logie Barrow, "The Homerton Social Democratic Club, 1881–1882," *History Workshop Journal* 5 (Spring 1978): 196.

15. *Comprehensionist* (London), June 1872, British Library.

16. *Comprehensionist*, July 1872.

17. *Comprehensionist*, July 1872.

18. *National Reformer*, August 18, 1872.

19. *Bee-Hive*, October 19, 1872; *National Reformer*, October 20, 1872.

20. *National Reformer*, March 9, 1873.

21. *National Reformer*, March 16, 1873; "From Our London Correspondent," *Royal Leamington, Warwickshire, & Centre of England Chronicle*, March 22, 1873.

22. *National Reformer*, May 4, 1873; "From Our London Correspondent," *Royal Leamington, Warwickshire, & Centre of England Chronicle*, March 22, 1873.

23. *National Reformer*, July 6, 1873.

24. *National Reformer*, July 13, 20, 1873.

25. "From Our London Correspondent," *Royal Leamington, Warwickshire, & Centre of England Chronicle*, July 19, 1873.

26. *National Reformer*, July 27, 1873.

27. "From Our London Correspondent," *Royal Leamington, Warwickshire, & Centre of England Chronicle*, August 30, 1873.

28. *National Reformer*, September 21, 28, 1873.

29. "From Our London Correspondent," *Royal Leamington, Warwickshire, & Centre of England Chronicle*, September 20, 1873.

30. *National Reformer*, November 23, December 7, 1873.

31. "From Our London Correspondent," *Royal Leamington, Warwickshire, & Centre of England Chronicle*, December 13, 1873.

32. Adolphe S. Hoadlingley, *The Biography of Charles Bradlaugh* (London: Remington, 1880), 297–98.

33. *National Reformer*, January 18, 1874.

34. *National Reformer*, January 18, 1874.

35. Texas longhorns carried ticks that infected Kansas farm cattle with splenic fever. In an effort to halt the spread of what was then known as "Texas Fever," in 1867 the Kansas leg-

islature passed a quarantine law that effectively banned longhorns from the eastern half of the state. Robert W. Richmond, *Kansas: A Land of Contrasts*, 4th ed. (Wheeling IL: Harlan Davidson, 1999), 121–22.

36. *National Reformer*, January 25, 1874.

37. *National Reformer*, February 1, 1874.

38. *National Reformer*, January 25, February 1, 8, March 15, 1874.

39. *National Reformer*, March 22, 1874.

40. *National Reformer*, March 29, 1874; "From Our London Correspondent," *Royal Leamington, Warwickshire, & Centre of England Chronicle*, March 18, 1874.

41. *National Reformer*, March 29, 1874; "From Our London Correspondent," *Royal Leamington, Warwickshire, & Centre of England Chronicle*, March 18, 1874.

42. *National Reformer*, March 29, 1874; "From Our London Correspondent," *Royal Leamington, Warwickshire, & Centre of England Chronicle*, March 18, 1874.

43. *National Reformer*, April 12, 1874; "From Our London Correspondent," *Royal Leamington, Warwickshire, & Centre of England Chronicle*, May 2, 1874.

44. C. Maurice Davies, *Heterodox London; or, Phases of Free Thought in the Metropolis*, vol. 2 (London: Tinsley Brothers, 1874), 234–35.

45. Davies, *Heterodox London*, 236–37.

46. Davies, *Heterodox London*, 238.

47. *National Reformer*, April 26, May 24, 1874; *Seneca Weekly Courier*, May 4, June 19, 1874.

48. "From Our London Correspondent," *Royal Leamington, Warwickshire, & Centre of England Chronicle*, June 27, 1874.

49. "From Our London Correspondent," *Royal Leamington, Warwickshire, & Centre of England Chronicle*, July 18, 1874.

50. *National Reformer*, August 2, 1874.

51. Cutler, *History of the State of Kansas*, 2:942; "Sother Items," *Seneca Weekly Courier*, August 14, 1874.

52. *National Reformer*, August 2, 23, 1874.

53. J. A. DeForest, Wetmore, to Thomas A. Osborn, Topeka, April 3, 1875, Correspondence, Thomas A. Osborn Administration, Records of the Governor's Office, Library and Archives Division, Kansas Historical Society; "Relief in Nemaha County," *Seneca Weekly Courier*, June 11, 1875; Kansas State Census, 1875, Nemaha County, enumerated March 1, 1875, Kansas Historical Society.

5. Hold Up the Lamp of Hope

1. Shipley, *Club Life and Socialism*, 50–58; Martin Crick, *The History of the Social-Democratic Federation* (Keele: Ryburn Pub., Keele University Press, 1994), 20.

2. *Royal Leamington, Warwickshire, & Centre of England Chronicle*, January 2, 1875.

3. *Royal Leamington, Warwickshire, & Centre of England Chronicle*, April 3, 17, 1875.

4. James F. Murray, "Special Resolutions of the Co-operative Colonization Company, Ltd.," May 5, 1875, Records of the Mutual Land, Emigration, and Co-operative Colonization Company, Ltd., BT 31/1457/4367, National Archives, Kew, London.

5. *National Reformer,* November 7, 14, 1875.

6. *National Reformer,* December 5, 12, 1875.

7. *National Reformer,* December 12, 19, 1875.

8. "From Sother," *Seneca Weekly Courier,* February 18, March 17, 1876.

9. *Seneca Weekly Courier,* July 21, 1876; *National Reformer,* August 6, 1876.

10. *National Reformer,* August 20, September 3, 24, 1876; Register of Deeds, Seneca, Kansas, November 8, 1876, book no. 26, 198.

11. "From Sother," *Seneca Weekly Courier,* October 20, 1876.

12. "From Sother," *Seneca Weekly Courier,* March 17, April 20, July 20, August 17, 1876; Register of Deeds, Seneca, book 26, 198, book N, 384, book K, 48; John Ostertag and Enid Ostertag, eds., *The 1887 Nemaha County Atlas* (St. Joseph MO: John and Enid Ostertag, 1993), 92.

13. Registrar of Joint Stock Companies, Companies' Registration Office, London, to Secretary (or Manager), Co-operative Colonization Company, London, February 14, March 21, 1883, January 15, 1884, Records of the Mutual Land, Emigration, and Co-operative Colonization Company.

14. Rueben F. Smith, *Smith's Guide to Northern and Northwestern Kansas, along the Central Branch Union Pacific R.R.* (Atchison: Campion Book and Job Printing House, 1877), 46.

15. Roy R. Bell, *Goff: The First Hundred Years* (Holton KS: Bell Graphics, 1990), 7–12.

16. *Seneca Weekly Courier,* August 31, 1877.

17. See appendix A.

18. John Stowell, *Don Coronado through Kansas, 1541, Then Known as Quivira: A Story of the Kansas, Osage, and Pawnee Indians* (Seneca KS: Don Coronado Press, 1908), 90–91.

19. Quoted in Henry George Jr., *The Life of Henry George* (New York: Cosimo Classics, 2006), 230.

20. George, *Life of Henry George,* 232–33.

21. George, *Life of Henry George,* 293–94, 307.

22. Clyde E. Reeves, "Henry George's Speaking in the Land Reform Movement: The West Coast 'Training Phase,'" *American Journal of Economics and Sociology* 24 (January 1965): 54.

23. John Radford, "King or People? Has Representative Government Failed? Shall We Stand by the Republic or Go Back to Monarchy?" *Wetmore Spectator,* December 16, 1882.

24. O'Brien, *Human Slavery,* 107.

25. Henry George, *Progress and Poverty* (1879; reprint, New York: Robert Schalkenbach Foundation, 2008), 530–31, 538.

26. Radford, "King or People?"

27. George, *Progress and Poverty,* 538.

28. Radford, "King or People?"

29. Radford, "King or People?"

30. Shipley, *Club Life and Socialism,* 69–70.

31. Crick, *History of the Social-Democratic Federation,* 20.

32. Henry Mayers Hyndman, *The Record of an Adventurous Life* (New York: Macmillan, 1911), 258–59.

33. Shipley, *Club Life and Socialism*, 71.

34. Hyndman, *The Record of an Adventurous Life*, 226.

35. Shipley, *Club Life and Socialism*, 13–14.

36. Richmond, *Kansas*, 178–79.

37. Cutler, *History of the State of Kansas*, 2:957–58.

38. *Wetmore Spectator*, March 10, April 14, 1883.

39. *Wetmore Spectator*, June 9, 23, 1883

40. H. C. DeForest, Wetmore, to Governor George W. Glick, Topeka, June 13, 1883, Correspondence, George W. Glick Administration, Records of the Governor's Office, Library and Archives Division, Kansas Historical Society.

41. *Wetmore Spectator*, July 7, 14, 21, 1883, September 5, 1885.

42. *Wetmore Spectator*, September 12, 1885.

43. *Wetmore Register*, August 7, 1886.

44. Bartels, *Missouri Pacific*, 45.

45. Leon Fink, *Workingmen's Democracy: The Knights of Labor and American Politics* (Urbana: University of Illinois Press, 1985), 9, 22, 23.

46. R. Alton Lee, *Farmers vs. Wage Earners: Organized Labor in Kansas, 1860–1960* (Lincoln: University of Nebraska Press, 2005), 37.

47. Fink, *Workingmen's Democracy*, 119.

48. Lee, *Farmers vs. Wage Earners*, 48–50; Fink, *Workingmen's Democracy*, 120–21.

49. *Wetmore Spectator*, May 19, 1883, November 13, 1886; *Wetmore Register*, August 7, 1886; *Goffs News*, December 8, 1887; *Nemaha County Spectator*, September 2, December 16, 1887.

50. John Stowell, "A Letter to Jay Gould," *Nemaha County Spectator*, March 16, 1888.

51. "Gould Wires Us," *Nemaha County Spectator*, March 23, 1888.

52. John Stowell to Jay Gould, Esq., *Nemaha County Spectator*, March 23, 1888.

53. Jay Gould, "Jay Gould Heard From," *Nemaha County Spectator*, April 13, 1888.

54. O'Brien, *Human Slavery*, 141.

55. *Nemaha County Spectator*, August 22, December 26, 1890, June 12, 1891.

56. O'Brien, *Human Slavery*, 112.

57. *Nemaha County Spectator*, January 27, March 16, 1888; Grant W. Harrington, ed., *The Annals of Brown County, Kansas: From the Earliest Records to January 1, 1900* (Hiawatha KS: Grant W. Harrington, 1903), 252.

58. Scott G. McNall, *The Road to Rebellion: Class Formation and Kansas Populism, 1865–1900* (Chicago: University of Chicago Press, 1988), 3–4.

59. O. Gene Clanton, *Kansas Populism: Ideas and Men* (Lawrence: University Press of Kansas, 1969), 50–51.

60. "The People Meet, an Enthusiastic Convention Held," *Hiawatha Journal*, July 24, 1890.

61. Brooke Spear Orr, "Mary Elizabeth Lease: Gendered Discourse and Populist Party Politics in Gilded Age America," *Kansas History* 29 (Winter 2006–2007): 252.

62. "Mrs. Lease Orates," *Hiawatha Journal*, September 18, 1890.

63. "Meeting at 44," *Hiawatha Journal*, October 23, 1890.

64. Quoted in Clanton, *Kansas Populism*, 80, 81.

65. "Alliance Convention," *Horton Commercial*, March 5, 1891; "The Congressional Alliance," *Hiawatha Journal*, March 12, 1891.

66. *Horton Commercial*, April 23, May 28, 1891; *Nemaha County Spectator*, May 29, June 5, 1891.

67. "The People's Party Convention," *Hiawatha Journal*, September 3, 1891.

68. Radford, "Communicated," *Horton Commercial*, October 6, 1892.

69. O'Brien, *Human Slavery*, 127.

70. Radford, "Communicated," *Horton Commercial*, January 26, 1893.

71. John Radford, "Ed. Commercial," *Horton Commercial*, February 16, 1893.

72. *Horton Commercial*, February 23, March 2, 1893.

73. Clanton, *Kansas Populism*, 132–36.

74. John Radford, "The Last Hour of the People's House," *Advocate* (Topeka), March 8, 1893; *Horton Commercial*, March 9, 1893.

75. *Advocate*, March 8, 1893.

76. *Horton Commercial*, June 1, 1893; advertisement, "Ornamental & Letter Engraving," *Populist* (Topeka), June 16–October 13, 1893.

77. *Goff's Advance*, March 22, 1906.

78. Benjamin Beeby, "Another Pioneer Gone," *Goff's Advance*, May 10, 1906.

Conclusion

1. O'Brien, "Mr. O'Connell and the Lambeth Radical Association."

2. Malcolm Chase, *The People's Farm: English Radical Agrarianism, 1775–1840* (London: Breviary Stuff, 2010), 157.

3. Thomas Spence, "A Further Account of Spenconia (1794)," in *Pigs' Meat*, ed. Gallop, 88.

4. Bronterre O'Brien, "The March of Despotism," *Poor Man's Guardian*, March 23, 1833.

5. Bronterre O'Brien, "The Repeal Question," *Poor Man's Guardian*, May 3, 1834.

6. O'Brien, "Social Occupations: Profit-Mongering, Popular Rights, &c."

7. O'Brien, *Human Slavery*, 102.

8. O'Brien, *Human Slavery*, 100, 107.

9. O'Brien, *Human Slavery*, 112.

10. O'Brien, *Human Slavery*, 100–103.

11. Bronterre O'Brien, "The National Reform League," *Reynolds's Political Instructor*, December 29, 1849.

12. *Bronterre's National Reformer*, January 7, 1837.

13. O'Brien, *Human Slavery*, 107–108.

14. Edward Grainger Smith, London, to David C. Butler, Omaha, December 28, 1868, Butler Papers.

15. Henry Clinton, "Associated Homes

16. Dolores Hayden, *Seven American Utopias: The Architecture of Communitarian Socialism, 1790–1975* (Cambridge: MIT Press, 1981), 300.

17. Peter Hall, Dennis Hardy, and Colin Ward, "Commentators' Introduction," in *To-Morrow: A Peaceful Path to Real Reform*, by Ebenezer Howard (London: Routledge, 2003), 4.

18. Bevir, "The British Social Democratic Federation, 1880–1885," 11.

19. Parssinen, "Thomas Spence," 135.

20. Quoted in Chase, *The People's Farm*, 142.

21. Bevir, "The British Social Democratic Federation, 1880–1885," 9–11.

22. John Radford, "Communicated," *Horton Commercial*, January 26, 1893.

23. Clive Wilmer, introduction to *News from Nowhere, and Other Writings*, by William Morris (London: Penguin, 2004), xix–xx.

24. Wilmer, introduction, xx; A. L. Morton, *A People's History of England* (London: Lawrence & Wishart, 1989), 385–88.

25. Nelson A. Dunning, ed., *Farmers' Alliance History and Agricultural Digest* (Washington DC: Alliance, 1891), 318.

26. Lawrence Goodwyn, *The Populist Moment: A Short History of the Agrarian Revolt in America* (New York: Oxford University Press, 1978), 91.

27. O'Brien, *Human Slavery*, 108.

28. O'Brien, "Social Occupations: Profit-Mongering, Popular Rights, &c."

29. O'Brien, *Human Slavery*, 139.

30. O'Brien, "Mr. O'Connell and the Lambeth Radical Association."

31. Jim Bissett, *Agrarian Socialism in America: Marx, Jefferson, and Jesus in the Oklahoma Countryside, 1904–1920* (Norman: University of Oklahoma Press, 2002), 183.

32. Bissett, *Agrarian Socialism*, 68.

33. O'Brien, *Human Slavery*, 126.

34. Bissett, *Agrarian Socialism in America*, 181.

35. Fogarty, "American Communes, 1865–1914," 150.

Selected Bibliography

Unpublished and Archival Sources

Address by the Promoters of the Mutual Land, Emigration, and Colonization Company, to the Working Classes of Great Britain, and to the Parties About to Emigrate. London: Published at the Office of the Company, 1868. British Library Collection.

Clinton, Henry. "Associated Homes: An Address to the Shareholders of the Mutual Land, Emigration, and Co-operative Colonisation Society," 1870. FWA Case A g 18, Family Welfare Association Library, Senate House Library, University of London.

Congressional Globe and Appendix, 42d Cong., 2d sess., pt. 2. Washington: Office of the Congressional Globe, 1872.

Governor David C. Butler Papers, Series 1, General Correspondence, Nebraska State Historical Society.

Governor's Office, George W. Glick Administration, Correspondence Received, 1883–85, Library and Archives Division, Kansas Historical Society.

Governor's Office, Thomas A. Osborn Administration, Correspondence Received, 1873–77, Library and Archives Division, Kansas Historical Society.

Josiah Warren Papers, Labadie Collection, University of Michigan.

Kansas State Census, Manuscript Census, Nemaha County, 1875, 1885, Library and Archives Division, Kansas Historical Society.

Molineux, C. Rex. "The English Colony at Llewellyn Castle & the Molineaux's," Seneca, Kansas, September 18, 1989.

Murray, Charles. *A Letter to Mr. Jacob Holyoake; Containing a Brief Review of that Gentleman's Conduct and Policy as a Reformer, with Special Reference to His Reply to Mr. Linton, and the "Boston Liberator": His Criticism upon the Stranger of the "Leader" Newspaper, and Defence of the Cobden Policy; with the Writer's Opinion upon Free-Trade Measures, and on the Position and Interests of the Middle and Working Classes; &c. &c. &c.* London: Samuel Bovingdon, Sherrard Place, Golden Square, 1854. British Library Collection.

"National Reform League Demonstration," Official Program, February 11, 1867. British Library Collection.

New World, November 1870. FWA Case A g 18, Family Welfare Association Library, Senate House Library, University of London.

New York Passenger Lists, 1820–1957, May 17, 1869, *Paraguay* [database online]; available from Ancestry.com.

O'Brien, J. Bronterre. *Propositions of the National Reform League for the Peaceful Regeneration of Society*. London: Working Printers' Co-operative Association, 1850. British Library Collection.

Records of the Mutual Land, Emigration, and Co-operative Colonization Company, Ltd. BT 31/1457/4367, National Archives, Kew, London.

Register of Deeds, Seneca, Kansas, November 8, 1876, books no. 19, 26, book N, book K, Nemaha County Courthouse.

Troka, Genevieve, California State Archives, Sacramento, to Gary R. Entz, McPherson, Kansas, August 21, 2000.

U.S. Department of the Census. Manuscript Census, Nemaha County, Kansas, 1870.

Published Sources

Ackroyd, Peter. *London: The Biography*. New York: Anchor Books, 2003. NC

Adams, W. E. *Memoirs of a Social Atom*. London: Hutcheson & Co., Paternoster Row, 1903; reprint, New York: Augustus M. Kelley, 1968. NC

Anderson, George L. "Atchison and the Central Branch Country, 1865–1874." *Kansas Historical Quarterly* 28 (Spring 1962): 1–24.

Arnstein, Walter L. *Britain Yesterday and Today: 1830 to the Present*. 3rd ed. Lexington MA: D. C. Heath, 1976.

Ashraf, P. M. *The Life and Times of Thomas Spence*. Newcastle upon Tyne: Frank Graham, 1983.

Ashton, Owen R., Robert Fyson, and Stephen Roberts, eds. *The Chartist Legacy*. Rendlesham: Merlin Press, 1999. NC

Ashton, Owen R., and Paul A. Pickering. *Friends of the People: Uneasy Radicals in the Age of the Chartists*. London: Merlin Press, 2002. NC

Bailie, William. *Josiah Warren: The First American Anarchist*. Boston: Small, Maynard, 1906.

Barker, Ambrose G. *Henry Hetherington, 1792–1849: Pioneer in the Freethought and Working-Class Struggles of a Hundred Years Ago for the Freedom of the Press*. London: Pioneer Press, 1938. NC

Barrow, Logie. "The Homerton Social Democratic Club, 1881–1882." *History Workshop Journal* 5 (Spring 1978): 188–99.

Bartels, Michael M. *Missouri Pacific, River and Prairie Rails: The MoPac in Nebraska*. David City NE: South Platte Press, 1997.

Beer, Max. *Fifty Years of International Socialism*. London: George Allen & Unwin, 1935.

Belchem, John. *"Orator" Hunt: Henry Hunt and English Working-Class Radicalism*. New York: Clarendon Press, 1985.

Bell, Roy R. *Goff: The First Hundred Years*. Holton KS: Bell Graphics, 1990.

Bellamy, Joyce M., and John Saville, eds. *Dictionary of Labour Biography.* Vol. 6. London: Macmillan Press, 1982. NC

──────. *Dictionary of Labour Biography.* Vol. 11. London: Macmillan Press, 1993. NC

Bevir, Mark. "The British Social Democratic Federation, 1880–1885: From O'Brienism to Marxism." *University of California Postprints,* paper 2584 (1992).

Birch, Brian P. "Popularizing the Plains: News of Kansas in England, 1860–1880." *Kansas History* 10 (Winter 1987): 262–74.

Bissett, Jim. *Agrarian Socialism in America: Marx, Jefferson, and Jesus in the Oklahoma Countryside, 1904–1920.* Norman: University of Oklahoma Press, 2002.

Boon, Martin J. *Home Colonization.* London: Edward Truelove, 1869.

──────. *A Protest against the Present Emigrationists.* London: Land and Labour League, 1869. British Library.

Boston, Ray. *British Chartists in America, 1839–1900.* Manchester: Manchester University Press, 1971.

Boyle, J. W., ed. *Leaders and Workers.* Cork, Ireland: Mercier Press, 1966.

Breuilly, John, Gottfried Niedhart, and Anthony Taylor, eds. *The Era of the Reform League: English Labour and Radical Politics, 1857–1872. Documents Selected by Gustav Mayer.* Mannheim, Germany: Palatium Verlag im J & J. Verlag, 1995.

Briggs, Asa. *A Social History of England.* New York: Viking Press, 1984.

Bristow, John T. *Memory's Storehouse Unlocked: Pioneer Days in Wetmore and Northeast Kansas.* Wetmore KS: John T. Bristow, 1948.

"The British Section of Icarian Communists." *Bulletin of the International Institute of Social History* 1 (August 1937): 84–88.

Bronstein, Jamie L. *Land Reform and Working-Class Experience in Britain and the United States, 1800–1862.* Stanford: Stanford University Press, 1999.

Buonarroti, Philippe. *Babeuf's Conspiracy for Equality.* Translated by Bronterre O'Brien. London: H. Hetherington, 1836; reprint, New York: Augustus M. Kelley, Bookseller, 1965.

Canavan, Bernard. "The Edgeworths of Edgeworthstown: A Rediscovered Heritage." *History Workshop Journal* 43 (Spring 1997): 240–48.

Chase, Malcolm. *Chartism: A New History.* Manchester: Manchester University Press, 2007.

──────. *The People's Farm: English Radical Agrarianism, 1775–1840.* London: Breviary Stuff Publications, 2010.

Claeys, Gregory, ed. *The Chartist Movement in Britain, 1838–1850.* Vol. 6. London: Pickering & Chatto, 2001.

Claeys, Gregory. *Citizens and Saints: Politics and Anti-Politics in Early British Socialism.* New York: Cambridge University Press, 2002.

Clanton, O. Gene. *A Common Humanity: Kansas Populism and the Battle for Justice and Equality, 1854–1903.* Manhattan KS: Sunflower University Press, 2004.

──────. *Kansas Populism: Ideas and Men.* Lawrence: University Press of Kansas, 1969.

Clark, John G., ed. *The Frontier Challenge: Responses to the Trans-Mississippi West.* Lawrence: University Press of Kansas, 1971.

Cobbett, William. *Rural Rides*. London: Penguin, 2001.

Cole, George D. H. *Chartist Portraits*. London: Cassell, 1989.

——. *The Life of Robert Owen*. Hamden CT: Archon Books, 1966.

Colley, Linda. *Britons: Forging the Nation, 1707–1837*. 2nd ed. New Haven: Yale University Press, 2005.

Collins, Henry, and Chimen Abramsky. *Karl Marx and the British Labour Movement: Years of the First International*. New York: St. Martin's Press, 1965.

Crick, Martin. *The History of the Social Democratic Federation*. Keele: Ryburn Pub., Keele University Press, 1994.

Cronin, Mike. *A History of Ireland*. New York: Palgrave, 2001.

Cutler, William G. *History of the State of Kansas*. Vol. 2. Chicago: A. T. Andreas, 1883.

Davies, C. Maurice. *Heterodox London; or, Phases of Free Thought in the Metropolis*. London: Tinsley Brothers, 1874.

Dunning, Nelson A., ed. *Farmers' Alliance History and Agricultural Digest*. Washington DC: Alliance, 1891.

Edgeworth, Maria, and Richard Lovell Edgeworth. *Essays on Practical Education*. 3 vols. 3rd ed. London: R. Hunter, 1822.

Edwards, Rebecca. "Mary E. Lease and the Populists: A Reconsideration." *Kansas History* 35 (Spring 2012): 26–41.

Entz, Gary R. "Paradise on the Plains: The Development of Communal Alternatives in Kansas, 1850–1900." PhD diss., University of Utah, 1999.

Epstein, James, and David Karr. "Playing at Revolution: British 'Jacobin' Performance." *Journal of Modern History* 79 (September 2007): 495–530.

Faherty, Ray. "Bronterre O'Brien's Correspondence with Thomas Allsop: New Evidence on the Decline of a Chartist Leader." *European Labour and Working Class History Newsletter* 8 (November 1975): 7–15.

Fernbach, David, ed. *The First International and After*. Vol. 3, *Karl Marx: Political Writings*. New York: Vintage Books, 1974.

Fink, Leon. *Workingmen's Democracy: The Knights of Labor and American Politics*. Urbana: University of Illinois Press, 1985.

Finn, Margot C. *After Chartism: Class and Nation in English Radical Politics, 1848–1874*. Cambridge: Cambridge University Press, 1993.

Fitzgerald, Daniel C. *Faded Dreams: More Ghost Towns of Kansas*. Lawrence: University Press of Kansas, 1994.

Flett, Keith. *Chartism after 1848: The Working Class and the Politics of Radical Education*. Monmouth: Merlin Press, 2006.

Fogarty, Robert S. *All Things New: American Communes and Utopian Movements, 1860–1914*. Chicago: University of Chicago Press, 1990.

——. "American Communes, 1865–1914." *Journal of American Studies* 9 (August 1975): 145–62.

Freitag, Sabine, ed. *Exiles from European Revolutions: Refugees in Mid-Victorian England*. New York: Berghahn Books, 2003.

Fuller, John. *The Art of Coppersmithing: A Practical Treatise on Working Sheet Copper into All Forms.* Mendham NJ: Astragal Press, 1993.

Gallop, G. I., ed. *Pigs' Meat: Selected Writings of Thomas Spence, Radical Pioneer Land Reformer.* Nottingham: Spokesman, 1982.

Gammage, Robert G. *History of the Chartist Movement, 1837–1854.* 1894; reprint, London: Merlin Press, 1976.

Gates, Paul Wallace. *Fifty Million Acres: Conflicts over Kansas Land Policy.* Norman: University of Oklahoma Press, 1954.

George, Henry. *Progress and Poverty.* 1879; reprint, New York: Robert Schalkenbach Foundation, 2008.

George, Henry, Jr. *The Life of Henry George.* New York: Cosimo Classics, 2006.

Gildart, Keith, and David Howell, eds. *Dictionary of Labour Biography.* Vol. 12. New York: Palgrave Macmillan, 2005.

Goodway, David. *London Chartism, 1838–1848.* Cambridge: Cambridge University Press, 1982.

Goodwyn, Lawrence. *The Populist Moment: A Short History of the Agrarian Revolt in America.* New York: Oxford University Press, 1978.

Grant, H. Roger. "Portrait of a Workers' Utopia: The Labor Exchange and the Freedom, Kan., Colony." *Kansas Historical Quarterly* 43 (Spring 1977): 56–66.

Hall, Catherine, Keith McClelland, and Jane Rendall. *Defining the Victorian Nation: Class, Race, Gender, and the Reform Act of 1867.* Cambridge: Cambridge University Press, 2000.

Hall, Robert G. *Voices of the People: Democracy and Chartist Political Identity, 1830–1870.* Monmouth: Merlin Press, 2007.

Hardy, Dennis, and Lorna Davidson, eds. *Utopian Thought and Communal Experience.* Enfield: Middlesex Polytechnic, 1989.

Harrington, Grant W., ed. *The Annals of Brown County, Kansas: From the Earliest Records to January 1, 1900.* Hiawatha KS: Grant W. Harrington, 1903.

Harrison, J. F. C. *Quest for the New Moral World: Robert Owen and the Owenites in Britain and America.* New York: Charles Scribner's Sons, 1969.

Harrison, Royden. *Before the Socialists: Studies in Labour and Politics, 1861–1881.* Aldershot: Gregg Revivals, 1994.

———, ed. *The English Defence of the Commune (1871).* London: Merlin Press, 1971.

Hayden, Dolores. *Seven American Utopias: The Architecture of Communitarian Socialism, 1790–1975.* Cambridge: MIT Press, 1981.

Hetherington, Henry. *The Poor Man's Guardian, 1831–1835: A Reprint of the Original Journal with an Introduction by Patricia Hollis.* 4 vols. London: Merlin Press, 1969.

Hine, Robert V. *California Utopianism: Contemplations of Eden.* San Francisco: Boyd and Fraser, 1981.

Hoadlingley, Adolphe S. *The Biography of Charles Bradlaugh.* London: Remington, 1880.

Howard, Ebenezer. *To-Morrow: A Peaceful Path to Real Reform.* London: Routledge, 2003.

Hyndman, Henry Mayers. *The Record of an Adventurous Life.* New York: Macmillan, 1911.

Institute of Marxism-Leninism of the C.C., C.P.S.U. *Documents of the First International: The General Council of the First International, 1868–1870.* Moscow: Progress; reprint, London: Lawrence & Wishart, 1963.

Jephson, Henry. *The Platform: Its Rise and Progress.* 2 vols. London: Macmillan, 1892.

Jones, Gareth Stedman. *Languages of Class: Studies in English Working-Class History, 1832–1982.* New York: Cambridge University Press, 1983.

Kanter, Rosabeth Moss. *Commitment and Community: Communes and Utopias in Sociological Perspective.* Cambridge: Harvard University Press, 1972.

Lancaster, Joseph. *Improvements in Education, as It Respects the Industrious Classes of the Community.* 3rd ed. London: Darton and Harvey, 1805; reprint, Clifton NJ: Augustus M. Kelley, 1973.

Lee, R. Alton. *Farmers vs. Wage Earners: Organized Labor in Kansas, 1860–1960.* Lincoln: University of Nebraska Press, 2005.

Lovett, William. *The Life and Struggles of William Lovett: In his Pursuit of Bread, Knowledge & Freedom, with some short Account of the different Associations he belonged to & of the Opinions He Entertained.* London: MacGibbon & Kee, 1967.

McAdam, Doug. *Political Process and the Development of Black Insurgency, 1930–1970.* Chicago: University of Chicago Press, 1982.

McCord, William. "Building Utopias: Successes and Failures." *International Journal of Comparative Sociology* 33 (September 1992): 151–67.

McNall, Scott G. *The Road to Rebellion: Class Formation and Kansas Populism, 1865–1900.* Chicago: University of Chicago Press, 1988.

Marx, Karl, and Frederick Engels. *Letters to Americans, 1848–1895: A Selection.* New York: International, 1953.

Maw, Ben. "Bronterre O'Brien's Class Analysis: The Formative Phase, 1832–1836." *History of Political Thought* 28 (Summer 2007): 253–89.

———. "The Democratic Anti-Capitalism of Bronterre O'Brien." *Journal of Political Ideologies* 13 (June 2008): 201–26.

Miller, Kenneth E. "Danish Socialism on the Kansas Prairie." *Kansas Historical Quarterly* 38 (Summer 1972): 156–68.

Miller, Timothy. *American Communes, 1860–1960: A Bibliography.* New York: Garland, 1990.

Morris, William. *News from Nowhere, and Other Writings.* London: Penguin Books, 2004.

Morton, A. L. *A People's History of England.* London: Lawrence and Wishart, 1989.

Niemi, William L., and David J. Plante. "Democratic Movements, Self-Education, and Economic Democracy: Chartists, Populists, and Wobblies." *Radical History Review,* no. 102 (Fall 2008): 185–200.

O'Brien, James Bronterre. *Bronterre's Life and Character of Maximilian Robespierre.* London: J. Watson, 1838.

———. *A Dissertation and Elegy on the Life and Death of the Immortal Maximilian Robespierre. Revealing, for the First Time, the Real Causes and Authors of His Death; with True Portraitures of the Three Assemblies that made the Revolution — the States-Gen-*

eral, the Legislative, and the Convention: and of their Historic Celebrities; Showing how Completely History has Misrepresented the Originals: as also an Ode to Louis Napoleon Bonaparte. London: Holyoake & Co. and E. Truelove, 1859.

———. *The Rise, Progress, and Phases of Human Slavery: How It Came into the World, and How It Shall Be Made to Go Out.* London: William Reeves, 185 Fleet Street, E.C., 1885.

Olson, James C., and Ronald C. Naugle. *History of Nebraska.* 3rd ed. Lincoln: University of Nebraska Press, 1997.

Orr, Brooke Speer. "Mary Elizabeth Lease: Gendered Discourse and Populist Party Politics in Gilded Age America." *Kansas History* 29 (Winter 2006–2007): 246–65.

Ostertag, John, and Enid Ostertag, eds. *The 1887 Nemaha County Atlas.* St. Joseph MO: John and Enid Ostertag, 1993.

Parssinen, T. M. "Thomas Spence and the Origins of English Land Nationalization." *Journal of the History of Ideas* 34 (January–March 1973): 135–41.

Peel, Frank. *The Rising of the Luddites, Chartists, and Plugdrawers.* 2nd ed. Heckmondwike: Senior and Co., Printers, 1888.

Picard, Liza. *Victorian London: The Life of a City, 1840–1870.* New York: St. Martin's Press, 2005.

Pitzer, Donald E., ed. *America's Communal Utopias.* Chapel Hill: University of North Carolina Press, 1997.

Plotz, John. "Crowd Power: Chartism, Carlyle, and the Victorian Public Sphere: Crowds as Speech." *Representations* 70 (Spring 2000): 87–114.

Plummer, Alfred. *Bronterre: A Political Biography of Bronterre O'Brien, 1804–1864.* Toronto: University of Toronto Press, 1971.

———. "Place of Bronterre O'Brien in the Working-Class Movement." *Economic History Review* 2 (1929): 61–80.

Podmore, Frank. *Robert Owen: A Biography.* Honolulu: University Press of the Pacific, 2004.

Prothero, Iorwerth. "Chartism in London." *Past and Present* 44 (August 1969): 76–105.

———. *Radical Artisans in England and France, 1830–1870.* Cambridge: Cambridge University Press, 1997.

Read, Donald. *Cobden and Bright: A Victorian Political Partnership.* London: Edward Arnold, 1967.

Reeves, Clyde E. "Henry George's Speaking in the Land Reform Movements: The West Coast 'Training Phase.'" *American Journal of Economics and Sociology* 24 (January 1965): 51–68.

Richmond, Robert W. *Kansas: A Land of Contrasts.* 4th ed. Wheeling IL: Harlan Davidson, 1999.

Rose, J. Holland. "The Unstamped Press, 1815–1836." *English Historical Review* 12 (October 1897): 711–26.

Rose, Jonathan. *The Intellectual Life of the British Working Classes.* New Haven: Yale University Press, 2001.

Rowe, D. J. "The Chartist Convention and the Regions." *Economic History Review* 22 (April 1969): 58–74.

———, ed. *London Radicalism: A Selection from the Papers of Francis Place*. London: London Record Society, 1970.

———. "The London Working Men's Association and the People's Charter." *Past and Present* 36 (April 1967): 73–86.

Royle, Edward. *Radicals, Secularists, and Republicans: Popular Freethought in Britain, 1866–1915*. Manchester: Manchester University Press, 1980.

Schafer, Delbert Frank. "James Bronterre O'Brien: A Working-Class Radical, 1831–1842." MA thesis, University of Oklahoma, 1967.

Shapin, Steven, and Barry Barnes. "Head and Hand: Rhetorical Resources in British Pedagogical Writing, 1770–1850." *Oxford Review of Education* 2, no. 3 (1976): 231–54.

Shepperson, Wilbur S. *British Emigration to North America: Projects and Opinions in the Early Victorian Period*. Minneapolis: University of Minnesota Press, 1957.

———. *Emigration and Disenchantment: Portraits of Englishmen Repatriated from the United States*. Norman: University of Oklahoma Press, 1965.

———. *The Promotion of British Emigration by Agents for American Lands, 1840–1860*. Reno: University of Nevada Press, 1954.

———. *Six Who Returned: America Viewed by British Repatriates*. Reno: University of Nevada Press, 1961.

Shipley, Stan. *Club Life and Socialism in Mid-Victorian London*. London: Journeyman Press and the London History Workshop Centre, 1983.

Shortridge, James R. *Peopling the Plains: Who Settled Where in Frontier Kansas*. Lawrence: University Press of Kansas, 1995.

Skelly, Colin. "An 'Impossibilist' Socialist? William Morris and the Politics of Socialist Revolution versus Social Reform." *Journal of William Morris Studies* 15 (Summer 2003): 35–51.

Smith, Rueben F. *Smith's Guide to Northern and Northwestern Kansas, along the Central Branch Union Pacific R.R.* Atchison: Champion Books and Job Printing House, 1877.

Spater, George. *William Cobbett: The Poor Man's Friend*. 2 vols. Cambridge: Cambridge University Press, 1982.

Stack, David, ed. *James Bronterre O'Brien*. Vol. 4 of *Lives of Victorian Political Figures II*. London: Pickering & Chatto, 2007.

Starr, Kevin. *Americans and the California Dream, 1850–1915*. New York: Oxford University Press, 1973.

Steiner, Bernard C. *Life of Reverdy Johnson*. Baltimore: Norman, Remington, 1914.

Stephen, Leslie, and Sidney Lee, eds. *Dictionary of National Biography*. Vol. 14. London: Oxford University Press, 1921–22.

Stern, Madeleine B. *The Pantarch: A Biography of Stephen Pearl Andrews*. Austin: University of Texas Press, 1968.

Stowell, John. *Don Coronado through Kansas, 1541, Then Known as Quivira: A Story of the Kansas, Osage, and Pawnee Indians*. Seneca KS: Don Coronado Press, 1908.

Sutton, Robert P. *Communal Utopias and the American Experience: Secular Communities, 1824–2000.* Westport CT: Praeger, 2004.

———. *Les Icariens: The Utopian Dream in Europe and America.* Urbana: University of Illinois Press, 1994.

Taylor, Bayard. *Colorado: A Summer Trip.* New York: G. P. Putnam, 1867.

Taylor, Blanche M. "The English Colonies in Kansas, 1870–1895." *Historical Magazine of the Protestant Episcopal Church* 41 (March 1972): 17–35.

Tennal, Ralph. *History of Nemaha County, Kansas.* Lawrence: Standard, 1916.

Thompson, Dorothy. *The Chartists: Popular Politics in the Industrial Revolution.* New York: Pantheon Books, 1984.

———, ed. *Small Chartist Periodicals.* New York: Garland, 1986.

Thompson, E. P. *The Making of the English Working Class.* New York: Vintage Books, 1966.

Tice, John H. *Over the Plains and on the Mountains; or, Kansas and Colorado Agriculturally, Mineralogically, and Aesthetically Described.* St. Louis: Industrial Age Printing Co., 1872.

Travis, Paul D. "Changing Climate in Kansas: A Late 19th-Century Myth." *Kansas History* 1 (September 1978): 48–58.

Tristan, Flora. *Flora Tristan's London Journal, 1840.* Translated by Dennis Palmer and Giselle Pincetl. Charlestown MA: Charles River Books, 1980.

Tuchman, Barbara W. "Perdicaris Alive or Raisuli Dead." *American Heritage* 10 (August 1959): 18–21, 98–101.

Turner, Michael J. "Chartism, Bronterre O'Brien, and the 'Luminous Political Example of America.'" *History* 97 (January 2012): 43–69.

Twain, Mark. *Roughing It.* Vol. 1. New York: Harper and Brothers, 1913.

Wake, R. *The United States as a Field for Emigration: With a Description of Nebraska: Hints to Emigrants & c.* London: J. Clarke, 1867.

Waldron, Nell Blythe. "Colonization in Kansas from 1861 to 1890." PhD diss., Northwestern University, 1932.

Webb, Robert K. "Working-Class Readers in Early Victorian England." *English Historical Review* 65 (July 1950): 333–51.

White, Jerry. *London in the 19th Century: A Human Awful Wonder of God.* London: Vintage Books, 2008.

Whitehead, Andrew. "The English Colony at Llewellyn Castle." *Kanhistique* 13 (October 1987): 14–15.

———. "The *New World* and the O'Brienite Colony in Kansas." *Bulletin for the Society for the Study of Labour History* 53 (Winter 1988): 40–43.

———. "Red London: Radicals and Socialists in Late-Victorian Clerkenwell." *Socialist History* 18 (2000): 1–31.

Winther, Oscar O. "The English in Nebraska, 1857–1880." *Nebraska History* 48 (Autumn 1967): 209–33.

Wishart, David J., ed. *Encyclopedia of the Great Plains.* Lincoln: University of Nebraska Press, 2004.

Wright, D. G. *Popular Radicalism: The Working-Class Experience, 1780–1880.* New York: Longman Group, 1988.

Wunderlich, Roger. *Low Living and High Thinking at Modern Times, New York.* Syracuse NY: Syracuse University Press, 1992.

Zornow, William Frank. *Kansas: A History of the Jayhawk State.* Norman: University of Oklahoma Press, 1957.

Index

⸺◈◈◈⸺

Bala, 18

ballot-box democracy: Bronterre O'Brien on, 22, 212; Knights of Labor on, 190; O'Brienites on, 51, 58, 59, 62, 182–83, 204, 214; political pragmatists on, 12–13; radical reformers on, 26–28, 31. *See also* democracy; universal suffrage; voting

Baltic (steamship), 160

banks, 152, 198

barges, 198

Barrow, Logie, 141

BBC World Service News, xvi

Beeby, Benjamin, 206

Beeby, William, 140, 146–47, 151–52, 162, 177, 206

Bellamy, Edward, 11, 216, 225

Bell, Roy R., xvi

Bevir, Mark, 217, 218

Bielby, Jane, 123

Bielby, Mary Anne, 123

Black Friday stock market crash, 190. *See also* stock market

Bonham Road, 40

Boon, Martin, 57, 58, 101–3, 169

boycotts, 191. *See also* strikes

Boyer, Paul, 12

Bradlaugh, Charles, 129, 154–56, 159, 225–26

Brentwood NY, 50, 51

Bright, John, 34

Brisbane, Albert, 13–14

Bristow, John T., 1–10, 180–81, 226, 231

Bristow, Martha, 1

Bristow, William, 1

British National Agricultural Labourers' Union, 169–70

Brown County KS, 196, 198, 199, 219

buckwheat, 137. *See also* agriculture; grain

building skills, 81–82, 84, 85, 89, 95–96, 98, 101–3, 110, 114, 133, 168

Burlington, CO, 15

Burton, Henry, 125

Butler, David C., 68–69, 70–73, 77

Cabet, Étienne, 11, 20, 38–40, 48, 178, 211

Calabria (steamship), 126

California, 49, 53, 63, 179–80, 216, 224, 225

California State Legislature, 63, 64, 139, 179–80. *See also* legislation

Canada, 6, 86, 169–70

capitalism: Charles Murray's warning about, 147–48; in cities, 120; colony as alternative to, 11, 124; and emigration, 102; and farming, 223; during Industrial Revolution, 24; and IWMA, 57, 59; John Radford on, 201; and labor exchanges, 211; of middle class, 34; O'Brienites on, 13, 179, 189–90; Robert Owen on, 25; in United States, 41. *See also* commercial activity; corporations

Carpenter, William, 29

Castle Garden NY, 86–87, 98, 104, 118, 126, 162, 240n31

cattle. *See* livestock; Texas longhorn cattle

CBUP. *See* Union Pacific Railroad, Central Branch

Cedarvale Commune. *See* Progressive Communist Community

Cedarvale KS, 14–16, 185

Centralia KS, 131

Central National Association, 43

Chaikovsky, Nicholas, 14, 185

Chartism: associations of, 57; of Bronterre O'Brien, 15, 21–22, 24, 31–34, 37–38, 43, 45, 46, 51; and democratic reform in Europe, 36; drift toward Marxism, 42, 211; on education, 46; of Edward Grainger Smith, 65; fading of, 213; of George White, 94; history of, 179; national conventions, 32–37, 46, 52, 65; of National Reform League, 80, 169; and O'Brienites, 19, 39, 61, 63, 169, 193, 209; and origin of colony, 12, 20; and Populist movement, 199, 200; and study of colonies, xiv. *See also* People's Charter

Chartist Cooperative Land Society, 35

Chase, Emma, 6

Chase, Malcolm, 42

Cherokee County, 111–12

Cherokee Neutral Tract, 111–12

Chicago-Colorado Colony, 15

Chicago IL: Charles McCarthy in, 162, 186, 187, 189; colonists in, 118; cost of shipping to, 155; Ebenezer Howard in, 216; Great Fire in, 132, 137; Haymarket Affair in, 192; John Fuller in, 141

cholera, 48

Christianity, 39, 193

Cincinnati, OH, 50

cities, 120, 202. *See also* urban dwellers

Civil War, 13, 59, 65–66, 87–88. *See also* United States

Clarksville TN, 1

class struggle: Bronterre O'Brien on, 46, 52, 67, 172; and emigration, 102, 107; Karl Marx on, 22, 59; O'Brienites on, 13, 183–84; Populist Party on, 198; Robert Owen on, 25

Clay County KS, 16–18

Clemens, Samuel, 1

Clerkenwell district, 63–64, 101, 129. *See also* London

Clerkenwell Green, 185

Clinton, Henry, 119–23, 215–16

coal, 16, 67

Cobbett, William, 25–28, 30, 44–45, 102, 210, 223

Cobden, Richard, 34

Coburn, Willis, 1, 9

collective ownership, 16, 84–85, 222–24. *See also* private ownership

collective power: Bronterre O'Brien on, 22; Frederick Wilson on, 151; in landowner- ship, 216; and moral persuasion, 195; op- position to, 49; of Workingmen's Coop- erative, 82, 84, 86, 97, 108, 136, 176

colonization: Bronterre O'Brien on, 23; Charles Murray on, 148; George White on, 94; James Murray on, 142–43, 148;

John Radford on, 80; Mutual Land com- pany on, 76–78, 124, 137, 138; promotion at home, 102, 172

Colorado, 15, 87, 155

Colorado: A Summer Trip (Taylor), 67

Colorado Cooperative Company, 224

commercial activity, 120, 121, 136, 150, 165. *See also* capitalism

Common Sense (Paine), 28

communal studies, xiv–xv

communism, 14, 15, 49, 57, 59, 185

The Communist Manifesto (Marx), 42, 59

communitarianism: experiments in, 11–13, 18–20, 49, 100, 141, 234n32; and labor ex- changes, 16; O'Brienites on, 63, 213; of Robert Owen, 25. *See also* cooperative colonies

Complete Suffrage Movement (CSM), 34. *See also* universal suffrage

Comprehensionist, 142–44

Coney, John, 85, 240n31

Congregationalists, 131–32, 177

Congress of Advanced Minds of the World, 54

Conover, Jane, 6

Conover, William, 6

cooperative colonies: Alexander Dupree on, 146; characteristics of, 224; establish- ment in Kansas, 13–18, 215–16; of Étienne Cabet, 38–40; failure of communal, 5, 217; Frederick Wilson on, 141–42, 150, 151; growing of livestock, 155; James Murray on, 142–44, 148; Mutual Land company on, 68; National Reform League on, 48– 49, 63–65, 213–14; opposition to, 51; Rob- ert Owen on, 25–26; study of, xiv, 20; in United States, 94–95; Workingmen's Co- operative as model of, 68, 119, 131, 133, 135, 138, 139, 143–44, 146–48, 159. *See also* communitarianism; Workingmen's Co- operative Colony

Co-operative Colony Aid Association, 15

105, 108, 110, 183, 197, 214, 222; in Crimean
War, 46–48; emigration from, 78–81, 101–
2, 137, 150; former colonists from, 218–19;
during Franco-Prussian War, 129; and
gold rush, 49; information about United States in, 65–66; IWMA in, 57; knowledge of colony from, 2–4; labor history in, xv; lack of reform in, 65, 78–79, 136,
142; land for agriculture in, 137–38, 155;
landownership in, 52–53, 156, 159; lists of
emigrants from, 227–31; Mutual Land
company in, 74; national debt of, 212; and
NRL cooperative, 48; NRL's agenda for, 44;
O'Brienite ideas in, 23, 61, 168, 169, 201,
209, 220, 226; political reform in, 29–31;
radical reform organizations in, 26–28,
38, 51; recruitment of immigrants in, 111–
12; recruitment of shareholders in, 103;
Reverdy Johnson in, 72; socialist party
in, 169, 184–85
Great Plains, 65–66, 99, 102–3, 112, 127, 134–
35, 137–38, 156, 164–65. *See also* American West
Great Salt Lake, 138
Great Southwest Strike, 191, 219. *See also*
strikes
Gronlund, Laurence, 11, 224–25
Guthrie OK, 206

Harney, George Julian, 37
Harper County KS, 18
Harris, George, 51, 57–61, 81–83, 95, 98–
99, 169
Harrison Township KS, 3, 92, 166, 241n45
Harvey, Thomas, 111
hay, 103, 131, 140, 173
Haymarket Affair, 192
Henry (passenger ship), 39, 40
Hertfordshire, 119–20
Hetherington, Henry, 27, 29
Hiawatha KS, 197–99, 201
Hill, Robert, 7–8, 81, 85, 115
Hill, Sophia, 115

Histed, Judge, 187
Holyoake, George Jacob, 15, 54
Home Colonization, 44
Homestead Act, 70, 73, 77, 215
homesteaders, 66, 77, 175
Horsham, Sussex County, 5
Horton KS, 196, 197, 199, 206
House of Commons, 31, 60
Houston TX, 40, 41
Howard, Ebenezer, 216–17
Hoxie, H. M., 191
Hugo, Victor, 56
human rights, xv, 28–29, 35–36
Hunt, Henry, 25–28, 30, 223
Hyde Park, 126, 129, 130
Hyndman, Henry Mayers, 184, 216–18,
220, 221

Icarian colonies, 20, 38–40, 48, 224. *See
also* France
Illinois, 118, 131, 138, 191
immigration, xiv–xv, 14, 18, 88, 91, 94, 155,
176. *See also* emigration
Independent Labour Party, 221
Indiana, 20, 25, 49, 50, 105, 118, 146
Indianapolis IN, 105
Indians, 70. *See also* Kickapoo Indian
Reservation
individualism, 49–50, 60, 143. *See also* sovereign rights
industrialization, 24, 102, 182, 183, 202. *See
also* Knights of Labor
industry, 30, 222, 225. *See also*
manufacturing
Insurance Commissioner, 63
Internal Revenue Service, 88
international affairs, 12, 46, 57, 129–30
International Democratic Association, 130
internationalism, 36, 220
International Working Men's Association
(IWMA): Charles Murray with, 126; during Franco-Prussian War, 129; General
Council of, 12–13, 57–59, 61, 62, 101, 130;

labor disputes, 189–95. *See also* employment; working class

labor exchanges: John Rogers on, 97; Josiah Warren on, 50; monetary system of, 16, 45, 76, 108, 211, 212, 215; and subtreasury plan, 221, 222; at Workingmen's Cooperative Colony, 115, 119, 127. *See also* currency reform; working class

Labour Exchange, 25–26

Labour Party, 221

Lambeth Loyal Association, 28

Lancaster Castle Prison, 33

land: allotment policy, 133, 137–38, 154–56, 159, 160, 162–63, 171, 176; availability in Kansas, 3, 86, 87–90, 111–12, 117, 155, 219; description of Kansas, 67, 85–86, 90–96, 105–6, 111–12, 114, 117, 134–37, 149, 153, 155, 163, 169–70; division of colony, 174–77; and grasshopper plague, 164–65; improvements to, 118–19; in Ireland, 29–30, 183; Mutual Land company's purchase of, 82, 84–85, 92–99, 104, 113–14, 120, 126, 149, 151, 154, 157, 158, 241n45; NRL's acquisition of U.S., 65–78

Land and Labour League (LLL), 101–2, 217

land nationalization: Bronterre O'Brien on, 23, 29–31, 34–38, 42, 44, 50, 52–53, 209–10, 212, 213, 217, 222–24; and home colonization, 172; idealistic views of, 40; Mutual Land company on, 69, 137–39; O'Brienites on, 57, 58, 62, 100–102, 148, 179–80, 218, 219. *See also* landownership; rents

landownership: and agriculture price drop, 197; in California, 63; in cities, 120; colony management of, 99, 100, 215; of defunct colony, 174–78, 218; Frederick Wilson on, 150, 151; Henry Hunt on, 26; James Murray on, 142–43; and liberal political economy, 209–10; in Marxism, 222, 223; Mutual Land company on, 68, 69, 73, 76, 107–9, 148–49, 156, 216; Populist Party on, 198, 202; and subtreasury plan, 221–

22; Thomas Spence on, 28–29, 216–17. *See also* collective ownership; land nationalization; leasing; private ownership; rents

Land Reform League of California, 180

Latter-day Saints. *See* Mormons

LCRR. *See* London Confederation of Rational Reformers (LCRR)

Lease, Mary Elizabeth, 12, 198–99

leasing: Bronterre O'Brien on, 30–31; James Murray on, 142; of John Stowell's land, 118; Mutual Land company on, 108–9, 113–14, 137–38, 150, 156; Sargoods on, 104; Thomas Spence on, 28–29; at Workingmen's Cooperative, 69. *See also* landownership; rents

Leavenworth KS, 1, 119, 206

legislation: on alcohol in Kansas, 186–89; Bronterre O'Brien on, 25, 26, 30, 52–53; and landownership, 107; NRL's seven points on, 43, 57; and Populist movement, 198, 202, 219–20; for quarantine, 155, 243n35; for reform, 60–62, 190–91, 203; on U.S. land policy, 179–80. *See also* California State Legislature; marriage laws

Le Havre, France, 83

Lewelling, Lorenzo, 201–6, 220

libraries, 46, 121

limited liability, 120–21

Lincoln, Abraham, 72, 88, 182

Lincoln NE, 71

Little Blue River, 87

Little Pulteney Street, 169

Liverpool, 48, 89, 117, 118, 126, 160

livestock: for agricultural work, 119, 172–73; infrastructure for, 114; marketability of, 119, 155; purchase of, 98, 101, 110, 127, 164; quarantine of, 155, 243n35. *See also* animals

Llano del Rio, 20, 216, 217, 225

Llewellyn Castle, 2–7, 10–11, 226. *See also* Workingmen's Cooperative Colony

lockout, 191. *See also* strikes

Milner, George, 57, 169

mineral wealth. *See* natural resources

miners, 63, 64

Mississippi River, 198

Missouri, 48, 67, 96, 105, 191, 194, 197–98. *See also* Kansas City MO; St. Louis MO

Missouri, Kansas, and Texas railroad line, 191

Missouri Pacific Railroad, 190, 192, 193

Missouri River, 198

Missouri River, Fort Scott, and Gulf Railroad, 112

mobilization, 19–20, 209

Modern Times, 20, 50, 51, 58, 60

Molineaux, Alfred, 10

Molineaux, C. Rex, xvi

Molineaux, John: as colonist, 7–8, 10, 162–64, 166, 170, 172, 175; emigration of, 159–61; farming of, 177; on fundraising, 157; house of, 176

Molineaux, Joseph, 161

monogamy, 14. *See also* marriage laws

Moore, Thomas, 138

moral guidelines: Bronterre O'Brien on, 22, 33, 38; of Elizabeth Thompson's colony, 16; and emigration, 78–79; Frederick Wilson on, 151; of Knights of Labor, 190; and People's Charter, 32, 42–43; of pioneers, 79; in railroad labor dispute, 195; in United States, 94; William Lovett on, 26; of Workingmen's Cooperative, 98, 148

Morgan, William, 169, 218

Morley, Josiah, 81, 85, 96, 113–15

Mormons, 69, 94–95, 138

Morris, William, 220–21

Mortlake, 89

Murray, Charles: anti-capitalist rhetoric of, 147–48; in British socialist party, 184–85; death of, 221; and death of Bronterre O'Brien, 55–56; debate with George Jacob Holyoake, 15; formation of Mutual Land company, 67; in IWMA, 57, 130;

on John Days, 63–64; to Kansas, 125–26; in Land and Labour League, 102; leadership of, 4–5, 7, 52–55, 80, 125–27, 131, 133, 139–40, 145–46, 153, 155, 162, 217; in Manhood Suffrage League, 169; and Nicholas Chaikovsky, 14; on pioneers' travel, 83–84; recruitment of shareholders, 97–98; resignation of, 152; on Sargoods' criticism, 106–10; on selection of colonists, 81, 89; in Social and Political Education League, 184; in Social Democratic Federation, 218; on Sother, 132; speeches of, 135–37, 171; on village plan, 150; and William Morgan, 169

Murray, George, 48–49, 63, 77

Murray, James: in British socialist party, 184–85; at Chartist uprising (1848), 52; on criticism of colony, 107; death of, 221; information request to, 160, 161; international politics of, 130; on land acquisition, 88–89; on land allotment, 156; leadership of, 4–5, 53–54, 80, 165; in Manhood Suffrage League, 169; optimism of, 136, 148; and origin of colony, 3; promotion of colonization, 138, 148, 171; publication of labor periodical, 123–24; on reform bill, 60; writings of, 142–44, 145

Murray, James (Reverend), 28;

Mutual Land, Emigration, and Colonization Company: acquisition of land, 68–73, 77, 88–99, 241n45; Articles of Association, 80, 109, 121, 136, 156, 171, 174; Charles Bradlaugh on, 154–56; and Congregationalist settlement, 132; criticism of, 104–5, 110–13, 154–56, 159; on deserters, 85, 240n31; dissolution of, 176; on Edward Smith's death, 125; on emigration, 78–79, 160, 171–72; finances of, 73–76, 82–85, 89, 94, 97–98, 100, 103–6, 109–11, 114, 116–17, 119, 125–28, 130–33, 136, 145–47, 149–53, 155, 157, 158, 161–62, 165, 174–75; formation of, 3, 67–68, 168, 215; on Frederick

agriculture, 135; benefits of, 68, 78; disillusionment of, 123, 151, 166; on Edward
Smith's death, 125; emigration of, 79, 81,
83–85, 90, 131, 168, 178, 240n31; fees of, 74–
76; and fence building project, 103; under Frederick Wilson, 160–62, 165, 170,
172, 174–75; of joint-stock limited-liability
company, 120–21; land of, 69, 70, 77, 88–
89, 94, 95, 104, 106, 108–9, 114, 137–38, 150,
154–56, 171, 174–76; lists of, 227–31; and
Sargoods' attack, 107; support of colony,
80, 97–98, 116, 119, 120, 128, 133, 136, 144–
46, 148, 149, 152–53, 157–58, 173; voting
rights of, 160, 171. *See also* Mutual Land,
Emigration, and Colonization Company
Sherman Station, 95–96, 118, 132. *See also*
Sother KS
Shipley, Stan, 169, 184
Shreveport LA, 40
Silkville. *See* Kansas Cooperative Farm
(Silkville)
silver, 198, 210, 221. *See also* metals, scarce
slavery, 41, 59. *See also* wage-slavery
Smith, Edward Grainger: and acquisition
of land for colony, 65, 68–73, 77, 78, 82,
86–96, 98, 99; Charles McCarthy with,
132; on colony expansion, 122–23; death
of, 124–25, 151, 217; on emigration, 75; en
route to United States, 83–85; financial
assistance to, 101; illness of, 116–18; on
land allotment, 137; leadership of, 5, 80–
81, 116–17, 124–25, 127, 140, 153, 215; Sargoods' attack on, 103–7, 109, 110, 113–15;
on selection of colonists, 76
Smith, Elijah, 131
Smith, Elizabeth, 89, 95, 117, 124
Smith, Reuben, 177
Smokey Hill River, 87
Social and Political Education League,
184–85
Social Democratic Federation (SDF), 12,
184–85, 216–18, 220–21
Social Democratic Party (Denmark), 14

socialism: and agriculture, 223; Bronterre O'Brien on, 22, 36, 45, 46; in Europe, 36, 38; and home colonization, 102;
and IWMA, 57, 58, 130; of John Radford, 9,
203–4; of Kansas cooperatives, 14–15; of
Knights of Labor, 190; and landownership, 224; of National Reform League, 68;
of O'Brienites, 218, 220, 221; O'Brienites'
familiarity with Marxist, 12–13; in political pragmatic colonies, 224; promotion
in Great Britain, 184–85; study of British,
xiv–xv, 20, 209. *See also* progressive socialist communities; scientific socialism;
utopian socialism
Socialist Labor Party, 15
Socialist League, 220–21
Socialist Party, 169, 184–85, 223
social justice: Josiah Warren on, 50–51; National Reform League on, 43–44, 61; pioneers' responsibility for, 82, 85; through
emigration, 39; through government, 38;
in United States, 41, 42, 181
social movements, 19–20, 209
Society of Spencean Philanthropists, 29
Soho, 4–5, 45. *See also* London
soil, 92, 137. *See also* agriculture
Sother KS, 96, 131–32, 135, 166, 177. *See also*
Sherman Station
Sother, Thomas M., 132
South Africa, 169
sovereign rights, 79. *See also* individualism
speculators, 70, 71, 77, 89, 117, 177, 189, 195,
198
speeches, 43, 46, 184–85, 196, 198–99, 201
Spencean Clubs, 29
Spence, Thomas: influence of, 30, 31, 223;
on land reform, 35, 44, 216–17; on private
ownership, 210; socialist ideas of, 11, 28;
theories of, 25
spiritualism, 14, 54, 159
Stack, David, 36, 55
Stahl, George C., 177
Standard Oil Company, 186

wheat, 119, 127–28, 137, 150. *See also* grain

Whig Party, 60, 72

White, George, 94–95

Whitehead, Andrew, xvi, 10

White Star Line, 160

Wichita ks, 18, 198–99

Willingwell Association, 172, 174

Willits, John F., 199

Wilson, Frederick: on emigration, 160; and failure of colony, 170–72, 174, 218; leadership of, 152–55, 157–59, 162, 168–70, 173; optimism of, 148–51, 167–68; ownership of colony, 3, 158, 165, 170, 174–76; proposals of, 141–42, 144–45; publications of, 141, 142, 144; resignation of, 165

Wilson, Mr. (U.S. surveyor), 86

woman's suffrage, 58. *See also* universal suffrage

Woodhull, Victoria, 58

Woodlawn Cemetery, 207

Worcester, William, 176

working class: and British political reform, 30; Bronterre O'Brien on, 22; Charles Davies on, 160–61; Charles Murray among, 126; at Chartist Convention (1848), 37; during Crimean War, 46, 52; and currency reform, 27; education of, 39, 42, 45–46, 52, 53, 58, 80, 182–84, 211–13, 220, 221; and emigration, 102; exploitation of, 52–55, 59, 67, 120, 147–48, 185; financial sacrifice of, 82; former colonists from, 218–19; and gold rush, 49; grievances of British, 4–5, 41; Henry Hunt's influence on, 26; during Industrial Revolution, 24; intellectual matrix of, 29; interest in Workingmen's Cooperative, 89, 171, 172; and iwma, 57, 59; James Murray on, 142; and labor exchanges, 16; in Land and Labour League, 101–2; and landownership, 50, 209–10, 216, 223; and Mutual Land company, 67, 78–79, 124, 162; and National Reform League, 44, 53–55, 62; O'Brienites' advocacy for, 179, 181, 183; origin of revolution

in, 32; Owenism of, 25–26; on Paris Commune, 130; and People's Charter, 31, 38; and Populist movement, 200–203; and reform bills, 60; Reverdy Johnson on, 72; Sargoods' warning to, 105, 110; settlement in United States, 63–66, 70, 71–75, 79, 99; and subtreasury plan, 221, 222; support of colony, 98, 103, 128, 137; in United States, 111, 197, 214; in utopian village plan, 122; Workingmen's Cooperative for, 11, 19. *See also* factory workers; labor; labor disputes; labor exchanges; urban dwellers

working hours, 194

Working Man, 60

Workingmen's Cooperative Colony: abandonment of, 131; acquisition of land for, 65–73, 77, 78, 82, 86–92, 112, 241n45; assimilation of colonists from, 21; birth at, 123; and Cedarvale Commune, 185; contracts of colonists in, 82, 84, 106, 107, 109, 113; contributions of, 12; descendants of, xvi, 3, 10; expansion of, 89, 116–17, 126, 131, 135, 146–47, 151–55, 158–59, 165; failure of, 3–5, 7–8, 10–11, 19, 21, 145, 166–68, 170–75, 177, 217–18, 225–26; financial assistance for, 101, 103, 116, 131, 145–46, 152–53, 157, 165, 166; founding principles of, 9, 23–24, 215; Frederick Wilson on, 141–42, 172; goals of, 2, 6, 10–11, 19–20, 22, 68–69, 73, 83, 100, 108, 109, 111, 163–65; hardships of, 7, 102–3, 110, 115–16, 123–25, 127, 131, 136–41, 147–51, 154–56, 164–65, 172–73; housing at, 2, 96, 101, 110, 121–23, 144, 162, 176, 226; institutional foundation of, 43, 44; John Bristow's knowledge of, 1–10; land plan for, 28–29; leadership of, 4–5, 9–10, 14, 53, 73–75, 116–19, 124–25, 127, 131–33, 141, 142, 149, 167–68; neighbors of, 92; original colonists of, 3–9, 69–71, 76–99, 109–10, 132, 186, 206–7, 240n31; and other colonies, 15–16, 18–19, 216; and Paris Commune, 130; as political pragmatic colony, 224–25; population of, 217; promotion of ef-